Managerial Accounting in the Hospitality Industry

Peter J. Harris, MSc, MHCIMA, CDipAF, FBHA
Principal Lecturer, School of Hotel and Catering Management
Oxford Polytechnic

Peter A. Hazzard, MSc, FCMA
Formerly Principal Lecturer, Department of Accountancy and Business
Polytechnic of West London

Stanley Thornes (Publishers) Ltd

First published by Northwood Publications Ltd 1972
Second edition 1977
Third edition 1979

First published as *Accounting and Financial Management in the
Hotel and Catering Industry:* volume 2, by Hutchinson Education 1983
Fourth edition published 1987
Reprinted 1988

Reprinted 1990 by
Stanley Thornes (Publishers) Ltd
Ellenborough House
Wellington Street
CHELTENHAM GL50 1YD

First published as *Managerial Accounting in the Hospitality Industry*
by Stanley Thornes (Publishers) Ltd. 1992.

Reprinted 1994

A catalogue record for this book is available from the British Library.

ISBN 0 7487 1567 3

Typeset in Linotron Palatino by
Northern Phototypesetting Co. Ltd., Bolton
Printed and bound in Great Britain at Redwood Books, Wiltshire

Managerial Accounting in the Hospitality Industry

Contents

Preface to the Fifth Edition

Previously published as *Managerial Accounting in the Hotel and Catering Industry,* this book has been substantially revised, expanded and updated in order to keep abreast of current accounting developments and their applications in the hotel, restaurant and catering industry.

In accordance with previous editions, the needs of students, managers, executives and the independent operator have been carefully borne in mind throughout this work.

Notable changes to this edition are as follows:

1. The addition of a new chapter entitled Building Computer Spreadsheet Models. The chapter explains how to build and operate a spreadsheet without previous experience. It also explains the principles of spreadsheet model design and illustrates this with a restaurant example.
2. Four chapters have been entirely re-written, namely: Chapter 7, Budgets for Planning and Control; Chapter 14, Measuring Financial and Operating Performance; Chapter 15, Sources of Finance; Chapter 17, Capital Investment Decisions.
3. The questions and problems sections at the end of many chapters have been revised, extended and updated.

Finally, we should like to thank those who have drawn to our attention errors in the earlier editions and made suggestions for inclusion in this edition. As always, users' comments are welcome.

P.J.H.
P.A.H.

April 1992

Certain questions at the end of chapters are reprinted by kind permission of:

Hotel, Catering and Institutional Management Association	(HCIMA)
Chartered Institute of Management Accountants	(CIMA)
Chartered Association of Certified Accountants	(CACA)
British Association of Hotel Accountants	(BAHA)

Chapter One

Accounting: A Background

Accounting has for centuries been concerned with *recording*, *summarizing* and *reporting* in money terms the transactions of an organization, although the scope has gone beyond these three basic procedures in modern times.

An example of simple accounting familiar to all readers is the 'statement of account' you receive from the bank. This statement is a copy of the bank's account with you and contains a *record* of the bank's transactions with you showing as a debit each amount paid to you – which you have withdrawn – and as a credit each amount received from you and paid into your account. The balance, being the amount of your money held by the bank – a credit balance – is a form of *summary*, and the whole is *reported* to you, the holder of the account, for information. The main and more complex accounting procedures of the bank would be to summarize all accounts and compile a report to shareholders containing a statement of profit made in the period and a balance sheet of the bank's financial position at the end of the period. Your credit balance would be amongst those shown as a liability in the balance sheet because the bank is liable, or obliged, to pay you the balance on request.

Accounting for exchange of money and services rendered presents few problems. Accounting for individual hotels and restaurants is not generally complicated as the unit is relatively small, whereas accounting for the large catering group with its centralized food production and freezing facilities introduces complications of valuing food stocks, pricing inter-group trading and other problems.

Financial, cost and management accounting

Accounting is wide in its meaning although recording of transactions in monetary terms is its central feature. Three recognized branches of accounting are:

(a) *financial accounting* which is specially concerned with reporting the financial affairs of an organization to interested outside parties;

(b) *cost accounting* which is concerned with the ascertainment of costs and the analysis of savings or excess costs compared with some standard;

(c) *managerial accounting* which deals with providing managers with reports about their organization.

All three branches are closely related to one another and operate under an overall framework of *financial management*.

Accounting and accountants

How is the qualified accountant concerned with hotel accounting? Accountants may be classified in many ways but for the present purpose can be placed into two categories:

(a) those who are practising accountants, that is they are either partners or employees in practising firms acting as auditors of companies, preparing accounts for small organizations like independent hotels, or providing taxation services and other similar work.

(b) Those employed by an industrial or commercial organization such as an hotel group who are concerned with recording the group's financial transactions and advising management on a wide range of money matters associated with the financial health of the organization.

The important difference between these categories is that whereas the first accountant audits the books of a number of client companies in the course of a year, the accountant employed by the commercial company is concerned entirely with his own company's operations and is part of the management team. The hotel accountant, for instance, identifies himself with the hotel operations exclusively.

Whilst these two kinds of accountant are involved with the accounting functions of recording, summarizing and reporting, mention might be made of the financier who, not necessarily an accountant, manages the company's finances from his position on the board of directors. He is sometimes criticized for the power he wields though this is often not justified because the importance of maintaining the large company in good financial health, vis-à-vis the stock market for instance, cannot be overstated. There would be understandable concern if a top financier flitted from company to company in different industries without really appreciating the managerial aspects peculiar to each industry. The majority of accountants and financiers in the hotel and catering industry are steeped in the industry to good effect.

Accounting and hotel catering managers

How is the hotel and catering manager concerned with accounting? The independent hotel whose owner also manages the unit will usually retain the services of a practising accountant who advises on day-to-day accounting records and produces annual accounts for legal purposes. Ideally more frequent accounts would be prepared for management control purposes. It is important for the proprietor to have a sound grasp of accounting and financial matters, for the accountant would be available to advise on only the more important decisions.

The manager of a medium sized hotel which is part of a group is immersed in financial activities from participation in preparing annual budgets to justifying the financial results of his operation. An understanding of accounting records and of the likely effect of alternative courses of action on hotel profit is also required.

The large hotel may have its own accountant, but being a large unit decisions are more onerous and the responsibility greater. Working with the accountant as a member of a team requires the manager to understand clearly the financial implications of decisions he takes. Whilst important decisions such as expansion of operations may be taken centrally he is closely involved in estimating the financial outcome of plans.

The hotel and catering manager, therefore, cannot avoid being involved one way or another in the financial side of his operation. A more positive attitude is currently evident as managers accept they are in business to contribute to the profitable operation of their organization.

Accounting: development

Well before the fourteenth century in England, accounting systems recorded and reported financial transactions as a check that stewards and agents had carried out their tasks in connection with secular and religious estates. The steward's accounts were submitted to the owner and subject to audit by him. The stewardship function has to this day been an important influence on the information provided to owners concerning the manner in which their resources have been managed.

Whilst estate accounting was operating in England, accounting for merchants' activities took place in Venice and this involved a double-entry system described by Pacioli in 1494 which was to become the basis of modern accounting systems. This system of accounting was given official recognition in the 1856 Companies Act requiring that books of companies had to be kept on a double-entry basis. Earlier in 1844 a Joint Stock Companies Act required the regular balancing of books and a 'full and fair' annual balance sheet without, however, giving guidance as to the basis of valuing assets or requiring a profit and loss account. Not until the Companies Acts of 1928 and 1929 was a profit and loss account required, assets divided between fixed and current and the basis of their valuation indicated.

Accounting has developed along two main streams, one of which was in response to the demand of owners and shareholders of companies for annual information on the financial state of the organization and protection against fraud. This stream, associated with the financial accounting and the stewardship function can be clearly identified with the professional or practising accountants and their audit work.

The other stream associated with cost accounting and management accounting, has developed to meet the demands of management for relevant information in decision making, which in turn has been influenced by the economist. This accounting is supplementary to and often integrated with financial accounting. Development here has been on an industry basis because each trade or industry is unique in its market, cost structure and planning needs, giving rise to special information requirements. Mass production in the early 1900s with its constant repetition of operations lent itself to the introduction of labour and machine time standards and standard costing. Hotel and catering, like many other industries, can only avail itself of standard costing to a limited extent, yet with increasing emphasis on labour saving methods and centralized food production, the industry is benefiting from this technique. Economics is contributing a great deal to this stream of accounting as accounting becomes more of an inter-disciplinary activity. In comparison with such techniques as standard costing, the use of budgets in businesses since the early 1900s has spread into all industries, because budgeting is concerned with the making of economic plans and this is regarded as essential in any well organized business.

More recent developments have been in uniform or standard systems of accounting which are introduced within an industry to provide a structure for assembling management information in a common form which then facilitates comparisons between firms. A standard system of hotel accounting was published in 1969 followed by one for catering in 1971. However, *The Uniform System of Accounts for Hotels*, published by the New York Hotel Association, has been adopted by the large hotel groups and all the evidence suggests that this system will become more widely used in this country.

The managerial approach

It is easy to fall into the trap of equating an appreciation of accounting with a superficial study of accounting practices and procedures. It is nonetheless difficult to know where to draw the line between gaining a fundamental appreciation of accounting and becoming familiar with the fuller aspects of accounting required by accountants. The object of this work is to help hotel and catering managers and potential managers to understand and use to advantage aspects of accounting they will meet in the administration of their undertakings.

The approach used here is the balance sheet approach rather than the double-entry book-keeping approach. Broad concepts are initially presented rather than minute detail, for otherwise there is a real danger of being confused by a mass of accounts.

Managers, by constantly making decisions, aim to achieve planned results using limited resources. Whilst this is done through people, the measurement of results and the resources used is mainly in money terms. Accounting, as noted earlier, is concerned with recording, summarizing and reporting, and the latter in particular provides the manager with financial information on resources and the results of his decisions. It is important therefore, that the manager should know how resources are obtained and used in his business and how the results are measured. The same basic concepts involved in this measurement apply to the small restaurant and the large hotel group.

The most essential financial information about an organization is contained in balance sheet form which shows whence resources have been obtained and how they are currently used to generate profit. Only with an understanding of the balance sheet and of profit is it advisable to consider the particular hotel and catering accounting applications which occupy much of this work.

Chapter 2 introduces the balance sheet and profit statement without attempting to raise important issues which affect their preparation and interpretation. These issues are taken up in Chapter 3 to give the reader a chance to understand the assumptions which underpin these statements, and to meet the problems which arise in assessing profit and the measurement of balance sheet values.

Further reading

1. Sidebotham, R., *Introduction to the Theory and Context of Accounting*, Pergamon Press, Chapters 1 and 2.

2. Solomons, D., (Ed.) 'The Historical Development of Costing', *Studies in Cost Analysis* Sweet and Maxwell, pp. 3–49.

Chapter Two

Accounting: Fundamental Statements

The most prominent financial statement of a business is a 'balance sheet', which by definition shows the financial position at a particular point in time. It could indicate one business to be in a strong financial position and another to be in serious financial difficulties. By comparing balance sheets at different times it is possible to determine the profit made in the period, so long as the owner had not invested or withdrawn resources such as cash during the period.

Profit generation is nevertheless the foremost objective of a business and this requires the preparation of profit statements covering different parts of the business at relatively short time intervals.

By demonstrating the effect some typical transactions have on the financial position of a business, concentration is on the output of the accounting system. This has the advantage of avoiding involvement with processing transactions through numerous accounts. The main reason accounts are used in practice is to accumulate common items so that balance sheets may be produced as required, say quarterly, instead of after each transaction, an almost impossible and certainly unprofitable task.

Dual aspect of the balance sheet

Resources, debts and owner's interests are known respectively as assets, liabilities and capital.

(a) *Assets* are anything of value owned by a business, including resources and future economic rights such as money owed by customers.

(b) *Liabilities* are financial obligations to outside parties repayable at some future time, such as a loan received from the bank.

(c) *Capital* is the sum invested in a business by the owners, partners or in the case of a company, its shareholders. Capital represents the rights of owners to the assets after the prior claims of outside parties (liabilities) have been satisfied in the event of the business closing. It is variously called owner's equity, owner's worth or net assets.

The most acceptable form of accounting for these three elements is known as double entry accounting and this is best expressed as a simple equation:

Assets = Liabilities + Capital

For accounting records to remain in balance an increase in one asset must be accompanied by a corresponding decrease in another asset or an increase in liabilities and/or capital. The balance sheet is a financial statement which truly reflects this dual aspect.

Description of business activities during a quarter

The dual aspect of the balance sheet will be demonstrated by tracing the activities of a business for three months from its formation on January 1st. The formal statements reflecting the transactions are in Exhibit 2–1 which will be used to explain further accounting aspects later in this chapter.

Jan.   1 Business formed with £70,000 in cash.
       2 Premises (£62,000) and equipment (£8,000) purchased for cash.
         Banqueting business started.
      31 Banquets in the month made a profit of £2,000. Sales revenue and all expenses, mainly food, wages and hire charges were cash transactions.
         Owner's worth and bank balance have both therefore, increased by £2,000.
Feb.   1 Food stocks purchased on credit to supply further business. These stocks (£4,000) are financed for the moment by the suppliers who are therefore creditors.
      28 Banquets in the month have again made £2,000 profit. However, food was drawn from stock (£3,000) leaving £1,000 in stock.
         Both revenue and expenses other than food were cash transactions.
         Cash balance has risen by £5,000 in the month despite a profit at only £2,000 because no purchases of food were made.
March 1 Creditors were paid the sum owing to them. Cash falls by £4,000.
      31 The third month's banqueting has produced a profit similar to that of earlier months. Owner's worth has therefore risen by £2,000 to £76,000. Only 'other expenses' of £5,000 are on a cash basis this month, for clients have

Exhibit 2–1

(a) Balance sheets covering three months

	January 1st £	January 2nd £	January 31st £	February 1st £	February 28th £	March 1st £	March 31st £	March 31st minus January 2nd £
CAPITAL								
Capital	70,000	70,000	70,000	70,000	70,000	70,000	70,000	—
Profit	—	—	2,000	2,000	4,000	4,000	6,000	+ 6,000
Owner's equity	70,000	70,000	72,000	72,000	74,000	74,000	76,000	
LIABILITIES								
Creditors	—	—	—	4,000	4,000	—	3,000	+ 3,000
Overdraft	—	—	—	—	—	—	2,000	+ 2,000
Total	70,000	70,000	72,000	76,000	78,000	74,000	81,000	+11,000
ASSETS								
Premises	—	62,000	62,000	62,000	62,000	62,000	62,000	—
Equipment	—	8,000	8,000	8,000	8,000	8,000	8,000	—
Stock of food	—	—	—	4,000	1,000	1,000	1,000	+ 1,000
Debtors	—	—	—	—	—	—	10,000	+10,000
Cash at bank	70,000	—	2,000	2,000	7,000	3,000	—	—
Total	70,000	70,000	72,000	76,000	78,000	74,000	81,000	+11,000

19

Exhibit 2–1 *cont.*

(b) Profit statements for period

		January £		February £		March £	Quarter Jan./March £
Sales revenue	(cash)	10,000	(cash)	10,000	(credit)	10,000	30,000
Less: Food costs of sales (an expense)	(cash)	3,000	(ex stock)	3,000	(credit)	3,000	9,000
GROSS PROFIT		7,000		7,000		7,000	21,000
Less: other expenses (paid in cash)		5,000		5,000		5,000	15,000
NET PROFIT		2,000		2,000		2,000	6,000

(c) The relationship between profit and cash

Profit for the three months to March 31st   £ 6,000

But not all sales revenue has been received in cash.
On the other hand not all purchases have been paid for.
More food has been purchased than used in generating sales and profit.

	Cash Rise £	*Cash Fall* £
(Debtors)		10,000
(Creditors)	3,000	
(Stock)		1,000
	3,000	11,000
		less 8,000
		2,000

Resulting in net cash fall since trading started on January 2nd, requiring overdraft facilities.

been allowed credit (£10,000) and food costing £3,000 was bought on credit to maintain food stocks at £1,000.

The sequence of events in Exhibit 2–1 (pages 19 and 20) illustrates four basic accounting principles.

1. *Owner's worth (equity) is what remains at any time when total liabilities are deducted from total assets.* On February 1st, for instance, £4,000 deducted from assets of £76,000 gives owner's equity of £72,000.
2. *Owner's worth (equity) compared at different times represents profit generated.* If the owner has introduced or withdrawn assets in the period in question then this must clearly be taken into account. January 2nd when trading started compared with March 31st shows a profit of £6,000 as detailed in the profit statement.
3. *The generation of profit in a period does not rely upon business being conducted on a cash basis as in January.* Revenue and costs are accrued, that is to say they are recognized and recorded when they are earned and incurred, not as money is received or paid. In March £10,000 sales have been invoiced and are regarded as revenue although these sales are on credit.
4. *Profit represents sales less expenses incurred in generating those sales.* First, sales revenue is determined for the period and then expenses are said to be 'matched' with the sales revenue. In February although £4,000 food was purchased, only £3,000 of purchases went into the sales and became an expense for the period, apart from £5,000 for other expenses.

Profit v. cash

It is difficult to divorce profit management from cash management although the larger the enterprise the more each becomes a specialist activity. A fall in cash from a nil balance on January 2nd to an overdraft of £2,000 on March 31st is explained by reference to the balance sheets; Exhibit 2÷1 (c) lists the reasons. The main reason is that clients were allowed credit in March. If their accounts had been settled by March 31st for the full amount the cash balance would have been £8,000. However, if a reduction in the charge were made for prompt payment, say 1% off the total bill, then profit would have been reduced by £100.

It is necessary to carry stocks of food and other goods and if £1,000 worth of stocks is constantly needed then this has to be financed. The usual alternatives are creditors, and bankers in the form of overdraft for seasonal requirements. It is common for the hotel and catering establishments to carry relatively little stock and for creditors to more than balance the value of stocks carried as on March 31st. This has a favourable effect on the cash position.

Balance sheet structure

Assets, liabilities and capital are subdivided in a balance sheet into five main groups located as follows:

Balance Sheet

Long-term	Owner's capital + profits	Fixed assets, e.g. premises
	Long-term liabilities e.g. loans	
Short-term	Current liabilities e.g. creditors	Current assets, e.g. stock of food

Groups are primarily established in relation to whether an item represents an asset or a claim on the business, and secondly in relation to time.

Long-term items

Fixed assets are items owned by a business for use in the production of goods and services. They are expected to benefit the business over fairly long periods of time. The purchase cost of these items is called 'capital expenditure' compared with expenditure on assets purchased for consumption and on services which are called 'revenue expenditure'. Examples of fixed assets are land and buildings both freehold and leasehold, plant and equipment.

Long-term liabilities normally take the form of loans which by definition are repayable at some future time.

Capital is of a more permanent nature and reflects the owner's investment in the business. Profits may be withdrawn or retained in the business.

Short-term items

Current assets and current liabilities are of a less permanent nature. They comprise stocks, debtors, cash, creditors and overdraft which are needed to service the routine trading activities of buying, processing, serving and selling.

Current assets minus current liabilities is called net current assets or working capital. Components of working capital are constantly changing, forming some kind of cycle, although there is generally no clear start or finish to the cycle. Purchases are made on credit which generate both creditors and stocks. Meals are sold, some on credit. Cash is received from customers and paid to suppliers. Surplus cash is still working capital but may be used to purchase assets or be withdrawn from the business, both activities reducing working capital.

Balance sheet layout

Balance sheets originated as a list of balances remaining at the end of the year as shown in Exhibit 2–2. As presentation to interested parties became important, formats developed designed to help interpretation. Long- and short-term items were separated and a vertical form was introduced as in Exhibit 2–3. Current popular presentations emphasize that long-term finance is used to supply both fixed assets and net current assets as in Exhibit 2–4.

Figures used in these presentations relate to March 31st in Exhibit 2–1.

Exhibit 2–2

Balance sheet as a list of balances

Capital & Liabilities	£	Assets	£
Owner's capital	70,000	Premises	62,000
Profit	6,000	Equipment	8,000
Loan capital	—	Stocks	1,000
Creditors	3,000	Debtors	10,000
Overdraft	2,000	Cash	—
	81,000		81,000

The profit statement

Revenue recognition

Determining profit requires that revenue be identified in a period and the associated expenses deducted. Recognizing revenue is a relatively easy matter compared with the problems involved in working out the associated expenses.

Revenue is recognized as such and recorded when a sale has been agreed and the customer comes into possession of the goods. In a

Exhibit 2–3

Balance sheet in vertical form

	£
Capital	
Owner's capital	70,000
Profit	6,000
	76,000
Loan capital	—
Current Liabilities	
Creditors	3,000
Overdraft	2,000
	81,000

	£
Fixed Assets	
Premises	62,000
Equipment	8,000
	70,000
Current Assets	
Stocks	1,000
Debtors	10,000
Cash	—
	11,000
Total Assets	81,000

Exhibit 2–4

Balance sheet showing net current assets

	£	£
Capital Employed		
Owner's capital		70,000
Profit		6,000
		76,000
Loan capital		—
		76,000

REPRESENTED BY:

	£	£
Fixed Assets		
Premises	62,000	
Equipment	8,000	70,000
Current Assets		
Stocks	1,000	
Debtors	10,000	
Cash	—	
	11,000	
Current Liabilities		
Creditors	3,000	
Overdraft	2,000	
	5,000	
Net current Assets		6,000
		76,000

service industry such as hotel and catering, revenue is recognized when the service is rendered, such as:

(a) when a guest books into an hotel;
(b) when a customer is served with a meal in a restaurant or a drink in a bar.

Revenue and cash received

The relationship between revenue and cash received from sales is shown in three different situations:

(a) The quick turnover restaurant often allows no credit. Customers pay cash. Revenue earned in a period is the cash in the till which should agree with all bills issued.
(b) A banquet for a client company may be on a credit basis. The revenue is taken immediately to calculate profit but the balance sheet would show the amount owing as part of the debtors figure.
(c) Advance booking deposits may be received by an hotel in an accounting period before the client books in. This is not revenue in the period but is shown grouped with creditors.

Cost and expenses

The term *cost* refers to anything on which money is ultimately spent in running the business. This includes, for instance, weekly wages, equipment and food whether purchased for cash or on credit.

An *expense* is a cost which has benefited the firm in an accounting period. Food purchased for stock is a cost but becomes an expense in the period when used to prepare a dish for a customer.

Three expense categories are as follows:

(a) *Non-storable benefits.* This is the most easily understood category and covers items which are not stored, such as wages, insurance and rent. The category is mainly associated with services.
(b) *Stocks.* The cost of unused or unsold food and drink stocks will have been incurred in the expectation of future revenue. When this revenue is recorded such as meals or drink sold, the food and drink cost becomes an expense for the period.
(c) *Depreciation of fixed assets.* Fixed assets are those assets which in the normal course of business will provide benefits over several years. The amounts by which the cost is periodically reduced and charged against revenue is known as depreciation, an expense.

Relating expenses to the correct period is often not a simple matter in practice. In order to explain accounting procedures necessary to the understanding of balance sheets and profit statements, three *timing* categories may be identified:
(a) costs which become expenses in the same accounting period;
(b) costs becoming expenses in a subsequent period;
(c) expenses which are not payable until a subsequent period.
These are now explained using figures from Exhibit 2–1.

(a) *Costs and expenses in the same period*:
1. In Exhibit 2–1, other expenses were assumed to be wages,

salaries, monthly hire payments and similar expenses which relate to the month stated. These kind of expenses are no problem as far as timing is concerned.

2. Food and other items normally stored which are used up and sold in the same period in which they were purchased are expenses in that period, as in January.

(b) *Costs becoming an expense in a subsequent period*:
1. Stocks of food and other items used up and sold in a subsequent period are expenses in that period. Stocks are automatically charged as expenses to the correct period by either pricing issues of say food issued to the kitchen, or deriving the cost of food used by adding purchases in the period to opening stocks and deducting closing stocks.
2. Fixed assets such as purchased equipment, lose value with use and time requiring that the cost be allocated to accounting periods so as to charge a fair proportion to each period during the expected future life. This is *depreciation*, defined as a measure of the wearing out, consumption or other loss of value of a fixed asset whether arising from use, effluxion of time or obsolescence through technology and market changes. The equipment in Exhibit 2–1 might be expected to have a life of, say, five years. Equal amounts charged to each period, known as the straight line method of depreciation, would require £1,600 per annum or £400 per quarter. This would have the effect of reducing profit for the quarter to £5,600 and the balance sheet value of equipment to £7,600 at March 31st.
3. Prepayments are amounts due to be paid in one period for services relating wholly or partly to subsequent periods. If an annual insurance premium of £400 is payable in advance, this would be included in January's other expenses. However, only £100 would be regarded as expenses for this first quarter, the other £300 relating to later periods would appear as 'prepayments' on the asset side of the balance sheet at March 31st.

(c) *Expenses payable in a subsequent period*:
Accrued expenses or accruals are expenses which have been incurred in an accounting period but are not due for payment until a later period. A quarterly gas bill covering January/March will not be received and consequently not paid until April. As an expense for the first quarter the amount, say £400, will be added to other expenses and shown as accrued expenses in the balance sheet at March 31st under current liabilities. It is similar to a creditor who is owed for goods supplied and is sometimes grouped with creditors in published accounts.

Expenses matrix

To sum up, the matching of expenses with revenue requires that costs be classified as they are incurred into revenue and capital expenditure. Revenue expenditure is further separated into purchases for stock and all other expenses.

At the end of an accounting period the matching process requires adjustments so that the profit statement – the presentation form of the profit and loss account – contains only those expenses relating to the sales and to the period.

A summary of this procedure is presented in matrix form in Exhibit 2–5.

Exhibit 2–5

A Classification Of Hotel And Catering Expenses Related to Period Profit

TIMING of EXPENSES	FORMS OF EXPENSES		
	Revenue Expenditure		Capital Expenditure
	Purchases which go into stock, e.g. food and drink	Providing non-storable benefits, e.g. wages, insurance, electricity	Depreciation of fixed assets
Costs and expenses in the same period	Stocks used up in becoming sales	Most expenses are in this position requiring no adjustment	
Costs becoming expenses in a subsequent period	Stocks are an asset in the balance sheet until used, becoming an expense when sold	Payment in advance e.g. for insurance. Cost carried forward to the next period is an asset in the balance sheet and grouped with debtors	Each period's depreciation expense is accumulated and deducted from cost of asset in the balance sheet
Expenses payable in a subsequent period		Accruals for services e.g. electricity. Similar to creditors in the balance sheet	
CRITERIA for charging expense to a period's profit and loss account	Related to sales in the period	Related to the period benefited by the expense	

Note to Exhibit 2–5:
1. This classification is presented to aid the understanding of financial accounting. Classification for management accounting purposes is covered in Chapter 5.
2. Where food has been processed and remains in stock, for example frozen made-up dishes, then some depreciation and other expenses will be added to the food cost to arrive at the stock value.

The profit statement: presentation

The significance of a balance sheet has been demonstrated because it is a vital part of accounting and at the same time is helpful to the understanding of accounting profit. However, deriving profit for a period by finding the increase in owner's worth is, in practice, inadequate for several reasons. One reason for supporting the balance sheet with a detailed profit statement is that it helps management to plan and control the business. Being aware of the detailed revenue and expenses making up the profit helps in the planning of the next period's results and the control of individual costs such as food.

Profit, although calculated in accordance with the matching principle, is presented in different ways to satisfy the different needs, for instance, of shareholders, the Inland Revenue and management. The profit and loss account compiled by the double entry method is dealt with in Volume 1. The presentation of profit in the annual report and accounts of limited companies is shown in Chapter 19. For internal management purposes the presentation of profit, and in particular its constituent parts, is made in a 'profit statement' rather than the traditional profit and loss account. An account calls to mind the two-sided account used in double entry book-keeping; a statement on the other hand, breaks away from the two-sided account and seeks to show accounting information in a more meaningful manner for the non-accountant.

The simplest form of profit statement, in fact a summary, was shown in Exhibit 2–1(c) and is repeated here:

Profit statement for quarter to 31st March

	£
Sales	30,000
Less: Cost of sales	9,000
Gross profit	21,000
Less: Other expenses	15,000
Net profit	6,000

Attention is drawn again to the very important accounting

concept that profit results from sales revenue less the cost of generating the sales, and not less the cost of purchases. The example drawn from Exhibit 2–1(c) could have been restated:

Profit statement for quarter to 31st March

	£	£
Sales		30,000
Cost of food used in sales:		
Opening stock	—	
Purchases	10,000	
	10,000	
Less: Closing stock	1,000	
		9,000
Gross profit		21,000
Less: Other expenses		15,000
Net profit		6,000

For management accounting purposes, the form of profit statement which gives one figure for cost of food instead of stating opening and closing stocks is usually adopted. For routine accounting purposes, stocks are valued at the lower of cost or net realizable value in accordance with the prudence concept considered in Chapter 3. A more detailed profit statement, including the three adjustments* noted on page 26 is as follows:

Profit statement for quarter to 31st March

		£
Sales revenue		29,800
Less: Cost of sales		9,000
Gross profit		20,800
Plus: Other revenue		200
		21,000
Less Other expenses:		
Employee benefits	8,000	
Staff food and drink	1,250	
Administration	1,950	
Marketing	500	
Heat, light and power (including £400 gas*)	1,500	
Insurance* (£400 less £300)	100	
General expenses	300	
Repairs and maintenance	1,500	
Depreciation*	400	15,500
Net profit		5,500
Less: Appropriations		3,000
Retained profit		2,500

Two additional items have been shown on page 29. 'Other revenue' refers to revenue other than from the main operating departments, for instance income received from advertising space in reception. The 'Appropriations' item indicates the use of the profit that has been generated and could refer to cash drawn from the business by the owner. What is not appropriated for various purposes is retained in the business and increases owner's worth. However, in its present form the above profit statement is still of limited value operationally. Management require periodical profit statements which contain revenues and expenses expressed in terms of departmental responsibility and control.

A suitable format for an hotel profit statement is the one developed over a number of years for the Hotel Association of New York City and published in *A Uniform System of Accounts for Hotels* (8th revised edition, 1986). It contains an analysis of the main operating departments and identifies several intermediate profit levels. A profit statement based on the uniform system is given in Exhibit 2–6.

Exhibit 2–6   *Departmental Profit Statement*

Operating departments	Sales Revenues £	Cost of Sales £	Payroll and Related Expenses £	Other Expenses £	Profit (Loss) £
Rooms					
Food and beverage					
Other departments					
Total					

Less: Undistributed operating expenses
Administrative
Data processing
Marketing
Energy costs
Property operation

    Total

Profit before fixed charges
Less: Fixed charges
Rent, rates and insurance
Interest
Depreciation
Profit before taxes

Less: Taxes

Net Profit   £

Questions and problems

2–1 What are assets, liabilities and capital?

2–2 Explain how the 'dual-aspect' concept and the 'accounting equation' are interrelated.

2–3 Give the relationship of assets, liabilities and owner's worth in three different equations (express each item as a function of the other two).

2–4 What is a balance sheet?

2–5 Distinguish between the following items:
  (a) fixed assets and current assets;
  (b) long-term liabilities and current liabilities;
  (c) capital and long-term liabilities.

2–6 What is a profit statement?

2–7 Distinguish between the terms 'cost' and 'expense'.

2–8 What do you understand by the term 'depreciation' in respect of fixed assets.

2–9 In what way is a profit statement connected with a balance sheet?

2–10 How may a profit statement, which is acceptable to owners and outside interested parties, be modified so as to provide relevant operational information?

2–11 Distinguish between the terms 'revenue' and 'receipt'.

2–12 Tabulate balance sheets after each of the following transactions:
  (a) Commenced business with £200,000 in cash;
  (b) Bought premises for £140,000 cash;
  (c) Bought stock on credit for £30,000;
  (d) Paid expenses in cash, £3,000;
  (e) Sold stock which cost £16,000 on credit for £24,000;
  (f) Paid creditors amount due;
  (g) Collected £18,000 in cash from debtors.

Note: Your answer might start:

(£000)	(a)	(b)	(c)	etc.
Capital	200			
Profit and loss a/c				
Creditors				
	200			
Cash	200			
Premises				
Stock				
Debtors				
	200			

2–13 The following transactions relate to a new restaurant:

May 1 Bank account opened with £200,000 representing £180,000 capital and a £20,000 loan.

2 Bought premises and equipment for cash £195,000.

30 Food bought to date on credit £6,000.

31 Operations during May:

	£
Meal sales – cash	8,000
Cost of food used from stock	3,000
Wages and other expenses – cash	2,000

June 1 Food stocks bought on credit £7,000.

30 Operations during June:

	£
Meal sales – cash	9,000
Food costs – cash	1,000
– from stock	3,000
Wages and other expenses – cash	2,000

July 1 Paid creditors full amount outstanding.

2 Food stocks bought on credit, £9,000.

31 Operations during July:

	£
Meal sales – cash	2,000
– credit	8,000
Food costs – cash	1,000
– from stock	4,000
Wages and other expenses – cash	2,000

Prepare:
   (a)   tabulated balance sheets at each date;
   (b)   a balance sheet at 31st July showing net current assets;
   (c)   a profit statement for the quarter.

2–14   The following information relates to a catering establishment
       for the year ended 31st December 1992:

	£000s
Sales	300
Other expenses	42
Aggregate depreciation – fixed assets –	
31st December, 1991	120
Current liabilities	12
Owner's capital	330
Cost of goods sold	120
Annual depreciation expense	6
Current assets	18
Wages	72
Long-term liabilities	210
Fixed assets at cost	720

Prepare a trial balance, a profit statement for the year ended 31st
December 1992 and a balance sheet as at that date.

Further reading

1. Anthony, R. N., *Management Accounting Principles*, Richard D.
   Irwin, Inc., Chapters 2 and 3.
2. Bull, R. J., *Accounting in Business*, 5th edition, Butterworths
   (1984), Chapters 1–5.
3. Glautier, M. W. E., and Underdown, B., *Accounting Theory and
   Practice*, 3rd edition, Pitman Publishing (1986).
4. Zeff, S. A., and Keller, T. F., *Financial Accounting Theory*,
   3rd edition, McGraw Hill (1985).

Chapter Three

Accounting: The Conceptual Framework

Accounting is essentially a practical activity that has developed over the centuries. Of the concepts that have evolved some are enforceable by law whilst others are but recommended procedures. An understanding of accounting concepts is invaluable as they provide a guide to the purpose of the balance sheet and at the same time highlight the problems encountered in valuing business assets and the profit generated.

The term concept has a number of synonyms, one being principle, but no purpose would be served here attempting to compare them. Concepts are general ideas which have developed slowly through experience. Early accounting systems were intended to serve a limited range of purposes and had no need of the many concepts which are important today.

It is useful to place accounting concepts into two groups (see Exhibit 3–1).

(a) accounting system design concepts;
(b) accounting operational concepts.

An attempt has been made to place the first group into a logical sequence relating to the setting up of an accounting system. Initially concepts are considered which deal with the inputs to the system in the form of recorded transactions and end with outputs associated with the summaries produced. There is little room to argue here, for recording and summarizing the end of period accounts should be in line with these concepts. The three operational concepts, however, are open to different interpretations because of the subjective nature of the ideas.

Accounting systems design concepts

Business entity

This concept concerns the boundary around the area of economic activity of the business unit for which accounting reports are prepared. In starting a business a sole trader for convenience regards his business operations as a separate entity from his personal finances. All accounting records are maintained in relation to the business and not the owner. A limited company is a legal entity which is clearly defined and this ensures accounting arrangements are separate from the owners who are shareholders.

It is implied in setting up a business entity that business will be conducted which will require financial measurement. This is the main object of the accounting system.

Exhibit 3–1

Accounting: Systems Design Concepts

1. What is to be accounted for and reported upon?	1. Operations of a *business entity*.
2. Is it expected to have a long life?	2. Yes. A *going concern* is assumed.
3. What is to be recorded concerning the entity?	3. *Measurable business transactions*.
4. What unit of measurement is to be used?	4. A *monetary unit*, a relatively stable measure.
5. How are transaction amounts to be determined?	5. Using *objectivity*, i.e. unbiased and verifiable.
6. What is the essential structure of the main report?	6. A *dual aspect* of assets and liabilities forming a balance sheet.
7. How frequently are reports to be prepared?	7. At least annually, introducing a *time period*.
8. How are items to be related to time periods?	8. *Accruals* or *matching* concept.
9. What essential information is to be reported?	9. (a) The *worth of the entity* in the form of net assets. (b) *Profit* or *loss* made in the period measured in two complementary ways: (i) sales revenue less expenses; (ii) change in net assets over time, assuming no additional investment or distribution to the owner.

Accounting: Operational Concepts

1. What is the criterion for deciding whether some item is classed as an asset or an expense?	1. *Materiality*.
2. Is the book value of an asset overstating its future worth to the business?	2. *Prudence* or *conservatism*.
3. Can figures be sensibly compared over several years?	3. *Consistency*.

Going concern

A basic assumption is that in the absence of evidence to the contrary, a business will continue to operate into the foreseeable future. This affects the valuation of assets and liabilities for end of year reporting. Fixed assets for instance are used in the business to generate profit next year and should be valued in this light.

The going concern concept is therefore related to the accruals concept which requires a fixed asset cost to be allotted to the time periods benefiting from this item. A different and probably lower value would be placed on kitchen equipment, for instance, if it were valued on the basis of a forced sale because the business was about to close down.

Further concepts affect end of period values such as the prudence concept which takes into account inevitable future uncertainties. Nevertheless, the going concern is implicit in the valuation whatever further concept is superimposed on it.

Measurable business transactions

Relations between the business and parties outside the business are carried on by means of identifiable, separable and measurable transactions. Transactions are recorded in the books of account, summarized and presented to interested parties.

Monetary unit

This concept states that only those business transactions which can be expressed in monetary terms are recorded in the accounts. The reason is, of course, that money provides the only common language into which diverse events may be translated. This concept is basic to all accounting records. Although a common language, money no longer provides a stable measurement and throughout this work reference will be made to the effects of inflation which need to be allowed for in many business situations.

Objectivity

This concept requires that recorded accounting data be free from bias in so far as there has been objective establishment of value determined by the market place. Objective evidence for the purchase of bar fittings will be in the form of an invoice which may be verified.

Historical costs of purchases are recorded and processed through the accounting system, laying a firm foundation for the initial valuation of assets at the end of a period. However, this value, after allowing for depreciation, may be adjusted when assets are valued for balance sheet presentation purposes.

The dual aspect of assets and liabilities

This concept was illustrated in Chapter 2 where it was shown that;

Capital + Liabilities = Assets

To facilitate the preparation of a balance sheet a system of double entry is used by all but the smallest businesses. Indeed, the law requires that public companies maintain their accounts on the double entry principle, although small hotels and restaurants may use single entry when final accounts are prepared from so-called 'incomplete records'.

Time period

Three major reasons require businesses to account for their profit at least annually. They are:

(a) All businesses pay tax on profits and this requires an annual report of their financial affairs.
(b) Legislation requires that company directors present annual accounts of their stewardship for the benefit of shareholders.
(c) Managing a business effectively demands frequent knowledge of how operations are financially progressing so as to maintain control.

Although the income tax year ends on 5th April the twelve month accounting period of the business is determined by its owners or directors. Control of the business might require shorter accounting periods of quarters, months or weeks.

At the end of the accounting year, accounts including a balance sheet and profit and loss account are prepared, and they are called either end of year accounts or final accounts.

Accruals or matching concept

This concept, which is automatically complied with when annual accounts are prepared, was considered in the last chapter. Revenue and costs are accrued, that is recognized and recorded as they are earned and incurred, not as money is received or paid. The profit statement for a period shows the profit which is the value of sales less the matching expenses, and it is noted that cash movements *do not* affect profit directly.

Owner's worth and profit concept

Concepts so far have concerned the inputs of the accounting system which, having been summarized, become the outputs of the system, providing the owner with financial information regarding the worth of his business and the profit generated.

The dual aspect of accounting being established, it has been seen that annual balancing is necessary in the life of a business. This gives rise to the concept of accruals or the matching concept which, in association with the dual aspect concept, determines the basis for finding at any time:

(a) the worth of the entity in the form of net assets;
(b) profit or loss made in a period, measured in two ways:
    (i) sales revenue less expenses incurred, and
    (ii) change in the value of net assets over time (assuming no additional investment or distributions to the owner).

This concept results from assembling the previous system design concepts into a structure and reflects the relationships associated with the balance sheet and profit and loss account.

Accounting operational concepts

Materiality

This concept recognizes that precision in reporting financial results is not always desirable because of the cost to achieve it may far outweight the benefits. At the end of the year a tin of spices in the kitchen store is conceptually an asset because it will be used to benefit sales in the next period. However, in practice, because of its low relative value it might for accounting purposes be regarded as an expense when purchased. The effect on profit therefore is one criterion of materiality, although there is no hard and fast rule to adopt.

Conservatism or prudence

This concept states that it is better to understate asset values and consequently profit than to overstate them because understatement has fewer unpleasant effects than overstatement. Railway companies in the last century often did not depreciate locomotives and even appreciated their values by adding repair charges. This is clearly wrong, for profits were thereby overstated and excessive dividends paid, reducing the real net asset value of the companies.

The application of this concept is a reaction to the uncertainty of the future. Future profits should not be anticipated, but possible future losses should be provided for. An hotel shop with jewellery stock which cost £3,000 but is now out of fashion might be expected to sell it for only £2,000 next year. Balance sheet value for this stock should therefore be only £2,000.

Consistency

Data cannot easily be compared unless they have been drawn up on a consistent basis. For accounting reports to be of material benefit to the user, the practices and procedures adopted to prepare them should be consistent from period to period. Modifications to practices, however, are sometimes necessary and such changes should be communicated to all interested parties.

Comments on concepts

Accounting world-wide is experiencing rapid changes to both inputs and outputs of accounting systems. Input changes are associated with computer technology, although such changes have not affected the accounting system design concepts. Such concepts are so fundamental that they help to retain the balanced overview so necessary when systems change. They still are essential to the stewardship function.

Some changes to the outputs of accounting systems have been brought about by demands for more valuable financial information. Whilst some of these changes have been adjustments to final accounts, others have meant the preparation of additional statements and the disclosure of information not previously made available to those outside the company. Disclosure of additional information has not been restricted to financial information.

Although the concepts of money measurement and objectivity remain firm as essential to the recording of transactions, money measurement using historical cost has become unsatisfactory from the presentation point of view because of rapid inflation in the mid 1970s. The concept of consistency has been adhered to by recording historical cost but inflation has distorted values over the years, making supplementary statements to final accounts desirable.

Methods of overcoming this problem have been proposed, but in 1986 no one method for a long-term solution had been recommended and approved by either professional accounting bodies or government. Low inflation in the mid eighties made a solution reporting inflation-adjusted accounts less urgent. Reference is made to this in Chapter 19.

Accounting information is used for a wide range of purposes, many of them economic, and concepts need to be used which are relevant to the purpose. Whilst the objectivity concept recognizes an asset's original cost which is relevant for taxation purposes, other concepts such as prudence admit other values which reflect its worth to the business.

Concepts considered in this chapter concern the preparation and presentation of annual accounts. Much of this work deals with the financial aspects of the planning and control of business operations which the annual accounts measure in total. These matters require the use of further concepts which are covered in Chapter 5.

Questions and problems

3–1 What do you understand by the term 'business entity'?

3–2 In accounting only those business transactions which can be expressed in monetary terms are recorded. Why?

3–3 In what sense is the term 'objectivity' used in accounting?

3–4 Explain, using simple arithmetical examples, the 'accruals' or 'matching' concept.

3–5 How are the 'going concern' concept and the 'accruals' concept related?

3–6 Distinguish between 'accounting system design concepts' and 'accounting operational concepts'.

3–7 Do you consider an understanding of the conceptual framework to be important when dealing with practical matters of accounting? Why? Give examples.

Further reading

1. Sidebotham, R., *Introduction to the Theory and Context of Accounting*, Pergamon Press; Chapter 3.
2. As per Chapter 2 reading list.

Chapter Four

Introduction to Financial Planning and Control

Profit is achieved by the effective management of all available resources, which are basically people and finance, and an important aim of the accounting function is to supply information that will aid management in the effective use of such resources. A management accounting system, accordingly, provides information on which managers can better manage, and because it measures profit and decisions affecting profit, should embrace all matters stated in monetary terms.

Planning aspects

Much management accounting work involves the preparation of routine statements to show whether the business is running as planned, an important function, but one which is rendered relatively ineffective if the plan itself is poor. A frequent business failing is the inability to be adaptive at management level although first-class routine control information is provided at the operating level. The result is efficient performance of bad plans.

This situation may be illustrated by comparing the results of Restaurants A and B for a 12-month period (year 2) shown in Exhibit 4–1 (overleaf).

Restaurant A's management planned to improve profit from £10,500 in year 1 to £15,000 in year 2, but in the event, turnover fell short of budget and food costs increased to 52% of sales, resulting in a profit of £12,600.

Restaurant B's management pursued a policy of no change, concentrating its efforts on repeating year 1 results. Although food costs were controlled to 50% of sales, turnover increased and profit was £600 above year 1.

Which restaurant would you say was better managed?

To give a sensible answer requires a study of facts not present in this simple profit statement, although it might be said that if all other financial factors, such as working capital and property values, were identical, then Restaurant A's management did the better job in increasing profit by £2,100 in the year compared with B's increase of only £600.

Factors to be taken into account in assessing the results of A and B would include:

(a) If A's profit has been achieved without additional investment, e.g. by better service or a pricing policy change, then existing resources have been more effectively managed and A's management is probably better than B's.

(b) If A spent £60,000 on additional facilities in the year, the extra return of £2,100 (3½%) might be regarded as a disappointment. However, the payoff may be expected in year 3 and A's management may therefore be reasonably satisfied with year 2 results.

(c) How are future profits likely to be affected by decisions taken in the year? A decision not to redecorate might adversely affect year 3 turnover and therefore profit.

(d) Is the business in a position to settle its suppliers' bills as they fall due? A might not, even though an improved profit has been recorded. Sight of the balance sheet might help with this answer.

(e) From what sources have finances been obtained? One restaurant may be paying more for its capital than the other because of poor management.

(f) Has the increase in food costs of A been the result of a policy change, increased food prices, or increased wastage? If wastage was the cause then management has been at fault.

(g) What has been the rate of inflation in the year? If 6% occurred in year 2 B might be worse off than in year 1 because £630 extra profit would be required to offset the fall in the value of money.

Most of these questions and many more can be answered by means of a good management accounting system which helps to quantify the effect of management plans and results.

It might be argued that management of Restaurant B has failed to be adaptive in not benefiting sufficiently from an expanding market, partly through too much attention to the control side. In the 1960s, Trust Houses suffered on the one hand because there was no forward plan for the group as a whole, and on the other hand, the detailed control over hotel managers was so tight that it destroyed initiative.

It is clear in modern management where competition is keen, that the successful management is flexible in outlook, plans with care yet takes calculated risks, trying to anticipate its customers' requirements, the labour market and availability of finance.

How then can an understanding of the financial side of the business help the manager to plan more effectively? Basically in two ways:

(a) Participating in routine annual budgeting will highlight important relationships existing between management functions, co-ordination of which help in the smooth running of operations and optimization of profit.
(b) Participating in the preparation of statements showing the effect on overall business profit of alternative courses of action, will give the manager confidence in seeking profitable opportunities.

The extent to which (a) and (b) above are formalized depends upon the size of the business, for the smaller undertaking will require a simple system; yet these two parts of the planning operation, routine budgeting and *ad hoc* profit studies, are relevant to even the smallest business.

It will be seen that at any time a business opportunity may be discovered which, when evaluated in terms of return on investment, is either rejected or accepted as falling in line with laid down policy and built into the next budget.

Planning for profit involves not only seeing that there is a surplus of revenue over costs, but also that sufficient cash and stock is available when needed, and that finance is obtained from the right source, i.e. that expansion involving purchase of accommodation and other long-term assets is not paid for by short-term credit, but from long-term sources such as the issue of shares, debentures and

Exhibit 4–1

Profit Statement

	Year 1 Actual		Year 2 Budget		Year 2 Actual	
Restaurant A	£	%	£	%	£	%
Revenue	51,000	100	60,000	100	57,000	100
Food costs	25,500	50	30,000	50	29,400	52
GROSS MARGIN	25,500	50	30,000	50	27,600	48
Other costs	15,000	29	15,000	25	15,000	26
PROFIT	10,500	21	15,000	25	12,600	22
Restaurant B						
Revenue	51,000	100	51,000	100	52,200	100
Food costs	25,500	50	25,500	50	26,100	50
GROSS MARGIN	25,500	50	25,500	50	26,100	50
Other costs	15,000	29	15,000	29	15,000	29
PROFIT	10,500	21	10,500	21	11,100	21

retained profit. The oldest financial mistake in the world is borrowing short-term and investing long-term.

Control considerations

Whilst the importance of a good plan is stressed, *control* of costs, revenue, stocks, and cash is essential in order to avoid unnecessary loss and wastage leading to falling profit. Hotel and catering businesses are generally alive to the needs of good control routines, especially when concerned with the day-to-day control of food, sales and cash where underages and overages can be quickly identified and speedy action taken to bring the position back under control if at all possible. Such control procedures are largely to avoid fraudulent use of the assets involved, but are only a part, although an important part, of the overall control system of the business which aims to help supervisors and managers achieve planned results. Results need to be quantified for comparison with planned performance and may be, for example, number of portions for day-to-day control. Somewhere along the line the measurement must be in value as it flows through the management accounting system so that management can see the overall picture of departmental and company performance.

This overall picture is achieved by means of an operating statement which shows actual and budgeted departmental revenues and costs and other hotel income and costs; in other words it is a profit and loss statement used for control purposes. An attempt is made to use budgets to help those responsible to control revenue and costs at departmental and hotel levels. Exhibit 2–6 shows a pro forma operating statement with control levels as recommended by the Uniform System of Accounts for Hotels. Since any change in revenue or cost directly affects planned profit, investigation of the significant variances is most important to enable management to rectify the position if results are adverse or to exploit the position if results become favourable. A significant adverse food cost caused by a national price rise might call for selling price revision whereas a favourable turnover compared with budget, after investigation, may lead to the discovery of an untapped source of customers.

Control of assets such as cash and stocks is aided only to a limited extent by comparison between actual and budget figures, since this only indicates whether policy in relation to levels of cash and stock holding is being achieved. More important, as mentioned earlier, is the stewardship function in maintaining accurate records of purchases and sales and ensuring that adequate physical control is exercised to avoid fraud.

Monthly and cumulative operating statements showing value and percentages help to indicate how the business is performing against budget, and may be said to be an internal control mechanism.

In recent years control has been aided by comparison with other hotels of percentages and ratios designed to indicate one's position relative to other similar establishments. This external control facility illustrates the continuing communication between the planning and control functions, for the greatest benefit is the guide management receives in setting better targets in areas where the business is producing a relatively poor performance.

Questions and problems

4–1 Explain why a good financial plan is important to any business regardless of the size of the undertaking.

4–2 A profit plan needs to ensure not only that sufficient profit will result, but also that there will be enough stock and cash available. Is a lack of cash more critical than making a loss? Explain.

4–3 Using assumed figures, explain why a business which has fallen short of a planned profit may be in a more satisfactory position than another business which has successfully repeated last year's results.

4–4 Should the current year's profit be the sole criterion of a successful management? Explain.

Chapter Five

Cost Behaviour

There are several ways of classifying costs, each depending on the object of the exercise. For present purposes three will be discussed and illustrated in Exhibit 5–1.

Exhibit 5–1   Three Cost Classifications

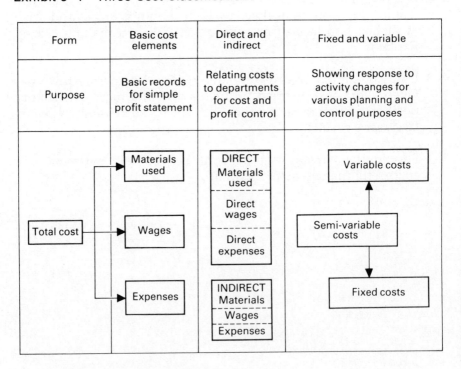

Basic elements of cost

This represents the most fundamental form of classification. Here costs are identified in terms of the basic resources of materials, labour and expenses necessary to produce a product, e.g a meal. Thus, in the case of a restaurant, materials in the form of food are purchased and subsequently labour effort and food production facilities, comprising chefs/waiters and equipment/kitchens, are expended to convert the raw material into a finished product. This form of grouping has traditionally been considered as a convenient way of assembling costs for general profit and loss presentation.

Direct and indirect costs

This method of classification is used for management control purposes. Direct costs are those which can be directly identified with a particular product, department or saleable service. Hence, the cost of direct materials, e.g. food, deducted from food sales provides the means to ascertain the all-important gross profit percentage figure which is one of the most widely used management control statistics in the catering industry. Residual figures like gross profit allow managers to monitor departmental profitability. Direct wages can frequently be identified with departments. For example, food production and service personnel are clearly associated with food departments, housekeepers and roomservice staff with accommodation departments, and so on. In the case of expenses, these tend to be mainly indirect costs termed 'overheads' (or 'burden' in the USA), which by definition cannot be identified with a particular product, department or service. Numerous costs fall into the overhead category, key examples being rent, rates, loan interest, and salaries. An example of a direct expense, however, is the one-off rental by an hotel of audio-visual equipment for a specific conference. It therefore becomes apparent that the classification of costs into direct and indirect groups provides a basis for assigning cost responsibility and accountability to departments or segments of a business.

Fixed and variable costs

This classification of costs is primarily used for management planning decisions. It is a crucial group in that it allows an insight into how costs behave in different circumstances. For instance, managers want to know how costs are likely to vary in response to a given change in activity.* In order to answer this and other similar kinds of question cost behaviour patterns are identified.

A variable cost is one which in total tends to vary in proportion to changes in volume of activity during a period, e.g. cost of food and beverages. So, in the case of a restaurant business where the food

---

* The term 'activity' refers to some productive activity such as dishes prepared, meals sold, rooms occupied.

cost is £2 per meal the variable cost of 5,000 and 10,000 meals sold will be £10,000 and £20,000 respectively (depicted in Exhibit 5–2).

Exhibit 5–2   Graph showing variable cost

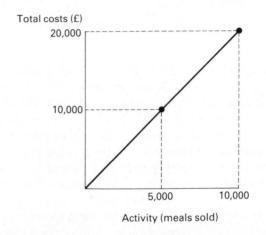

As fixed cost is one which in total accrues in relation to the passage of time and that, within limits, tends to be unaffected by fluctuations in activity (output or turnover) during a period, e.g. rates, insurance and salaries. Thus assuming the above restaurant incurs a fixed cost of £10,000 per annum the cost will tend to remain constant over the period regardless of whether the volume of meals sold is 5,000 or 10,000 (depicted in Exhibit 5–3).

Exhibit 5–3   Graph showing fixed cost

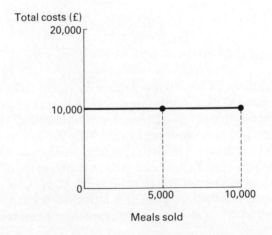

In addition to the wholly fixed and variable costs there are the semi-variable (or mixed) costs which contain both fixed and variable elements. This kind of cost is partly affected by fluctuations in volume during a period, but not proportionately so, e.g. wages, electricity, and laundry. Therefore, if the restaurant incurs an electricity cost of £1,000 at an activity level of 5,000 meals sold then it could expected to incur a cost of (say) £1,500 at a level of 10,000 meals (depicted in Exhibit 5–4).

Exhibit 5–4 Graph showing semi-variable cost

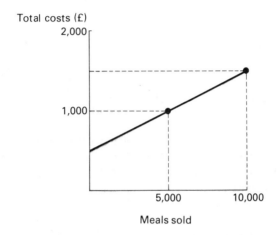

The relevant range

An important factor that should be taken into account in the analysis of cost behaviour is that the extent of the pattern (or line) of the cost function can only be ascertained from the data of a particular firm. Thus, the way in which a cost behaves outside the known data becomes a matter for conjecture. For example, in the case of fixed costs such as salaries, they may be applicable to an activity range of 5,000 to 10,000 meals sold per month, but it is possible they may change substantially if business increases or decreases beyond that range. The effect of this on the cost pattern is illustrated in Exhibit 5–5.

The relevant range concept is critical when management is contemplating significant reductions or increases in activity levels. However, where this is not so then, as in this case, the fixed cost is acknowledged to be £10,000 and will normally be depicted as per Exhibit 5–3.

An assumption frequently made in investigations of cost behaviour is that the cost functions are linear, i.e. take the form of a continuous straight line. If cost functions are curvilinear then cost computations can become extremely complex. Partly as a result of this, linear approximations, within the relevant range of activity

Exhibit 5–5   Graph showing the relevant range

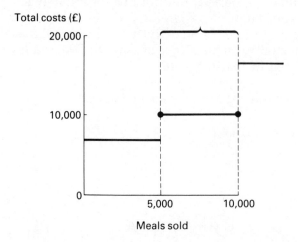

Meals sold

experienced by particular firms, are often used to simplify the calculations. Furthermore, the practice is not unreasonable, as a number of statistical studies have shown linear approximations to be realistic interpretations of cost behaviour patterns.

Total costs and unit costs

Another important aspect worthy of attention is the way in which costs are presented and interpreted. Until now discussion has centred on costs in 'total'. Fixed cost and variable cost imply *'total fixed cost'* and *'total variable cost'*. Interest has focused on how fixed and variable costs respond in total to changes in activity level. In addition, though, costs may be presented in terms of a single 'unit', e.g. cost per meal. So what are the implications of total cost and unit cost determination? This can be considered by utilizing data from the previous exhibits in Exhibit 5–6.

Exhibit 5–6   Total and unit costs

No. meals sold:	5,000	per unit	10,000	per unit
Variable costs:	£10,000	£2	£20,000	£2
Fixed costs:	£10,000	£2	£10,000	£1

Observation of Exhibit 5–6 shows that over the relevant 5,000 to 10,000 range of activity, variable costs increase, whereas fixed costs remain constant. However, over the same range variable cost *per unit* remains constant at £2 per meal, but fixed cost *per unit* reduces from £2 to £1 per meal. The variable cost per unit, e.g. food cost, remains at about £2 *per meal* regardless of the number of meals sold.

In contrast, the fixed cost *per unit*, e.g. salaries, grows smaller as it is spread over a larger number of meals. It is possible to summarize the total and unit responses of fixed and variable costs as shown in Exhibit 5–7.

Exhibit 5–7   Total and unit cost behaviour

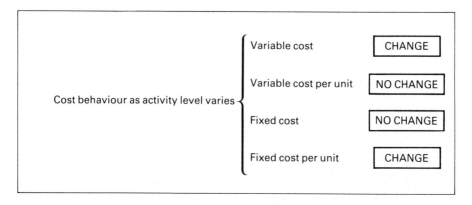

The recognition of 'total' and 'unit' costs is essential to the decision-making process, but care should be exercised in assessing and evaluating opportunities where the reports draw upon these measurements of cost, particularly when unit costs are present. Unit costs are average costs and there is the danger of interpreting total unit cost, i.e. fixed plus variable unit costs, as if they are exclusively variable. Emphasis has already been placed on the fact that fluctuations in activity will affect variable costs, but fixed cost will remain the same. Thus, in a case where activity is increasing then the total unit cost will *reduce* to the extent by which the fixed cost element is shared by a greater number of products. In other words, it is not possible to take the total unit cost predicted for one level of activity and simply multiply it by another level of activity and expect to obtain a meaningful cost prediction. The important point to bear in mind when dealing with unit costs is that they should be handled with caution.

Semi-variable cost patterns

In practice, semi-variable costs display a variety of behaviour patterns in response to changes in volume. One such is the step cost where, for example, an additional restaurant service person has to be engaged to serve a small range of extra covers, all for the extra wage. This gives rise to the 'step' effect as illustrated in Exhibit 5–8(a). Intepretation of the cost behaviour pattern in terms of it being a fixed or variable cost depends primarily on the width of the step.

Exhibit 5–8 Graphs showing step-variable cost

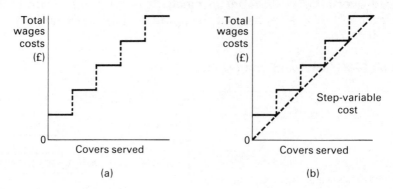

(a)　　　　　　　　　　　(b)

In the case of food service staff wages the underlying trend suggests the cost can be interpreted as a variable cost as illustrated in Exhibit 5–8(b). Where a cost displays a step which encompasses a larger proportion of the relevant range of activity then it would be appropriate to regard it as a fixed cost as illustrated in Exhibit 5–9.

Exhibit 5–9 Graph showing step-fixed cost

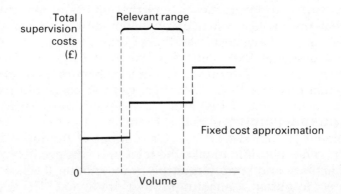

The above examples have highlighted two semi-variable cost patterns so as to illustrate how a pragmatic approach can be taken in the analysis of cost behaviour in order to classify costs into fixed and variable groups. The benefits from identifying the fixed and variable categories are numerous and are considered in Chapter 9, but the problem arises of actually placing *all* costs into these two categories. For decision-making purposes the third category, i.e. semi-variable costs, should be eliminated by apportioning them into their fixed and variable components.

Various methods are available for approximating semi-variable cost behaviour functions. These are discussed and evaluated in the following sections.

Accounts analysis method

With this method the historical accounting records are examined and each cost is arbitrarily classified into one of the three behavioural categories, i.e. fixed, semi-variable and variable. The classification is usually based on some predetermined independent variable, such as room occupancy or covers sold, and relevant range of activity. Using judgement and experience the costs in the semi-variable category are then apportioned, item by item, into their fixed and variable components. Often the person closely involved with a cost item can give a fair estimate of the cost behaviour, such as the house engineer estimating the variability in consumption of heat, light and power.

This is a highly subjective process of cost analysis as the classification is heavily reliant on personal judgement. The subjectivity can, however, be reduced to some extent by studying how the costs tend to respond over a number of periods before committing them to particular categories. Where costs, or cost components, are largely fixed or variable the method can be acceptable, but if this is not so semi-variable costs should be subjected to one or more of the objective statistical methods discussed later.

An important aspect with this approach is that the method can be used in two ways. It can form an end in itself in that approximate cost functions can be determined by examination and judgement, or it can provide the first stage for a more analytical approach to the study of cost behaviour.

High and low points method

The aim of this and other statistical methods discussed below is to measure the average change in one variable, designated the 'dependent variable' (y) e.g. cost, that is associated with a unit increase in the value of another variable, known as the 'independent variable' (x), e.g. number of rooms. The dependent variable is then expressed as a function of the independent variable.

The high and low points method is a fundamental statistical method which establishes a cost–volume relationship from past cost data.

To determine the fixed and variable elements of a particular cost two observations are identified at the two extreme activity levels within the relevant range. The points selected from the data are the highest and lowest points in terms of activity level. Normally these points also comprise the highest and lowest cost figures, but where this is not so the activity level is the deciding factor in making the selection.

The line that connects the points is assumed to be linear and the angle of the slope is taken to represent the variable cost per unit. It is also assumed that the extreme points of activity are representative of the intermediate points. In Exhibit 5–10(a) this is a valid assumption, but in Exhibit 5–10(b) it can be seen that the fixed cost can be substantially overstated.

Exhibit 5–10   Graphs showing high and low data points

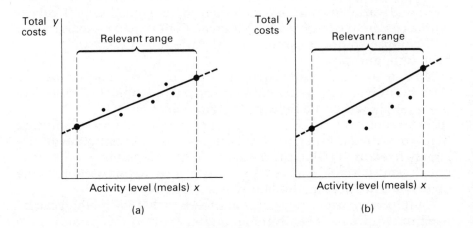

(a)   (b)

The procedure involved is equivalent to solving two simultaneous equations, based on the assumption that both data points fall on the locus of the true variable cost line. Below is an example using assumed data from the rooms department of an hotel:

Month	No. rooms sold	Overhead cost £
1	400	300
2	600	250
3	800	350
4	900	280
5	1,100	420
6	300	200
7	650	310
8	1,000	340

The first and most critical step is to plot the observations on a graph. This provides a visual insight into the data thereby giving an indication of the degree of association between variables and the linearity of the cost behaviour pattern. The plotted rooms and cost data are illustrated in Exhibit 5–11.

Exhibit 5–11   Graph showing hotel rooms and cost data

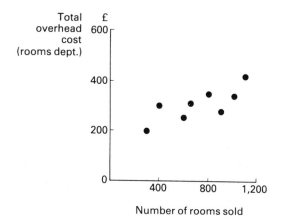

Number of rooms sold

It can be seen from the cost pattern that the room costs indicate a linear trend. The calculations are set out and explained below:

	Activity level (number rooms sold)	Total cost (overhead) £
High (month 5)	1,100	420
Low (month 6)	300	200
Difference	800	220

$$\text{Variable overhead cost per unit} = \frac{£220}{800}$$

$$= £0.275 \text{ per room sold}$$

Fixed cost calculation: £
   Total cost for (say) month 5   = 420.00
   Variable cost for month 5 = 1,100 × £0.275 = 302.50

          Fixed cost   = 117.50

As mentioned earlier, the slope of the line is taken to represent the variable cost per unit, in this case the variable overhead cost per room sold. Thus, to ascertain a total cost estimate for a given level of activity the following formula can be used:

Total cost = Fixed cost + Variable cost per unit × No. units

The formula is in effect the equation for a straight line and is usually expressed in the following form: $y = a + bx$

Substituting the hotel rooms data the estimating equation will appear as follows:

$$y = £117.5 + £0.275 \times \text{No. rooms}$$

So, to estimate the rooms department total overhead cost for month 9 based on (say) a sales forecast of 700 rooms the equation is applied as below:

$$y = £117.5 + £0.275 \times 700$$

Estimate total cost $= £310$

The high and low points method is simple to apply, but it is statistically questionable. It only uses two extreme data points which may represent abnormal rather than normal conditions, and disregards all others.

Scattergraph method

Again, this is a statistically based method which uses historical data to determine cost behaviour. The important difference between the scattergraph method and the high and low points method lies with the sample data used to ascertain the cost function. In this case all the observations are plotted and a straight line is fitted visually midway through the points.

As with the previous method, the form of the line is assumed to be linear and the angle is taken to signify the variable cost per unit. Using the hotel rooms data the graph, with a line fitted by visual inspection, might appear as illustrated in Exhibit 5–12.

Exhibit 5–12   Graph showing hotel rooms and cost data with line by visual fit

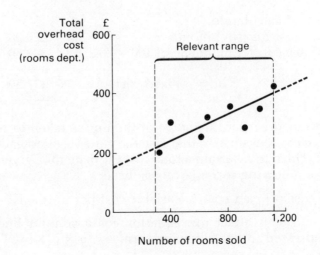

The fixed cost is the point at which the fitted line intersects the vertical axis. In this instance the freehand line shows a fixed cost of approximately £150. The total cost equation can now be estimated by ascertaining the total cost at any particular activity level and deducting £150 in order to give the variable cost element of the total cost. For example, at an activity level of 500 rooms, the total line indicates £280. Therefore variable cost is £280 − £150 = £130, the variable cost per room is £130/500 = £0.26, and the estimated total cost function becomes $y = £150 + £0.26x$.

A weakness of the scattergraph method is that without mathematically computing the line there are no objective tests than can be used to validate the fit in terms of it being the most accurate representation of the available data.

Linear regression method

An extension of the scattergraph approach, the mathematical technique knowns as 'the method of least squares' is used to determine the 'regression line of best fit' for a given set of data. It is based on the principle that the sum of the squares of the vertical distances from the regression line to the plots of the actual data points is less than the sum of the squares of the vertical distances from any other line which may be determined.

The linear regression equation which satisfies the above requirements is obtained from two 'normal equations' which must be solved simultaneously in order to derive values for a and b in the total cost function (represented by $y = a + bx$). The equations are as follows:

Equation 1: $\Sigma y = na + b\Sigma x$
Equation 2: $\Sigma xy = a\Sigma x + b\Sigma x^2$

where
a = fixed cost
b = variable cost per unit
n = number of observations
Σx = the sum of the observations of the independent variable (e.g. activity level)
Σy = the sum of the observations of the dependent variable (e.g. total cost)
Σxy = the sum of the product of each pair of observations
Σx^2 = the sum of the squares of the x observations.

The computations required to determine the total cost function for the hotel rooms department, using linear regression, are shown in Exhibit 5–13.

Exhibit 5–13

Month	Number rooms	Overhead cost			
	x	y	xy	x^2	y^2
1	400	300	120,000	160,000	90,000
2	600	250	150,000	360,000	62,500
3	800	350	280,000	640,000	122,500
4	900	280	252,000	810,000	78,400
5	1,100	420	462,000	1,210,000	176,400
6	300	200	60,000	90,000	40,000
7	650	310	201,500	422,500	96,100
8	1,000	340	340,000	1,000,000	115,600
	$\Sigma x = 5,750$	$\Sigma y = 2,450$	$\Sigma xy = 1,865,500$	$\Sigma x^2 = 4,692,500$	$\Sigma y^2 = 781,500$

Note: The y^2 column is not required for the regression equation computations, but it will be used later.

The computed figures can now be inserted in the equations as follows:

(1) $\quad 2,450 = 8a + 5,750b$
(2) $1,865,500 = 5,750a + 4,692,500b$

By multiplying equation (1) by 781.75, i.e. 5,750/8, the result is

(1) $1,760,937.5 = 5,750a + 4,132,812.5b$
(2) $1,865,500 \quad = 5,750a + 4,692,500b$

and by subtracting (1) from (2) gives:

$105,562.5 = 559,687.5b$
$\therefore b = 0.1886$

Substituting 0.1886 for b in (1) gives:

$2,450 = 8a + 1,084.45$
$\therefore a = 170.69$

The computed values of a and b can now be used to provide the straight line equation as:

$y = 170.69 + 0.1886x$

Therefore, the hotel rooms department overhead cost shows a fixed element of £171 and a (linear) variable element of £0.1886 per room sold. Note that it is acceptable to round-up the element of fixed cost as it is a 'total' figure and will, for practical purposes, not affect the amount. However, where 'unit' costs are determined the rounding of amounts below three or four decimal places can cause significant distortions to total cost forecasts. For instance, as part of the process of total cost calculation a variable cost per unit may be multiplied by anticipated sales volume figures of hundreds and frequently thousands of rooms which may result in the rounded-up amount being magnified to the extent that it provides a misleading set of total cost estimates. As always, unit costs should be handled with caution.

Correlation analysis

The use of linear regression allows a line of best fit equation to be computed which may be used to predict the future level of total costs. Having determined the equation the next step is to assess the quality of the fit of the line in relation to the particular set of data.

The quality or 'goodness of fit' of a regression line is measured by the coefficient of correlation, denoted by r, and can be computed from the following formula:

$$r = \frac{n(\Sigma xy) - (\Sigma x)(\Sigma y)}{\sqrt{[n(\Sigma x^2) - (\Sigma x)^2]}\sqrt{[n(\Sigma y^2) - (\Sigma y)^2]}}$$

The coefficient of correlation squared, r^2, is known as the 'coefficient of determination' and is an extensively used statistic in cost analysis. The coefficient of determination is a relative measure which indicates the percentage variation in total cost that is accounted for by the observed changes in activity levels. It varies from 0, which suggests no correlation, to ± 1, which indicates perfect correlation.

Exhibit 5–14 illustrates examples of different cost–volume relationships.

From this exhibit it is evident that the tighter the cluster of data points are along the regression line the better the fit and the higher the r^2 values. Negative correlation is shown, but rarely occurs in cost studies.

The computations required to determine the r^2 for the hotel rooms department overhead cost are as follows:

$$r = \frac{8(1,865,500) - (5,750)(2,450)}{\sqrt{[8(4,692,500) - (5,750)^2]}\sqrt{[8(781,500) - (2,450)^2]}}$$
$$= 0.791$$
$$\therefore r^2 = 0.624 \text{ or } 62.4\%$$

Therefore, about 62 per cent of the variation in the rooms department overhead cost can be explained by rooms sold. This does not suggest that the overhead cost is *directly* caused or affected by rooms sold, but that it can be explained by rooms sold. The remaining 38 per cent is explained by random variation and

Exhibit 5–14   Graphs showing various correlations

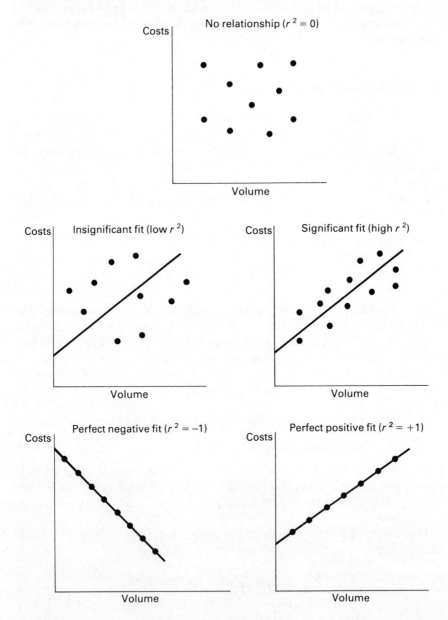

possibly other unknown variables. The result is statistically significant at a fairly high level of confidence and management could reasonably use rooms sold as a predictor of the hotel's room department overhead cost.* Ideally, r should be higher, e.g. 0.95,

---

* For illustration purposes the sample number of observations is small, i.e. 8, but in an industrial situation a large sample comprising 30 or more pairs of observations would normally be used.

giving $r^2 = 0.90$, but it is seldom the case that a single variable will explain such a high percentage of cost variation.

If, in the light of these results, management wished to identify more than 62 per cent of the overhead cost then it is possible to do so by the inclusion of additional independent variables to the regression equation, e.g. rooms department labour hours. The equation can be extended accordingly and takes the following general form:

$$v = a + b_1 x_1 + b_2 x_2 + \ldots + b_n x_n$$

This form of function is solved by using 'multiple linear regression' which provides the means to measure the joint effect of any number of variables on costs.

Other tests of reliability

The coefficient of determination provides an indication of the reliability of the estimate of a total cost function, but it does not give management an indication of the absolute size of a deviation from the regression line. This information is ascertained by determining the 'standard error of estimate' which gives the range of probable error associated with a particular total cost estimate, a useful indicator for budgeting and profit planning purposes.

In addition to producing a total cost estimate with a range of probable error, management may wish to know the reliability of the b coefficient, i.e. variable cost per unit. This can be assessed by computing the 'standard error of the regression coefficient' which gives the range of probable error associated with a particular b coefficient, useful for such purposes as product costing and pricing decisions.

Finally, it is essential for management to know if there is, in fact, any statistically significant relationship between the x and y variables. For example, the b coefficient for the hotel rooms suggests a change in overhead cost of £0.1886 for each additional room sold. The coefficient is an estimate of the 'population coefficient' and this particular sample may indicate a relationship, by chance, where none actually exists. In the event of there being no relationship then the b slope of the 'true' regression line would be zero, indicating the rooms department overhead is essentially a fixed cost.

The detailed method of these additional measures of reliability are beyond the scope of this book, but interested readers are referred to the references at the end of the chapter for further reading.* Problems incorporating these aspects have been included

---

* Particularly Horngren, C. T. and Foster, G., *Cost Accounting, A Managerial Emphasis*, 7th edn. Prentice-Hall International (1991), Ch. 25, pp. 783–805, and Drury, C., *Management and Cost Accounting*, Van Nostrand Reinhold (1985), Ch. 20, pp. 465–482.

along with the normal selection of questions and problems drawn from the main text.

Horngren points out that : 'A knowledge of how costs behave under a variety of influences is essential to intelligent predictions, decision making and performance evaluation.' This particularly includes various forms of costing, pricing, and budgeting and is fundamental to many other related aspects of financial planning and control of hotel and catering business activities discussed in subsequent chapters. Up until recent times many forms of cost analysis were laborious and uneconomic. However, with the developments in computer technology and the introduction of statistical software packages it is now commercially viable to pursue the understanding and use of cost estimation.

In the study of cost behaviour the critical area for managers to concentrate their efforts upon is not the derivation, manipulation and processing of the mathematical formulae, but the ability to evaluate the results and implications of the computed analyses.

Questions and problems

5–1   Explain what you understand by the 'elements of cost'.

5–2   Distinguish between 'direct' and 'indirect' costs and give examples of each.

5–3   Distinguish between 'fixed' and 'variable' costs.

5–4   What is a semi-variable cost?

5–5   Outline the various methods of identifying the fixed and variable elements of semi-variable costs.

5–6   A prospective client visited a banqueting suite to acquire a suitable menu quotation for his firm's annual dinner. For a single menu he was given the following quotations:

		selling price per head £
Menu 'D'	100 covers	3.00
Menu 'D'	150 covers	2.80
Menu 'D'	200 covers	2.65

Portion size and quality of the food and service were the same in all cases. Explain how it is possible for a banqueting suite to reduce the selling price per head simply because of an increase in the number of covers, and yet maintain the same net profit-to-sales ratio.

5–7 (a) Sketch a graph from which could be read the cost per unit at various levels of activity in respect of:

   (i) variable cost;
   (ii) fixed cost; and
   (iii) total cost.

   Label clearly each line on your graph.

   (b) 'Fixed costs are really variable. The more you produce, the less they become. ' Do you agree? Explain.

   (c) 'In the long term all costs are variable.' Explain.

   (d) Why is it necessary in practice to distinguish fixed costs from variable costs?

5–8 Below are details of a number of costs:
   1. Spirits used up at a constant cost per measure.
   2. Electricity charge consisting of a flat basic charge plus a variable charge after a minimum number of units have been used.
   3. Depreciation of equipment where the charge is calculated by the straight line method.
   4. Salaries of maintenance staff where 1 member of staff is required for 150 bedrooms or less, 2 members of staff for 151–300 bedrooms, 3 members of staff for 301–450 bedrooms and so on.
   5. Cost of wine in bulk, where the cost per litre decreases with each litre until a minimum cost per litre is reached.
   6. Laundry costs in an hotel which changes all its bedroom linen after each bednight.
   You are to match each cost with its relevant graph.

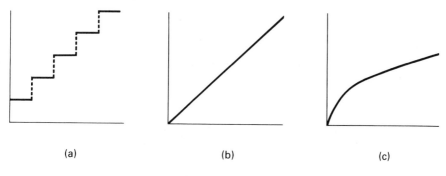

(a)   (b)   (c)

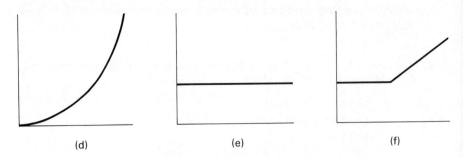

(d)   (e)   (f)

Note: The vertical (y) axis represents total cost and the horizontal (x) axis represents total activity.

5–9 Indicate which of the graphs best fits each of the items numbered below. The horizontal axis represents the total output/sales in units, e.g. rooms, meals, etc., and the vertical axis represents total cost. The graphs may be used more than once:

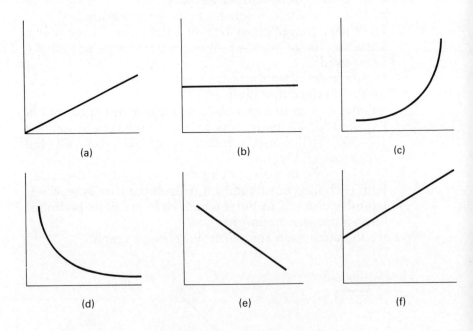

(a)   (b)   (c)

(d)   (e)   (f)

1. Total cost *per unit* of output/sales.
2. *Total* fixed cost.
3. Variable cost *per unit* of output/sales.
4. *Total* semi-variable (mixed) cost.
5. Fixed cost *per unit* of output/sales.
6. *Total* variable cost.

(HCIMA)

5–10 The actual number of rooms sold and the hotel maintenance cost incurred during the first four months of 1987 are as follows:

	No rooms sold	Hotel maintenance cost (£)
January	800	350
February	1,200	350
March	400	150
April	1,600	550

Required:

(a) Draw a scatter diagram.
(b) Compute the variable maintenance cost per room sold and fixed maintenance cost per month, consistent with the high and low method.
(c) Compute the variable maintenance cost per room sold and fixed maintenance per month, consistent with least squares regression analysis.
(d) Compute the coefficient of correlation (r) and the coefficient of determination (r^2).
(e) Discuss your results (a) to (d).

5–11 The financial controller of an hotel company believes there is some correlation between rooms sold per month and the actual monthly wages incurred by the rooms department. An assistant has suggested that a simple linear regression model be used to determine the wages cost behaviour of the rooms department. The regression equation shown below has been developed from 36 pairs of observations using the method of least squares. The regression equation and related measures are as follows:

$$y_c = £10,860 + £1.028 \text{ (NRMS)}$$

where y_c = total monthly rooms department wages, and NRMS = number of rooms sold.

Standard error of estimate: s_e	= 2,100
Standard error of coefficient: s_b	= 0.3787
Coefficient of correlation r	= 0.421

Required:

(a) Explain the meaning of '10,860' and '1.028' in the regression equation.
(b) Assume 6,000 rooms are budgeted to be sold for a given month. Compute the estimated cost of wages and the

range of values the actual wages cost can be expected to fall within if a 95 per cent confidence interval is specified.

(c) The financial controller wishes to use estimated numbers of rooms sold as the basis from which to predict the wages cost of the rooms department. Advise him.

(d) The rooms manager queries the regression equation given above. He argues that the rooms department wages cost is a discretionary fixed cost. Test the validity of his argument at the 95 per cent confidence level.

(e) When a simple linear regression model is used to make inferences about a population relationship from sample data, what assumptions must be made before the inferences can be accepted as valid?

5–12 Bayshore Hotel is aware that its energy costs are a semi-variable cost and over the last six months those costs have shown the following relationship with output:

Month	Rooms occupied	Total energy costs (£000s)
1	12	6.2
2	18	8.0
3	19	8.6
4	20	10.4
5	24	10.2
6	30	12.4

Required:

(a) Using the method of least squares, determine an appropriate linear relationship between total energy costs and rooms occupied.

(b) If total energy costs are related to both output and time (as measured by the number of the months) the following least squares regression equation is obtained:

Energy costs = 4.42 + 0.82 × Output + 0.10 × Month

where the regression coefficients (i.e. 0.82 and 0.10) have t-values of 2.64 and 0.60 respectively, and the coefficient of multiple correlation amounts to 0.976.

Compare the relative merits of this fitted relationship with the one you determine in (a) above. Explain how you might use the data to forecast total energy costs in month 7.

Further reading

1. Benston, G. J., 'Multiple regression analysis of cost behaviour', *The Accounting Review*, **41**, 4, pp. 657–672.
2. Drury, C., *Management and Cost Accounting*, Van Nostrand Reinhold (1985).
3. Harris, P. J., 'The application of regression and correlation techniques for cost planning and control decisions in the hotel industry', *International Journal of Hospitality Management*, **5**, 3 (1986), pp. 127–133.
4. Horngren, C. T. and Foster, G., *Cost Accounting: A Managerial Emphasis* (7th edn.), Prentice-Hall International (1991).
5. Kaplan, R. S., *Advanced Management Accounting*, Prentice-Hall International (1982).
6. Redlin, M. H., 'Energy consumption in lodging properties: applying multiple regression analysis for effective measurement', *The Cornell Hotel and Restaurant Administration Quarterly*, **19**, 4 (1979), pp. 48–52.
7. Spurr, W. A. and Bonini, C. P., *Statistical Analysis for Business Decisions* (revised edition), Richard D. Irwin, Inc. (1973).
8. Sizer, J., *An Insight into Management Accounting* (3rd edn.), Pitman (1989).

Chapter Six
Budgetary Preparation

An essential task performed by management is the planning of future business activities. This may involve identifying potential markets and developing suitable products and services to satisfy demand, or perhaps consolidating the current share of an existing market. Whatever the case, sound planning and monitoring of plans as they become reality is required if a business is at least to maintain its market position.

Planning can be divided into two main categories, namely long-term planning and short-term planning. Long-term planning, also referred to as 'strategic' or 'corporate planning', is concerned with the objectives of a business and the long-term plans to achieve the objectives. In the hotel and catering industry where capital investment is high for new projects, long-term plans for up to five and seven years are made. In general terms, however, long-term planning refers to periods beyond one year. Conversely, short-term planning is concerned with the present. Resources should be obtained and employed effectively within the framework of long-term planning decisions. The time period associated with short-term planning is one year. In order to obtain an overview of the relationship between long-term and short-term planning the process is presented in diagrammatic form in Exhibit 6–1.

Budgetary control

Reference to Exhibit 6–1 shows that budgetary control is born out of the short-term phase of the planning process. Having selected the course of action to be pursued this is translated into monetary terms and forms the basis of the annual budget. During the accounting period actual results are compared with budget and the differences, known as variances, are reported. Variances which are regarded as significant will be investigated with a view to taking corrective action and improving the situation for a future period. Thus, budgetary control is double-edged encompassing both a planning element and a control element. The present chapter concentrates on budgetary planning whilst the following chapter focuses on control.

Exhibit 6–1   Relationship between long-term and short-term planning

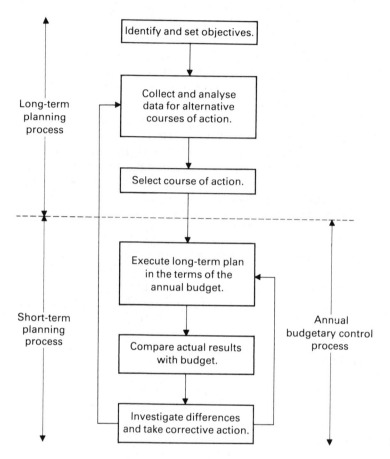

Advantages of budgeting

As with any system the benefits derived tend to correspond with the way in which it is implemented. Where budgets are administered with forethought and sensitivity the advantages are numerous:

(a) Budgets give a business direction. This flows from the fact that specific objectives are set which give management and staff something tangible to aim for.

(b) Budgeting compels management to plan. By thinking ahead it is likely that the best possible advantage can be gained from anticipating business conditions, and otherwise unforeseen problems can be avoided.

69

(c) Budgets provide management with a basis on which to measure subsequent performance. Although anticipating the future is fraught with problems, the preparation of budgets which take into account likely conditions is generally regarded as a more positive approach on which to compare actual performance. The alternative is the comparison of actual results with past performance which may contain inefficiencies and conditions irrelevant to the budget period.

(d) The budgeting process encourages communication between employees and the co-ordination of activities. It is said that no man (or woman) is an island, and seldom can this be truer than in the planning and organization involved in successfully producing and marketing a firm's products. The budget acts as a vehicle through which the activities of different parts of an organization can be integrated into an overall plan. For instance, departments such as production, purchasing and accounting will need to liaise to agree material specifications and stockholding requirements to satisfy forecast demand.

It is sometimes argued that budget preparation is too time consuming and costly to implement, but these are hollow arguments which are usually associated with autocratic or ill-conceived budgetary systems. In order to be viable in economic terms, the degree of sophistication of the budgeting process should correspond with the size, style and complexity of the particular organization.

Human factors

The human factor in a budgetary system is as complex as it is essential. A budget can be a useful device in influencing managerial behaviour and motivating managers to attempt to achieve predetermined targets. On the other hand, budgets can be divisive and prompt inefficiency and conflict between managers. Where managers have actively participated in budget preparation they are more likely to achieve the agreed objectives. This is particularly so if they believe that it will help them to manage their departments effectively. In these conditions the budget can act as a powerful, motivational device in providing a challenge which, if taken up positively is advantageous to the individual and the firm as a whole. Conversely, if budget preparation is mishandled and targets are totally imposed from above then the budget will usually be regarded as a threat rather than a challenge. In this kind of situation the targets are likely to be resisted and this may do more harm than good.

If top management wish to develop a budgetary system which will provide an effective vehicle through which to achieve stated objectives then they should demonstrate a genuine desire actively to involve managers in the process. Although this alone may not overcome the complexities that determine managerial behaviour, it should provide a positive working atmosphere in which to begin to understand matters such as personal aspirations and their relationship to achieving organizational goals!

Budget administration

In order to ensure the budgetary process operates efficiently budget approval procedures should be laid down.

The budget committee

The budget committee consists of senior managers who are responsible for the major functions in the organization. The committee will normally appoint a budget director or officer who will usually be an accountant. The budget director is responsible for co-ordinating the various budgets into the final budget for the whole organization. This provides the budget committee with an overview of the total annual budget whilst at the same time enables managers to see how their particular budgets relate to the overall planned position.

The work of the budget committee covers all aspects of the annual budget preparation and control. The committee set general guidelines which should be followed by individual managers producing their budgets. After the budgets are prepared they are submitted to the committee for approval. If a budget does not reflect a reasonable level of performance it will not be approved and the particular manager will be required to revise the content and resubmit it for approval. It is important that the manager who resubmits a budget should, to a large degree, agree with the amendments as it is he or she who has to achieve it. In cases where a manager remains unconvinced of proposed budget adjustments and the committee imposes changes, it is important that he or she at least feels that a fair hearing has been given. This is also important when disagreements occur between managers during budget preparation. In order to avoid a situation escalating into open conflict the budget committee should be seen to listen closely to both sides of the argument and arbitrate in an even handed manner. Budgeting is a bargaining process and, providing the budget reflects the organization's overall objectives, the budget committee should be prepared to give and take, and allow trade-offs between the different inputs submitted by managers.

After the budget committee has approved the individual budgets it will produce the final comprehensive budget known as the 'master budget'. This takes the form of a budgeted profit and loss statement and a budgeted balance sheet. The master budget is then passed to the board of directors for their approval.

When the organization enters the period covered by the budget the budget committee will receive monthly or quarterly reports, prepared by the accounting department, containing actual and budgeted results. The reports will be used by the committee to review performance and recommend corrective action as appropriate. The budget committee will also use the reports, together with its knowledge of the trading conditions experienced during the period of the budget, to formulate its guidelines for the coming year.

Budget manual

The budgeting process and procedures will normally be set out formally in a budget manual. The manual will describe the objectives, rules and regulations associated with the budgeting process and in addition, provide a useful source of reference to managers involved in the implementation of the budget programme. The detail includes instructions on what, when and how tasks should be carried out by managers. The manual should be circulated to all persons responsible for preparing budgets.

Limiting factors

A limiting factor may be described as a variable which impedes the operation or growth of business activities. In broad terms limiting factors include numbers of customers, materials, labour and capital. If unlimited amounts of these variables were available the profit potential of a firm would be infinite. However, all businesses suffer the shortage of one or more limiting factors and, therefore, prior to commencing budget preparation the limiting factors present in the particular firm should be identified. The main limiting factors associated with the hotel and catering industry are discussed below.

Sleeping capacity

Due to the nature of the accommodation product sleeping capacity is a particularly critical factor. 'Absolute perishability' is a characteristic of room letting. An unsold room is a sale lost for ever. Unlike many tangible products which if not sold immediately can be sold at some time in the future, there is only one opportunity to let a bedroom. Therefore, every unsold room has an immediate effect on annual profit.

Hotel and institutional sleeping capacity is essentially fixed. Once an establishment has been constructed it is a complicated and protracted process to change its capacity. Annual demand for hotel bedrooms may mathematically indicate that all the rooms available during a year can be let. The problem is that demand for accommodation fluctuates considerably leaving many rooms empty in some periods and potential guests being turned away in others. Hence, in a budgeting context, managers should pay close attention to how they can stimulate an even spread of demand for rooms.

Seating capacity

A somewhat similar situation to the accommodation problem can be identified in eating establishments, but they are not so severe. Restaurants and other types of dining facilities are relatively fixed in terms of capacity, but they do retain some flexibility in that seating arrangements can be altered to allow extra tables to be included at peak times. There is also the opportunity to adjust the numbers of covers on tables and also increase or reduce the length of tables to accommodate parties, etc. Nevertheless, as with room sales, the demand patterns must be taken carefully into consideration when budgeting food sales.

Bar capacity

Again, as with accommodation and eating establishments, drinking facilities are fairly fixed although by no means so critical as the previous two examples. When all the seats are taken in a bar customers are often prepared to stand, even in the most crowded conditions.

Customers

Sufficient numbers of customers is perhaps the most critical limiting factor to a business. Without an adequate demand for its products a firm will be starved of revenue and soon cease to exist. Thus, thorough market research studies and effective sales promotion activities should form the basis for developing forecasts of consumer demand patterns for incorporation in the sales budget. This factor, of course, goes hand in hand with the capacity factor.

Labour

The labour factor is double-edged. Not only have staff to be available for employment in sufficient numbers, but they also have to have the appropriate skills and experience. This is particularly important for the more upmarket establishments which require highly skilled chefs, waiters and bar staff. It can also prove difficult, however, to attract people to carry out the more mundane and laborious low-skilled tasks like washing-up and room servicing.

Capital

Obtaining funds to finance new projects or extend existing facilities is an important activity. This can take the form of long-term capital for construction purposes and short-term funds to finance working capital. If a firm enjoys a growth in demand with the potential to expand its activities, the failure to budget for adequate funds to finance operations can cause serious disruption and delay in realizing the benefits.

Management

The quality of management will often determine the degree of effect that the other limiting factors have on a business. The higher the quality of management the more effective they will be in running a business. Thus, it can be argued that the success or failure of a firm is ultimately in the hands of the managers.

Other factors

There are numerous other limiting factors present which could be discussed here, but the main ones, in so far as the hotel and catering industry is concerned, have been considered. Other factors would include availability of food and beverage materials, the kind of equipment in use or available, economic and political conditions, and so on.

Classification of budgets

Budgets can be grouped into two categories, namely 'operating budgets' and 'capital budgets'. Operating budgets relate to the anticipated revenue and expenditure associated with providing room, food and beverage products in the budget period, e.g. sales budget, food and beverage cost of sales budgets. Together the operating budgets form the budgeted profit and loss statement.

Capital budgets comprise capital items such as fixed assets, e.g. furniture and equipment, and working capital items, e.g. stocks, debtors and cash. The capital budgets are brought together to form the budgeted balance sheet. The diagram in Exhibit 6–2 illustrates the relationship of the various budgets which give the master budget.

Exhibit 6–2   Classification of budgets

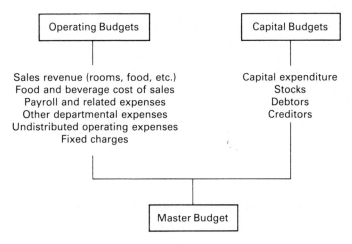

(Budgeted profit statement and balance sheet)

The various budgets presented in Exhibit 6–2 are for an hotel, but with modifications they can be related to any kind of hospitality concern.

Before discussing the methods of preparing the individual budgets an important principle should be borne in mind. Wherever feasible, *physical quantities* should be determined before calculating the revenue and cost values associated with them.

Sales revenue budget

This is the most important budget as it sets the pattern for *all* other budgets. Among other things it is particularly influenced by potential sales volume, sales mix and selling price policy.

Maximize gross profit/contribution margin

Sales revenue forecasts for rooms, food, beverages and other items are of only limited value until they are related to the cost of sales and resulting gross profit (or contribution margin when it is possible to identify fixed and variable costs). With the same number of rooms and floor space available as in the previous year management should plan to attract additional customers to fill spare capacity, or perhaps alter the proportions of space usage so that revenue which attracts higher gross profits is increased at the expense of space which returns lower gross profits.

Interdependence

When forecasting the total sales revenue for an establishment the *interdependence* of the various departments should be taken into account. For instance, in an hotel the estimated level of rooms revenue is likely to increase the level of food revenue because some guests can be persuaded to eat in. Estimate banqueting revenue may prompt an increase in rooms revenue because some members attending functions may have travelled long distances and wish to stay the night.

Sales forecasting considerations

Clearly, the importance of the sales revenue budget cannot be overemphasized. The care with which the estimates are developed will to some extent reflect in the costs and profits which accrue during the budget period. In order to assist in the preparation of a sales budget the following factors should be considered:

(a) past sales volume and mix;	(g) sales personnel;
(b) advance bookings;	(h) sales training;
(c) market research studies;	(i) sales promotion;
(d) capacity;	(j) competition;
(e) pricing policy;	(k) seasonality;
(f) relative product profitability	(l) local activities/events.

In addition to the above, account should be taken of the general economic, political and industrial outlook.

Food and beverage cost of sales budget

The cost of food, beverage and other sales are variable costs and can be determined by multiplying sales revenue by the expected percentage of cost to revenue. For instance, if food sales are forecast at £40,000 and the expected cost of sales is 40% of food revenue, then the budgeted cost will be £16,000 (i.e. £40,000 × 40%) leaving a gross margin of £24,000 or 60% of revenue. Because of the wide variety of continually changing menu items it is not normally practical to determine the physical quantities of food and beverage ingredients for the budget.

Payroll and related expenses budget

With this budget it is possible in some cases to compute the physical volume. This can be done by preparing staffing schedules which are based upon the forecast volumes of rooms and covers sold. The schedules are built up by determining the minimum number of permanent personnel which will need to be employed all year round and then ascertaining the additional staff required to service the level of business beyond which the number of permanent staff is not sufficient. The alternative approach is to calculate the figures in a similar way suggested for the food and beverage cost of sales budget by applying a predetermined percentage to revenue for each department.

Other departmental expenses budget

Again, this budget can be built up by estimating the costs associated with the level of volume, i.e. guest supplies determined by the number of rooms forecast in the sales budget. The alternative is to apply a percentage figure to revenue.

Undistributed expenses budget

This includes administrative and general, data processing, human resources (personnel), marketing, energy, and property operation department costs. The budgets are prepared by estimating the salaries and wages and other specific costs associated with the expected business. A fairly large proportion of these departmental budgets will contain permanent or predetermined costs.

Fixed charges budget

This budget is made up of management fees (contract), rates, interest and depreciation charges. The forecasts for rates and interest will, to a great extent, be determined by economic conditions, whereas the depreciation charge will be a matter of management policy. These costs are not directly related to sales revenue, but to the provision of the basic hotel and catering facility regardless of the level of business anticipated.

Cash budgeting

Cash is the life-blood of a business. Without sufficient amounts of cash to meet obligations a firm will soon find itself in serious financial difficulties.

A cash budget is a forecast of receipts and payments which is normally prepared on a monthly basis for the budget period. Sometimes there is confusion as to the difference between a cash budget and a budgeted profit and loss statement. A cash budget is solely concerned with the *timing* of cash receipts and payments during a period, whereas a profit and loss statement is concerned with the revenue and expenses which *accrue* during a period. This means that revenue and expenses are matched one with the other and dealt with in the period of the profit and loss statement irrespective of the period of receipt or payment. For instance, assume a budget period January–December. Part of the cash from estimated sales revenue generated in December will probably be collected in January and February the following year. The cash budget will show the anticipated amounts of cash expected to be received, from the December sales, under the appropriate months, i.e. December, January and February. The budgeted profit and loss statement will include the *total* sales revenue in December along with the other eleven months' revenue.

Only when all other operating and capital budgets have been prepared is it possible to produce the cash budget. The exception to this is where small businesses operate on a purely cash basis and, therefore, only need to prepare a cash budget.

Having prepared a cash budget it provides a useful overview of the inflow and outflow of cash during the budget period. From this management can be forewarned as to when cash shortages are likely to arise during the year, such as in peak periods, and, therefore, make appropriate overdraft arrangements in order to ensure the firm can meet its immediate commitments. A cash budget will also indicate when excessive surpluses of cash are likely to occur. With this knowledge managers can invest some of the surplus in secure short-term investments which are easily realizeable when cash is needed. (An example of a cash budget appears on page 80).

Budget preparation (existing business)

The following example shows that in the case of an existing

business the budgeting procedure begins with the present financial position, as shown by the balance sheet, then planned changes are applied and budgeted statements are derived. The assumed data for the Europe Hotel are set out below:

The balance sheet of the Europe Hotel at 31st March, 19X7 disclosed:

Liabilities	£000	Assets	£000	£000
Creditors	25	Cash at bank		3
Accrued expenses		Debtors		45
Heat and power	5	Food stocks		2
Loan interest	25	Beverage stocks		30
Long-term loan	400	Prepaid expenses		—
Owners' capital	1,600	Fixed assets at cost	2,947	
Retained profit	445	Less: Aggregate depn.	527	2,420
	2,500			2,500

The budget committee has agreed the following budgets for the three months ending 30th June 19X7.

Operating department revenue and expenses:

Month	Sales Revenue			Cost of Sales		Payroll and related expenses			Other expenses		
	Rooms	Food	Bev.	Food	Bev.	Rooms	Food	Bev.	Rooms	Food	Bev.
	£000	£000	£000	£000	£000	£000	£000	£000	£000	£000	£000
April	100	40	20	16	10	12	10	5	9	4	3
May	150	60	30	24	15	20	15	8	11	5	3
June	250	100	50	40	25	35	25	12	16	11	5

Undistributed operating expenses:

	Admin.		Marketing		Maintenance		Heat & Power	
	Payroll	Other	Payroll	Other	Payroll	Other	Payroll	Other
	£000	£000	£000	£000	£000	£000	£000	£000
April	2	1	1	1	2	1	1	2
May	2	1	1	1	2	2	2	3
June	2	1	1	1	3	2	3	4

Fixed charges per quarter:	£000
Rates and insurance	16
Loan interest (15% per annum)	15
Depreciation of fixed assets	30

Additional information:

(a) Half of all sales revenue is received in cash. The remaining half is on credit and is collected one month after the date in which the transaction was made.

(b) All food and beverage purchases are made on credit and the suppliers are paid in the month following the transaction.

(c) The gross profit on sales revenue is: Rooms 100%; Food 60%; Beverage 50%.

(d) Payroll and related expenses and other expenses are paid in the month in which they are incurred.

(e) Undistributed operating expenses are paid in the month in which they are incurred with the exception of heat and power which is paid one month in arrears.

(f) Rates and insurance are paid annually in advance on 1st April.

(g) Loan interest is paid half-yearly in arrears on 1st May and 1st November.

(h) The purchase and payment of a computerized reservation and accounting system is planned to take place during May, the cost and installation of which is estimated at £145,000.

(i) Food and beverage closing stock levels on 30th June 19X7 are expected to remain unchanged from the previous period.

The following statements have been prepared for the Europe Hotel: cash budget; budgeted profit statement; budgeted balance sheet.

The Europe Hotel
Cash Budget
for quarter ending 30th June 19X7

	April £000	May £000	June £000
Receipts:			
Total revenue: cash	80	120	200
credit	45	80	120
	125	200	320
Payments:			
Total purchases*	25	26	39
Payroll and related exp.	27	43	72
Other expenses	16	19	32
Admin. and general exp.	3	3	3
Marketing	2	2	2
Repairs and maintenance	3	4	5
Heat and power	5	3	5
Rates and insurance	64	—	—

cont.

cont.

Loan interest	—	30	—
Computerized system	—	145	—
	145	275	158
Month surplus/deficit	(20)	(75)	162
Opening balance	3	(17)	(92)
Closing balance	(17)	(92)	70

* *Note*: Where stock levels remain unchanged then purchases are equivalent to cost of sales.

Budgeted Profit Statement
for quarter ending 30th June 19X7

Operating departments	Sales revenue	Cost of sales	Payroll and related expenses	Other expenses	Profit (loss)
	£000	£000	£000	£000	£000
Rooms	500	—	67	36	397
Food	200	80	50	20	50
Beverage	100	50	25	11	14
Total	800	130	142	67	461

Less: Undistributed operating expenses:

Admin. and general expenses	6	3	9
Marketing	3	3	6
Repairs and maintenance	7	5	12
Heat and power	6	9	15
Total	22	20	42

Total profit before fixed charges	419

Less:

Rates and insurance	16
Loan interest	15
Depreciation of fixed assets	30
Total	61
Net profit	358

Budgeted Balance Sheet
at 30th June 19X7

Current liabilities:	£000	£000	Current assets:	£000	£000
Creditors	65		Cash at bank	70	
Accrued expenses:			Debtors	200	
Heat and power	7				
Loan interest	10	82	Stocks: Food	2	
			Beverage	30	
Long-term loan		400	Prepaid rates + ins.	48	350
Owners' Interest:			Fixed assets		
Capital 1/4/87	1,600		Existing assets	2,947	
Retained earnings	803	2,403	Computer system	145	
				3,092	
			Less: Accumulated depn.	557	2,535
		2,885			2,885

Budget preparation (new business)

When preparations are being made to open a new business the major problem usually encountered is the lack of historical operating data available for initial budget preparation. Ideally some form of market feasibility study should be undertaken in order to establish if there is sufficient potential demand to support the new venture.

If a formal study is carried out then the report will contain estimates of revenue, cost and profit data derived from the market research results, and thus facilitate the initial budget preparation. However, this will usually only apply to the larger national multiple unit firms which have the resources to commission such studies. The smaller local investor in a new business may not feel the need nor have the resources to engage in expensive feasibility studies. Whatever the case, it is quite possible to develop a realistic profit budget for the first year of operation.

Restaurant operations

In the case of a new restaurant the budgeted profit position can be built up by using local knowledge of the population and competition together with industrial averages and other statistics. With such information the expected revenue can be computed as follows:

$$\left(\begin{array}{c}\text{Seating}\\\text{capacity}\end{array}\right) \times \left(\begin{array}{c}\text{Seat}\\\text{turnover}\end{array}\right) \times \left(\begin{array}{c}\text{Days open}\\\text{per week}\end{array}\right) \times \left(\begin{array}{c}\text{Average}\\\text{spend}\end{array}\right) = \left(\begin{array}{c}\text{Weekly}\\\text{revenue}\end{array}\right)$$

e.g. 60 × 0.8 × 7 × £4.50 = £1,512

The estimated weekly revenues can be totalled to give monthly, quarterly and finally the annual revenue anticipated from the restaurant. Industry studies can now be applied in order to ascertain an approximate food cost percentage allowance (or budget) which can be spent on menu ingredients.

The amount of labour needed to assist with running the restaurant can be determined from anticipated opening hours and estimated numbers of customers. This, however, should be related to annual revenue as a percentage and compared with industry statistics. This will provide an indication as to whether the labour budget is a reasonable proportion of turnover.

Finally, all expenses other than food and labour are estimated and each one related to revenue as a percentage and again compared with industry averages. These will include items such as laundry, rates, advertising, repairs, heat, light and power.

The food, labour and other expense estimates (budgets) are then deducted from revenue to give estimated net profit for the period. The net profit can also be related to revenue and compared with the statistics.

Although most hotel and catering industry studies are based on a national sample, or at best on a regional basis, they do provide a useful approximation of the various revenues and costs that could be expected to occur. This together with a fairly detailed knowledge of local activities will provide the foundation on which to prepare the initial budget. Even when the business is established the statistics will form a useful yardstick on which to compare and control operations.

Hotel operations

The approach described above for a new restaurant can be extended to new hotel operations. The main difference is the determination of room revenue expected. This can be computed as follows:

$$\left(\begin{array}{c} \text{Estimate} \\ \text{room} \\ \text{occupancy} \end{array} \right) \times \left(\begin{array}{c} \text{Number of} \\ \text{rooms} \\ \text{available} \end{array} \right) \times \left(\begin{array}{c} \text{Average} \\ \text{room} \\ \text{rate} \end{array} \right) \times \left(\begin{array}{c} \text{Number} \\ \text{days per} \\ \text{week} \end{array} \right) = \left(\begin{array}{c} \text{Weekly} \\ \text{revenue} \end{array} \right)$$

e.g. $\quad$ 70% $\quad \times \quad$ 30 $\quad \times \quad$ £30 $\quad \times \quad$ 7 $\quad = \quad$ £4,410

Having built up the estimated annual revenue the associated expenses can be determined in a similar way as for a restaurant.

In an hotel business additional revenue will be generated in the restaurant and, where applicable, in the bar. The extent of this will depend largely on the way the total hotel product is managed. Where the rooms, restaurant and bar products are conscientiously harmonized then this will frequently attract a substantial level of business in the restaurant and bar. This in turn will provide a sound basis from which to prepare more accurate initial budgets for the restaurant and bar. It is, however, important to remember that where this is so, then a heavy burden of responsibility is laid upon the accuracy of the rooms revenue budget as all other budgets will largely be developed from the rooms budget.

Preparation of the profit statement will indicate whether or not the proposed business is generating an acceptable operating profit. In the event of the profit figure not being considered adequate, then the various elements should be reappraised with a view to seeking new ways of improving the position. When a satisfactory figure has been reached it is then appropriate to prepare a cash budget and budgeted balance sheet, as described earlier.

The development of all budgets is subject to numerous uncertainties and uncontrollable factors so great care should be taken with respect to the assumptions made prior to their preparation. The danger is that the procedures and formulas described above may be regarded as an end in themselves rather than a means to an end. Fallacious assumptions, concerning the level of anticipated business, which are rooted in ignorance are no basis on which to evolve meaningful budgets, particularly in the case of a new operation. At best they will usually constrain the development of the business and at worst could spell financial disaster.

Questions and problems

6–1   Explain the terms 'budgeting' and 'budgetary control'.

6–2   'Too many department heads think that budgets represent a penny-pinching, negative brand of managerial pressure.' *Cost Accounting: A Managerial Emphasis* by Charles T. Horngren. Discuss this statement.

6–3   Why is the sales budget considered to be such an important element in budgetary planning?

6–4   Explain how an hotel housekeeping budget may be prepared and how it fits into the overall budgetary control plan.

6–5   Your catering organization has decided to introduce a comprehensive system of budgetary control. As a first step it has been agreed to form a budget committee, and you have been requested to prepare a report for your managing director on the functions of such a committee and who should serve on it.

6–6   You have recently been appointed manager of a medium sized hotel. The firm operates a very simple system of budgetary control, in that at the beginning of each quarter the managing director, without consultation, sets financial targets in respect of revenue and of expenditure for all departments of the hotel. In order to stimulate the director's interest in management techniques and aids, you have been passing over to him your copies of *The Caterer's Journal* each month. In one edition there appeared the following flow chart depicting part of the budgeting process. The managing director has asked you to prepare a memorandum commenting on each of the stages on the flow chart. Your comments should indicate whether you think each stage is necessary, and in so far as

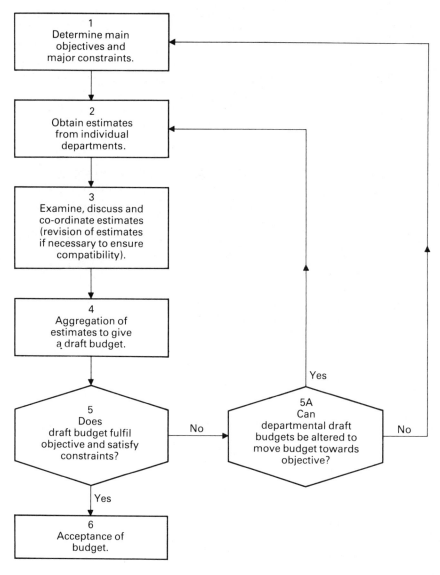

they appear to differ from the present system, what benefits could be expected to accrue if those stages with which you agree were introduced into the hotel.

6–7   A new hotel is to be opened for business on 1st August 1992. It is expected that the preceding month will be devoted to staff training and other start-up requirements.

The following is the forecast trading data and expenditure for the first year from 1st July 1992 to 30th June 1993.

Sales:	£600,000	
Pattern of sales:	July – September	20%
	October – December	20%
	January – March	15%
	April – June	45%
Credit sales:	20% of each quarter's sales, payable in the following quarter.	
Variable costs:	35% of total sales, payable within the quarter in which they are incurred.	

Fixed costs:

Salaries:	£96,000 a year, payable monthly.
Insurance:	£8,000 a year, of which £6,000 is payable in January and £2,000 in October, both policies expire on 30th June 1993.
Rates:	£25,000 payable in September, covering the period to 30th June 1993.
Maintenance, etc.:	£7,000 payable in December and £13,000 payable in January.
Depreciation:	£30,000 for the year.
Vehicle running costs:	The annual road tax of £600 and insurance of £1,200 are payable on the 1st July; petrol, oil and maintenance £7,200; depreciation £6,000. The tax and insurance are payable in July, and the petrol, etc. are payable equally each month.
Interest:	£60,000 a year, half of which is payable on 31st December 1992, and half on 30th June 1993, on a loan received on 1st July 1992.
Other costs:	£24,000 a year payable on an equal monthly basis.

You are required to:
(a) Prepare a cash budget on a quarterly basis for year to 30th June 1993.

(b) The budgeted net profit for the year is £112,000. Explain and reconcile the difference between the net profit and the closing cash balance on 30th June 1993.

(c) Comment on the results revealed in the cash budget.

6–8 A company, West Lodge Ltd, has been formed to take over an existing resort guest house as from 1st August 19X3. The capital of this company amounts to £100,000. The purchase price of the guest house will be £97,000, which represents the fixed assets only. The following targets have been set:

(i) Net profit for the year, after charging £5,000 depreciation on fixed assets, to be £12,000.

(ii) Gross profit will be 60% of *all* sales.

(iii) Labour costs will be 30% of sales with other overheads absorbing another 20% of sales. (Depreciation is included in this figure.)

(iv)] 75% of all sales will be received in cash in the month of sale with the balance being received a month later. (Sales to be evenly spread over the year.)

(v) Stock will be maintained at the level of two months' trading requirements.

(vi) Trade creditors will amount to £4,000 as at 31st July 1984.

You are required to:

(a) Calculate the cash requirement for the year to 31st July 19X4, and draw up a budgeted trading and profit and loss account for the year followed by a budgeted balance sheet.

(b) Make appropriate comments on the results you have produced including, where relevant, the assumptions on which they are based.

(HCIMA)

6–9 Restaurant Royale Limited is preparing its budgets for the quarter beginning 1st July. Stock on hand at the end of June is expected to be £72,000 and the balance at the bank £10,000. In view of the pressure on liquid resources the directors have decided to reduce the stock level at the end of each month to an amount sufficient to cover the following two months' sales. Purchases are paid for by the end of the following month; the amount payable for June's purchases is £36,000.

Budgeted sales (which provide a gross profit of 33⅓% on cost) are:

	£		£
July	40,000	October	48,000
August	42,000	November	52,000
September	46,000	December	44,000

Ten per cent of the sales are for cash and of the credit sales two-thirds are paid for during the month after the sale and the remainder during the following month. Credit sales during May amounted to £24,600 and during June £26,100.

The annual rental for the company's premises is £18,000 payable monthly. Other payments to be made are:

	July £	August £	September £
Salaries, wages and commission	4,800	5,100	5,500
Rates		800	
Other expenses	1,600	1,800	2,000

Required:

    (a) Prepare the company's cash budget for the quarter July–September inclusive.

    (b) Briefly mention the objectives of cash budgeting.

6–10 A. Walker, a successful restaurateur, is taking over another restaurant as a going concern on 1st July 19X4. He estimates that his balance sheet on the day he starts business will be:

Balance Sheet as at 1st July 19X4

		£
Fixed assets		34,000
Current assets		
Stocks	1,500	
Rates prepaid	50	
Cash and bank	500	2,050
		36,050
Capital		26,050
Loan		10,000
		36,050

Notes:

    (i) Mr Walker's sales will be £2,000 for July and are estimated to increase by 20% each month compared to the previous month. He estimates that 10% of his monthly sales will be on credit, and the remainder cash sales. Debtors will be expected to settle their accounts after two months.

    (ii) The restaurant will operate on a 45% cost of sales; 20% of food and beverages purchased will be paid for in cash, the remainder will be bought on credit and paid for after two months. Food and beverages will be replaced the month after consumption.

(iii) Wages and salaries £500 per month, payable in the month the expense is incurred.

(iv) General expenses (including interest on the loan) will be £300 per month. The expenses will be payable in the second month following that in which they were incurred.

(v) The loan will be repaid at £200 per month.

(vi) Rent (not included in general expenses) is £600 per annum and is paid in advance in two equal instalments in February and August.

(vii) Depreciate £4,000 worth of equipment by 20% per annnum.

(viii) Ignore VAT throughout.

You are required to:

(a) Prepare a monthly cash budget for the three months July to September.

(b) Prepare a profit budget (in total) for the three months July to September, and a balance sheet as at the 30th September.

(c) Comment on Mr Walker's financial position after three months' trading.

(HCIMA)

6–11 Antonia Wallace plans to commence business as a restaurateur on 1st January 1992. She will invest capital of £100,000 in cash immediately and any additional financial need will be met by a bank overdraft.

Her initial requirements are furniture and equipment £95,000, which will be depreciated at 20% per annum, and food stocks £5,000.

Meals are expected to sell at 200% above food cost and 40% of the sales will be on credit, the remainder being for cash. Expected sales are £9,000 for the first two months and £12,000 thereafter. Two months' credit will be allowed to customers, and one month's credit is expected from suppliers of food, furniture and equipment. It is intended to replace food stocks during the month in which the food is consumed.

Monthly payroll and other expenses of £4,000 will be paid in cash. This does not include rent of £15,000 for the first year which will be paid in January.

You are required to:

   (a) prepare a monthly cash budget for the four months ending 30th April 1992;
   (b) prepare a budgeted profit and loss statement for the four months ending 30th April 1992;
   (c) prepare a budgeted balance sheet as at that date.

6–12 The Revellers Restaurant is a seasonal licensed establishment. At 31st May 19X9 its balance sheet disclosed:

	£		£
Capital	40,000	Freehold property	26,200
Trade creditors	5,200	Plant, fixtures, etc.	12,000

	£		£	£
Rent received in advance	500	*Stock*: Food	800	
		Beverages	4,000	4,800
		Debtors	——	2,000
		Cash at bank		700
	45,700			45,700

The budget committee has provided the following forecasts and information for the three months to 31st August 19X9:

| | Sales | | Stock purchases of: | | Wages and other | Depreciation |
Month	Food	Beverages	Food	Beverages	expenses	of plant
	£	£	£	£	£	£
June	12,000	4,400	6,500	2,000	8,000	100
July	15,000	5,000	7,000	2,200	9,250	100
August	18,000	5,600	8,500	2,500	10,750	100

Additional information:
   (a) The gross profit on (i) food sales is 50%;
                                 (ii) beverage sales is 66⅔%.
   (b) Three quarters of the sales of food and beverages are for cash; the balance represents credit sales which are settled in the month after the date of the transaction.
   (c) All stock purchases are on credit; the suppliers are paid in the month after the date of the transaction.
   (d) Rent is received from shopkeeper tenants who pay at quarterly intervals in advance, on 1st August, 1st November, 1st February, and 1st May each year.
   (e) Wages and other expenses are all cash, except the

insurance premiums of £600 per annum which are paid in advance on 1st June each year.

(f) On 1st July, a loan of £2,400 is to be received from Finance Co. Ltd. The annual rate of interest payable is 10%, paid half-yearly in arrear.

(g) On 1st July kitchen plant is to be acquired at a cost of £3,400. The kitchen plant which it is to replace is in the balance sheet at a book value of £1,000. The supplier agreed to accept this kitchen equipment for a part exchange value of £750.

(NB: Items (f) and (g) are not included in the forecast of the budget committee.)

You are required to prepare:

  (i) the monthly cash budget for the period from June to August inclusive;

 (ii) the calculation of the value of the closing stock of food and beverages;

(iii) a budgeted departmental trading, profit and loss account for the three months ending 31st August 19X9 and the budgeted balance sheet as at that date.

(HCIMA)

Chapter Seven

Budgets for Planning and Control

The concern of this chapter is the manner in which budgets are used as tools of management. The preparation of departmental budgets and their assembly into a master budget profit and loss account was shown in Chapter 6; here, uses and limitations of the master budget are highlighted.

The master budget is essential for establishing a twelve-month business plan, but its variant, the flexible budget, will be seen to facilitate better short term financial control.

Master budget: a fixed budget

The master budget reflects planned operations at one particular level of activity. Each departmental budget is set at a realistic occupancy level which is expected to generate budgeted gross and net profit. An occupancy level will of course be set for monthly or quarterly periods in relation to seasonal demand.

The master budget profit and loss account and balance sheet is a target for the next 12 months' operations against which progress is monitored during the year. It already therefore serves one important purpose, it is a mechanism for integrating planned activities and their financial implications into a coherent operating plan for the business as a whole. Another purpose is to focus management's attention on a financial target for the coming year. Monitoring operating and financial progress month by month – actual versus budget – and on a cumulative basis, shows management how they are doing in relation to their annual profit target. As actual operations and financial results rarely match the budget month by month, management invariably need supplementary information to adjust plans in the light of the latest departmental results.

The flexible budget for planning

Departmental budgets that make up the master budget profit and loss account are not changed in any way during the budget year and so are called fixed budgets. Progress towards the annual profit target may be poor and lead to management asking 'what if' questions such as what will be the financial results if occupancy remains 10% below budget or special price changes are made to influence volume?

A knowledge of cost behaviour, i.e. how fixed, semi-variable and variable costs are affected by changing levels of activity, enables alternative departmental forecasts to be prepared to assist marketing efforts. These are forecasts based on different levels of activity. Revised short term budgets may be prepared to reflect revised short term targets. However, the master budget for the year would remain as a fixed target. A revised budget may be called a flexible budget. This is defined as a budget which, by recognising different cost behaviour patterns, is designed to change as volume changes.

In this way forecasts and revised, flexible budgets, may be prepared during a budget year for a dynamic management that seeks to remedy adverse operating conditions.

The flexible budget for control

A manager needs to compare regularly budget and actual results and take appropriate action in order to control progress. A cost in a departmental fixed budget may usefully be compared with actual cost if it relates to such items as basic salaries, heat and light, and maintenance. These are fixed costs and so should not be affected by small changes in sales activity; comparison of actual and budget will show savings or excess spending which the manager must accept. He will naturally request further information on actual costs if excess costs are high.

Fixed costs in a fixed, master budget are accordingly quite suitable to use for control purposes as they are expected to remain unchanged during the year. On the other hand, variable costs and sales revenue in the fixed budget are expected to change as output levels change. Variable costs in the form of food cost are particularly relevant.

Budgeted gross profit for a period extracted from the master budget has to be compared with actual gross profit to maintain control in attempting to achieve target gross profit. Significant differences that arise must be investigated for causes which might lead to remedial action.

Settles is a small outlet selling only one item. The simplest control statement for this concern is shown in Exhibit 7–1. Gross profit has fallen despite a 10% rise in sales volume. It is a simple example designed to highlight how financial information may be developed to assist managers in controlling their departmental performance.

Questions needed for control would include:
Is food cost under control despite rising to 66.8% of sales?

Exhibit 7–1

Settles
Financial Statement Period 12

	Per dish	Budget		Actual	
No. dishes		3,000		3,300	
	£	£	%	£	%
Sales revenue	1.60	4,800	100	4,980	100
Food cost	1.00	3,000	62.5	3,328	66.8
Gross profit	0.60	1,800	37.5	1,652	33.2

Price reductions took place in the period. What did this cost the firm?

Why has the increased volume not increased gross profit?

The first stage in providing better information is the introduction of a flexible budget (Exhibit 7–2). It indicates the gross profit that would have resulted from the actual quantity of sales, if sales price and food cost per dish had remained as planned. It shows physical quantity rising by 10% above budget, with 3,300 dishes sold compared with 3,000 in the fixed budget. This 10% rise influences gross profit directly as each component would be expected to rise by 10%. For example sales revenue would have been £4,800 × 110% = £5,280 and food cost £3,000 × 110% = £3,300.

Exhibit 7–2

Settles
Flexible Budget Worksheet Period 12

Activity 110%	Per dish	Fixed budget	Flexible budget	Actual	Variances
No. dishes		3,000	3,300	3,300	
	£	£	£	£	£
Sales revenue	1.60	4,800	5,280	4,980	300 (U) Selling price
Food cost	1.00	3,000	3,300	3,328	28 (U) Food cost
	0.60	1,800	1,980	1,652	

£1,800 v. £1,980

£1,800 v. £1,652 = 148 (U)

328 (U) Price/usage
= 180 (F) Sales margin volume

Management of Settles would have expected £1,980 gross profit from 3,300 dishes sold, that is, if sales price had not dropped and food cost remained at £1 per dish.

Variances are shown in a final column, the result of a difference between budget and actual or between two budgets. A variance may be favourable, labelled (F), indicating higher profit than in the fixed master budget. Unfavourable (U), shows a lower profit than in the fixed budget.

Another class of variance is either a sales margin volume or a price/usage variance as shown in Exhibit 7–2.

(a) *A sales margin volume variance* is so called because it represents the change in the gross profit margin that would be expected from a change in sales volume. This variance is the difference between the fixed budget gross profit and the flexible budget gross profit.

(b) *Price/usage variances.* These are differences between a flexible budget and actual results, occasioned by either a price change (here a selling price) compared with budget and/or a usage change compared with budget. Food cost variance may be a combination of both price and usage.

Settles' Period 12 Statement (Exhibit 7–2) is a worksheet rather than a presentation statement. However it does show that the drop in gross profit of £148 was caused by:

(a) *Selling price variance* (£300 unfavourable). This is the most significant variance. It is the difference between the flexible budget figure and the actual sales revenue. Actual revenue divided by actual units sold gives an average price of £1.509; clearly not a price applicable to all 3,300 units. Probably a price drop very early in the period.

(b) *Sales margin volume variance* (£180 favourable). This is the difference in gross profit between the fixed and flexible budgets. It shows that an extra £180 would have made from the 10% volume rise had price and cost of each dish not changed.

(c) *Food cost variance* (£28 unfavourable). Food cost £28 more than allowed for in the flexible budget for the quantity sold. Much less than suggested by the increase from 62.5% to 66.8% of sales. The high food cost percentage is partly due to the sales price fall.

An operating statement more suitable for presentation to management is shown in Exhibit 7–3 on page 96. Here variances can be grouped where cause and effect may be at work, for example the net effect of sales price fall and volume rise being £120(U). Alternatively they may be grouped to coincide with managerial responsibilities for budgets and variances.

The flexible budget and sales mix

The flexible budget will be seen as a particularly useful device for developing marketing information where a range of items are sold.

Exhibit 7–3

Settles
Operating Statement Period 12

Activity 110%	£	£
Budgeted gross profit		1,800
Sales variances		
Sales margin volume variance	180 (F)	
Selling price variance	300 (U)	
	120 (U)	
Food cost variance	28 (U)	
Total variances		148 (U)
Actual gross profit		1,652

Settles has expanded to become Settles Restaurant with results shown in Exhibit 7–4. Volume of sales has increased by 10%, food cost has risen from 37.5% to 42.9% of sales, and gross profit is £1,120 short of the fixed budget for the period. As demonstrated with Settles, more information is needed to discover reasons for this poor financial performance despite greater sales.

Exhibit 7–4

Settles Restaurant
Financial Statement Period 12

	Budget		Actual	
No. covers	3,000		3,300	
	£	%	£	%
Sales revenue	40,000	100	41,800	100
Food cost	15,000	37.5	17,920	42.9
Gross profit	25,000	62.5	23,880	57.1

Settles Restaurant has four menu items, item 4 being the dish from the Settles example. The fixed and flexible budgets for a period are shown in Exhibit 7–5; the difference in total gross profits of £80(U) representing a sales margin volume variance. Settles Restaurant is known to have increased covers by 10%, giving rise to an expected 10% increase in sales revenue. Average spend was budgeted at £40,000/3,000 = £13.33 and 3,300 covers should bring in 3,300 × £13.33 = £44,000 (rounded).

The column for actual sales value represents revenue from the actual sales of each menu item but ignoring any selling price changes in the period.

Exhibit 7–5

Settles Restaurant
Flexible Budget Worksheet

	Fixed budget				*Flexible budget*			
	Budgeted sales: Budgeted mix				Actual sales at budgeted prices: Actual mix			
No covers	Sales 3,000		Gross Profit		Sales 3,300		Gross Profit	
Menu item	Mix (%)	Value (£)	%	£	Mix (%)	Value (£)	%	£
1	12.5	5,000	78	3,900	12.5	5,500	78	4,290
2	23	9,200	50	4,600	50.5	22,220	50	11,110
3	52.5	21,000	70	14,700	25	11,000	70	7,700
4	12	4,800	37.5	1,800	12	5,280	37.5	1,980
	100	40,000	62.5	25,000	100	44,000	57	25,080

Sales margin volume variance
£80 (F)

Closer inspection shows that the actual mix of each item differs from the budget. Menu items 1 and 4 are unchanged but item 2 has risen at the expense of item 3. As menu item 3 has a higher gross profit percentage, 70% compared with 50%, overall gross profit has fallen compared with budget from 62.5% to 57%.

To find the financial extent of this deterioration in mix, a further flexible budget is placed between the fixed budget and the first flexible budget (Exhibit 7–6). This second flexible budget represents the gross profit that would have been expected had the mix of sales remained as in the budget. In other words, a mix variance has now been subtracted from the volume variance, leaving a residual sales margin quantity variance.

This new centre section showing the 10% rise in sales in budgeted mix is prepared by multiplying items in the fixed budget by 110%. The sales margin volume variance is split into sales margin quantity and sales margin mix variance. This is done especially to highlight the financial effect of a change of sales mix.

The sales margin quantity variance of £2,500 favourable indicates the extra gross profit that would have been made if the total actual sales had been in the budgeted mix. With the sales margin mix variance registering an unfavourable variance of £2,420, almost all the benefit of higher turnover has been lost. Only £28 gross profit remains above budget, that is the sales margin volume variance.

Selling prices and food cost variances

To complete the reconciliation between budgeted and actual gross profit, recorded sales and food costs feature in a fourth column in Exhibit 7–7. Only *total* sales, food costs and gross profit appear in this worksheet for two reasons. The mix of sales has now been accounted for and in this example actual food costs are not analysed over separate menu dishes. The additional information is the selling price variance and the food cost variance. The figures in the 'actual results' column come from Settles Restaurant in Exhibit 7–4.

Presentation of results

The management presentation is in the form of an operating statement (Exhibit 7–8). Management's attention is drawn to the unfavourable total sales variance of £2,120 resulting from a 10% increase in number of covers served. Three inter-related factors, sales quantity, mix and selling price would be closely scrutinised by sales management in order to plan a better financial performance in future. The food cost variance showing a saving of £1,000 might be a result of purchase price savings, less kitchen wastage, or portion control changes.

Exhibit 7–6

Settles Restaurant
Flexible Budget Worksheet

		Fixed Budget Budgeted sales: Budgeted mix				Flexible Budget Actual total sales: Budgeted mix				Flexible Budget Actual sales at budgeted prices: Actual mix			
		Sales		Gross Profit		Sales		Gross Profit		Sales		Gross Profit	
No. covers		3,000				3,300				3,300			
Menu item	Mix (%)	Value (£)		%	£	Mix (%)	Value (£)	%	£	Mix (%)	Value (£)	%	£
1	12.5	5,000		78	3,900	12.5	5,500	78	4,290	12.5	5,500	78	4,290
2	23	9,200		50	4,600	23	10,120	50	5,060	50.5	22,220	50	11,110
3	52.5	21,000		70	14,700	52.5	23,100	70	16,170	25	11,000	70	7,700
4	12	4,800		37.5	1,800	12	5,280	37.5	1,980	12	5,280	37.5	1,980
	100	40,000		62.5	25,000	100	44,000	62.5	27,500	100	44,000	57	25,080

Sales margin volume variance
£80 (F)

Sales margin quantity variance
£2,500 (F)

Sales margin mix variance
£2,420 (U)

99

Exhibit 7–7

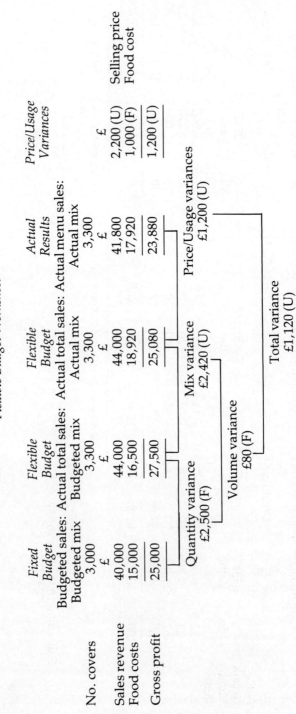

Settles Restaurant
Flexible Budget Worksheet

	Fixed Budget Budgeted sales: Budgeted mix	*Flexible Budget* Actual total sales: Budgeted mix	*Flexible Budget* Actual total sales: Actual mix	*Actual Results* Actual menu sales: Actual mix	*Price/Usage Variances*	
No. covers	3,000	3,300	3,300	3,300		
	£	£	£	£	£	
Sales revenue	40,000	44,000	44,000	41,800	2,200 (U)	Selling price
Food costs	15,000	16,500	18,920	17,920	1,000 (F)	Food cost
Gross profit	25,000	27,500	25,080	23,880	1,200 (U)	

Quantity variance £2,500 (F)

Mix variance £2,420 (U)

Price/Usage variances £1,200 (U)

Volume variance £80 (F)

Total variance £1,120 (U)

Exhibit 7–8

Settles Restaurant
Operating Statement Period 12

Activity 110%	£		£
Budgeted gross profit			25,000
Sales margin quantity variance	2,500	(F)	
Sales margin mix variance	2,420	(U)	
Sales margin volume variance	80	(F)	
Selling price variance	2,200	(U)	
Total sales variance	2,120	(U)	
Food cost variance	1,000	(F)	
Total variance			1,120 (U)
Actual gross profit			£23,880

Standard costing

This system may be regarded as an extension of budgetary control, providing more control information in the form of additional variances. It exists where firm standards of performance are capable of being set.

In fast food outlets where standardized products are sold, it is possible to establish standard ingredient prices designed to last for the budget year and a standard ingredient quantity per dish. This situation then, lends itself to a form of standard costing which assists many large manufacturers to control costs. The standard quantity of material required to produce each output unit is carefully set. A standard purchase price is also established for each material.

Standard material price times standard input quantity for each output unit results in a standard material cost per unit of output. This standard cost enables the flexible budget variance for material to be broken down into sub-variances of price variance and usage variance. Some industries extend standards to other costs, but only material (food cost) standards are generally practical in restaurants.

The following example gives an insight into standard costing for materials, using Settles' figures in Exhibit 7–2.

Assume 0.20 kg of the ingredient is needed per dish and its purchase price is £5.00 per kg. Records for the period in which 3,300 dishes were served showed 640 kg was used costing £3,328 (£5.20 per kg). It is known that the total food cost variance is £3,328 − £3,300, that is £28(U). This may be separated into sub-variances as follows:

Food costs (direct material):

(a) Standard cost for the period per the flexible budget:

$$3,300 \times 0.20 \text{ kg} = 660 \text{ kg} \times £5 \qquad = 3,300$$

(b) Actual purchase @ standard price:

$$640 \text{ kg} \times £5 \qquad = 3,200$$

(c) Actual cost $\qquad\qquad\qquad 640 \text{ kg} \times £5.20 = 3,328$

Usage variance (a) – (b): (660 kg – 640 kg) $\times$ £5 $\quad = \quad$ 100(F)

Price variance (b) – (c): $\quad$ (£5.00 – £5.20)$\times$ 640 kg $=\quad$ 128 (U)

Total material cost variance (a) – (c): $\qquad\qquad$ 28(U)

The variances reveal that although ingredients were overspent by £28, the cause was an increased purchase price of £128, largely offset by a saving of £100 in preparing food. Variances are often inter-related; here for instance, better quality purchases at a higher price may have resulted in less food waste.

Purchase price variance is best established at time of purchase, in which case purchase and usage quantities may not coincide. The total material cost variance would then be:

Usage variance =
(Standard quantity – Actual quantity)×Standard price,
plus
Price variance =
(Standard price – Actual price)×Purchase quantity.

Flexible budget for overheads

Some large organizations needing close control of overhead costs find it worthwhile to produce a flexible budget which takes account of the cost behaviour of each expense item. Exhibit 7–9 shows a control statement for a rooms department. Where an expense item is expected to change to some extent in relation to changes in sales, it has been adjusted to form a flexible budget. By admitting that certain costs must rise in sympathy with activity changes, due allowance is given for these and then attention is directed to changes not foreseen. These may be because of change in price, good or poor cost control, or difficulty in determining cost behaviour of the cost item.

As already demonstrated, the difference between the original budget and the flexible budget is a volume variance caused by the change in sales level.

It should be noted that the flexible budget costs are not part of the double entry accounting system but are memorandum figures prepared as and when required. It is usual to record information on cost behaviour at budgeting time to enable reasonably accurate flexible budgets to be prepared when necessary.

Exhibit 7–9

Room Department Cost Control Statement
(6 months ended . . .)

	Cost class	(1) Fixed budget	(2) Flexible budget	(3) Actual	(4) Variance (Col. 3–2)	(5) Remarks
		£	£	£	£	Increased turnover caused by . . .
Guest accommodation		20,000	22,000	22,000		
Room hire		1,000	1,100	1,100		
TOTAL SALES		21,000	23,100	23,100		
Gross Pay						
NI						
Holiday pay						
Staff meals						
Staff accommodation						
TOTAL WAGE & STAFF COST	SV	7,000	7,100	7,100	—	
NET MARGIN		14,000	16,000	16,000	—	
Department supplies	SV	1,500	1,600	1,700	(100)	Minor equip. for rooms
Flowers and decoration	F	300	300	320	(20)	Price increase
Magazines & periodicals	F	100	100	90	10	
Printing and stationery	SV	400	430	420	10	
Laundry & dry cleaning charges	SV	700	750	800	(50)	Under est. in quantity of dry cleaning
Cleaning contracts	F	500	500	500	—	
Linen	SV	100	105	105	—	
Uniforms	SV	200	200	200	—	
Utensils	F	200	200	200	—	
TOTAL ALLOCATED EXPENSE		4,000	4,185	4,335	(150)	
DEPARTMENTAL OPERATING PROFIT		10,000	11,815	11,665	(150)	

SUMMARY	£
Profit variance due to volume (Col. 2–1)	1,815
Profit variance due to price/usage (Col. 3–2)	(150)
TOTAL PROFIT VARIANCE FROM BUDGET (Col. 3–1)	1,665

Questions and problems

7–1 What is the basic limitation of an original/fixed budget when it comes to control of trading activities?

7–2 What is a control/flexible budget and how might it be applied to an hotel or catering organization?

7–3 'There is only one kind of budget which is any use for monitoring purposes and that is a control/flexible budget.'

   You are required to:
   (a) Comment on this quotation;
   (b) discuss the factors which you would take into account in deciding the volume base, e.g. meals, sales, revenue etc., you would select for measuring changes in activity; and
   (c) state what factors, other than the changes in the level of activity, would cause costs to vary.

7–4 Explain, in brief, the following terms:
   (a) standard cost;   (d) food usage variance
   (b) standard price;   (e) sales margin variance;
   (c) food price variance;   (f) sales mix variance.

7–5 Select a particular type of hotel or catering establishment and suggest which departments, and who within the departments, are concerned with setting standards.

7–6 Enumerate the likely causes of food cost variances and sales margin variances.

7–7 Explain the relationship between the food price variance and the food usage variance. Is it feasible for a favourable result achieved from one variance to contribute to an adverse result in another variance?

7–8 Distinguish between controllable and non-controllable costs giving examples of each.

7–9 Explain what you understand by 'responsibility accounting'.

7–10 The Noble Hotel, in common with other firms in the industry, is suffering from a depression in the market. Currently it is operating at a normal level of room occupancy of 70%, which represents 4,200 room lets, but the hotel sales manager believes that a realistic forecast for the next budget period would be 50% occupancy.

Below is the current flexible budget:

	Level of occupancy		
Operating costs:	60%	70%	80%
	£	£	£
Direct materials (food)	7,200	8,400	9,600
Direct labour	9,000	10,500	12,000
General admin. and marketing	10,400	10,400	10,400
Heat, light and power	6,440	6,680	6,920
Property operation	5,380	5,860	6,340
Depreciation and rates	5,000	5,000	5,000

Net profit is 20% of selling price.

Required:
(a) From the data given in the current flexible budget above, prepare a budgeted profit statement based on a room occupancy level of 50%. The profit statement should show clearly the contribution margin which could be expected.
(b) Explain *briefly* three problems which might arise from such a change in the level of room occupancy.

7–11 The data below relates to Period 4 of the staff dining hall of an industrial engineering company:

	Budget
No. covers sold	80,000
Average spend per head	£1.50
Food cost percentage of sales	60%
Fixed labour and overhead	£40,000

At the end of Period 4 the results were:

	Actual
No. covers sold	75,000
Sales revenue	£115,000
Food cost	£68,500
Fixed labour and overhead	£40,000

You are required to:
(a) Prepare a statement for Period 4 showing the fixed budget, flexible budget, actual results and variances.

105

(b) Comment on the results you have prepared in (a) above.
(c) Outline the principles of flexible budgetary control.

7–12 The information that follows relates to the employee feeding facility at an industrial company for a year:

	Budget
Number of covers sold	100,000
Average spend per head	£1.60
Food cost percentage of sales	40%
Variable labour cost percentage of sales	10%
Fixed labour cost	£30,000
Fixed overhead	£40,000

At the end of the year the total results were

	Actual
Number of covers sold	105,000
Sales revenue	£157,500
Food cost	£ 75,000
Variable labour	£ 14,000
Fixed labour	£ 25,000
Fixed overhead	£ 41,000

You are required to:

(a) prepare a statement for the year showing the fixed budget, flexible budget, actual results and variances;
(b) evaluate the results you have prepared in (a) above and suggest possible causes for the variances.

7–13 'Hobson's Choice' is a staff cafeteria with a limited menu. It has a system of budgetary control which has a weekly fixed budget as follows:

Sales:	4,000 meals with an average spend of £1.61 including VAT.
Cost of sales:	Meat ingredients averaging 0.4kg per meal at an average cost of £1.50 per kg. Vegetable ingredients, averaging 0.5kg per meal at an average cost of £0.40 per kg.

The actual results for the week ending Sunday 1st June 1986 are:

Sales:	4,200 meals at an average price of £1.84 including VAT.
Cost of sales:	Meat 1,640kg at £1.80 per kg. Vegetables 2,200kg at £0.36 per kg.

You are required to:
  (a) Prepare comparative trading statements for a fixed budget, a flexible budget, and the actual results.
  (b) Calculate the variances and reconcile the budgeted gross profit with the actual.
  (c) Comment on the variances you have produced.
  (d) Discuss the usefulness of variance analysis in the hotel and catering industry.

(HCIMA)

7–14 The following information relates to the food and beverage budget of the Berkshire Banqueting Suite for 1st quarter of 1986:

Budgeted number of covers	Menu A	3,000
	Menu B	4,000
	Menu C	5,000
Budgeted selling prices per cover	Menu A	£4
	Menu B	£5
	Menu C	£3
Budgeted food cost per cover	Menu A	40%
	Menu B	30%
	Menu C	50%

Semi-variable cost behaviour attributable to various levels of activity are estimated to be:

$Y_c = 1,000 + 0.15$ (covers)

Fixed costs for the quarter are £20,000. Budgeted activity is 60% of banqueting capacity.

Actual results were:

Number of covers sold (sales mix)	Menu A	12%
	Menu B	40%
	Menu C	48%

Food cost £15,700
Semi variable costs £2,100
Activity was 50% of capacity at budgeted selling prices.

Required:
(a) Prepare a statement for 1st quarter of 1986 showing the fixed budget, flexible budget, actual results and variances.
(b) Comment on the results you have prepared in (a) above.

7–15 The following data relates to Period 7 of a restaurant:

	Budget
No. of covers sold	60,000
Selling price per cover	£8
Food cost percentage of sales	40%

Semi-variable overhead costs from past periods indicate:

Period	Covers sold	Overhead (£)
1	70,000	105,000
2	55,000	85,000
3	45,000	80,000
4	62,500	100,000
5	85,000	110,000
6	75,000	90,000

Budgeted fixed overhead for Period 7 is £124,750.

The actual results for Period 7 are detailed below.

	Actual
No. of covers sold	65,000
Sales revenue	£500,000
Food cost	£220,000
Semi-variable overhead	£95,000

Required:
(a) Prepare a statement for Period 7 showing the fixed budget, flexible budget, actual results and variances.
(b) Briefly support your basis of cost analysis for the semi-variable overhead.
(c) Comment on the results.

7–16 The Restview Restaurant prepared a budget from which standards are established, For a week in June the budgeted standards set, and the actual results achieved are as follows:

	Budgeted		*Actual*
	£		£
Sales: 1,500 dishes		1,560 dishes	
at £1.06	1,590.00	at £1.10	1,716.00
Less: Cost of sales	795.00	*Less*: cost of sales	783.20
Gross profit	795.00		932.80

The standard costs per dish (only two ingredients are used) were calculated as follows:

		Standard cost per dish
Ingredient A	500 g at £0.50 per kg	£0.25
Ingredient B	250 g at £1.12 per kg	£0.28

The actual costs were as follows:

	Actual price	*Actual food used*
Ingredient A	£0.52 per kg	800 kgs
Ingredient B	£1.02 per kg	360 kgs

You are required to:
  (a) calculate the following variances:
      (i) sales variances,
      (ii) ingredient price variances, and
      (iii) ingredient usage variances.
  (b) reconcile the budgeted profit with the actual profit, and
  (c) briefly comment on the significance of the variances.

(HCIMA, adapted)

7–17 (a) What are standard costs and why is their use superior to comparisons of actual costs with past costs?
      (b) A restaurant in a large leisure complex, which operates a system of standard costing, showed the following information:

Standard Cost Card

Ingredients:

		£
A	160g at £3.00 per kg	0.48
B	50 g at £0.80 per kg	0.04

	0.52
Standard margin (GP) 60%	0.78
Standard selling price	1.30

Budgeted sales for the period 7,000 dishes

Actual data for the period:

Ingredient	Food used kg	Price paid £
A	955	3,200
B	320	280

Number of dishes sold 6,500
Sales revenue £8,325

You are required to:
  (a) Prepare: (i) sales variances;
                (ii) food cost variances; and
               (iii) a statement reconciling budgeted and actual gross profit.
  (b) Give a *very brief* explanation to management suggesting the possible causes of each variance.

(HCIMA)

7–18 The sales and cost budget for a fast food establishment for the month of November is as follows:

Food item	Units	Sales value £	Standard cost £
'Artie Berger'	10,000	10,000	9,000
'Brunchie'	5,000	8,000	6,000
'Crunchy'	10,000	12,000	10,800
'Dunkie'	5,000	18,000	14,200
		£48,000	£40,000

After completion of the sales analysis for November, the following statement of actual values is compiled:

Food item	Units	Sales value £
'Artie Berger'	9,200	9,200
'Brunchie'	7,000	11,000
'Crunchy'	12,000	14,600
'Dunkie'	2,000	7,800

Calculate the variation in profit from that budgeted, and show how much is due to the factors of sales price, quantity and mix.

7–19 'Super Snacks' is a fast food operation which offers a choice of two snacks. The business operates a system of standard costing and below is the information relating to one month's activities.

	Budget/ standard	Actual
Number sold:		
Boomerang	10,000	13,200
Torpedo	20,000	18,400
Selling price:		
Boomerang	£1.00	£0.90
Torpedo	£0.75	£0.75
Ingredient quantity:		
Boomerang	200 g	210 g
Torpedo	125 g	130 g
Ingredient price:		
Boomerang	£3.00/kg	£3.00/kg
Torpedo	£4.00/kg	£3.85/kg
Standard cost:		
Boomerang	£0.60	—
Torpedo	£0.50	—

You are required to:
   (a) prepare a detailed variance analysis; and
   (b) explain, as if to a layman, the reasons for providing the information you have prepared in (a) above.

(HCIMA)

Chapter Eight
Behavioural Aspects of Budgeting

Introduction

A routine budgetary control system involves:

- (a) preparation of a master budget;
- (b) recording costs and revenues of budget centres;
- (c) reporting variances from plan;
- (d) taking action on significant variances.

Budgets are an aid to planning and especially useful as a co-ordination mechanism. With the aid of a computerized management information system the mechanistic side of budgetary control can be relatively trouble-free. The system of budgetary control relies heavily upon the individual in an organization to make the system work successfully – for one budget might motivate, but a different budget could demotivate the same person.

The attitude of top management to the preparation and use of budgets can influence the behaviour of individuals. In this chapter we shall look briefly at the behavioural aspects of budgets.

Responsibility centres

A responsibility centre is concerned with making individuals responsible for the financial performance of their own responsibility centre – of which there are three kinds:

- (a) cost centre;
- (b) profit centre;
- (c) investment centre.

A *cost centre* is a segment of an organization where individuals are accountable for the expenses under their control. It may be a department, manufacturing process or an individual carrying out a management function – wherever there is a need for costs to be separately budgeted and where costs may conveniently be separately indentified and controlled.

A *profit centre* is where the manager is responsible for the profit generated. He controls revenues as well as costs.

An *investment centre* is a centre where profit is measured in relation to investment, for example a firm in its own right.

Control of cost centre costs

The existence of a defined target such as a budget is likely to motivate individuals to perform better than in the absence of such a target. To perform better in a cost centre context is to reduce spending. With no budget to restrain spending, costs would inevitably rise unnecessarily.

The budget level itself can have a significant effect on spending. A budget with a generous cost allowance encourages managers to spend it all – whether it be necessary or not – in order to ensure a further generous allowance next year. This is called a 'loose' budget and is not effective in controlling costs.

On the other hand, an extremely 'tight' budget may lead to the manager giving up hope of keeping within the budget and ignoring the budget altogether.

A middle position represented by the fairly tight budget, or at least one that is attainable with some effort, has been shown to be the most effective in cost control.

Research has shown the importance of taking into account 'aspiration levels' (personal targets or goals) in setting corporate budgets, the art of budgeting being to get personal and corporate targets close together. Two conclusions are:

(a) targets are good for motivating high performance, including keeping costs under control or increasing profit;
(b) budgets which are fairly tight have more positive effect than either loose or extremely tight ones – even if the tight cost budget is exceeded occasionally.

Participation in budgeting and overcoming 'slack'

It has been found that managers who participate in the preparation of their own budgets are more likely to accept them and work towards their achievement than if the budget were to be imposed by higher management without consultation. Participation should involve a full discussion of anticipated costs for which the manager is responsible.

Unless a budget is imposed there could be slack built into it. Slack or padding is the difference between the minimum expense and actual expense of carrying out planned activities. Many managers are instinctively inclined to create slack as a defence against adverse variances being reported. A 'loose' budget is the result.

Practical ways of reducing slack include:

(a) Not tightening the next budget if the present budget is underspent;
(b) rewarding managers who achieve permanent cost savings.

Controllability of costs

The concept that managers should only be charged with responsibility for costs they are able to control is difficult but possible to put into practice. Some cost control categories can be identified:

(a) Many costs are controllable by some person in the organization, e.g. salesmen's travelling expenses being controlled by the sales manager.
(b) The control of some costs such as material costs may be shared by individuals. Standard costing can help separate material price – the responsibility of the buyer – from the quantity used which is controlled by the chef.
(c) Some insignificant costs would be accepted by the chef even if he were unable to control them.
(d) Who controls maintenance costs? The general manager would certainly control such costs, but can responsibility be placed further down the line? The maintenance foreman is responsible for carrying out the work efficiently but the amount of work could rise through misuse of equipment by another department.

A general principle is that responsibility for the control of a cost is accepted by the person who has a significant influence over it. Routine reports may be constructed to show separately those costs which the recipient is required to control, and those he cannot control (non-controllable costs).

A responsibility accounting system is operated within the budgetary control system and its requirements are:

(a) the individual in charge is held to be responsible for the activities within his jurisdiction, and the effort used in attaining his objectives is to be measured in terms of controllable and non-controllable costs.
(b) the organization chart of the firm, supported by a schedule of cost responsibilities is the basis on which reports are prepared and recognition of controllable and non-controllable costs and revenue made.

An example of this is shown in Exhibit 8–1. Here it can be seen that all costs are controllable by the general manager, whereas certain costs are not controllable at the lower levels of management e.g. in this case repairs are not controllable by the restaurant manager.

Exhibit 8–1 Hotel organization chart (extract)

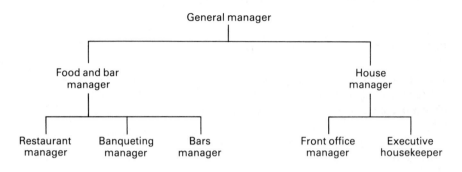

Schedule of cost responsibilities (extract)			
	Restaurant manager	Food and bev. manager	General manager
Wages of waiters	C	C	C
Flowers	C	C	C
Laundry	C	C	C
Breakages	C	C	C
Music	N/C	C	C
Repairs	N/C	C	C
Stationery	N/C	N/C	C
Cleaning Contract	N/C	N/C	C

C = Controllable
N/C = Non-controllable

Controlling significant variances

Random variances need no control. Adverse and favourable variances are likely to cancel out. Each organization decides what is to be regarded as a *significant* variance which needs investigating in order to find the cause and then to possibly prevent it happening again. Typical criteria are:

(a) variances exceeding 10% of budget or standard;
(b) variances exceeding a specific amount;
(c) repetition of an adverse variance.

115

Management influence on variances

Three styles of management influence the action taken on variances according to research by Hopwood (1976).

Inactive style

This refers to a management which plays lip-service only to the budgetary control system, rendering it ineffective. The system is mechanistic only.

Authoritative style

Undue emphasis is placed on cost control to the exclusion of more positive aspects. All adverse variances are associated with failure. This can result in tension and worry and lead to manipulation of accounting reports by managers. Short-term cost savings may lead to serious overspending in the long run. Skimping of hotel maintenance is an example of this.

Profit-conscious style

This is a style where positive, flexible attitudes towards variances are encouraged. Carefully used, this style can motivate managers to improving personal and company performance.

Profit centres

The advantage claimed for profit centres – where managers are responsible for sales as well as costs – is the encouragement it gives to managers to perform well. Cost control of cost centres tends to restrict a manager's activities whereas profit responsibility tends to improve status and encourages a more positive attitude to financial matters.

Investment centres

Large companies with varied activities are often divisionalized, usually along product or service lines. The central feature of a division is the delegation of decision making and the operational authority given to divisional managers with overall control retained at the centre.

If the manager of a division has control over fixed assets, stocks and other investments then the investment centre form of responsibility centre makes sense. If the assets in divisions are controlled by head office then the centre may be more suited to be a profit centre.

Advantages claimed for divisionalization include:

(a) managers are more motivated to perform well because of the greater authority they enjoy;
(b) autonomy of the divisional managers reduces communication problems;
(c) top management has more time to concentrate on strategic matters.

Divisional performance

This term concerns the methods used for measuring performance of divisional managers. The most common method is the return on investment (ROI) – the percentage of annual profit in relation to investment in the division. If the manager truly has control over profit and investment then the benefits of using the measure are similar to those for individual companies.

A second measure is known as residual income (RI). This is the profit remaining after the division has been charged with the cost of invested capital. This is an absolute measure compared with ROI which is a relative measure.

Problems of definition can arise with divisions. For the purpose of performance comparison it is necessary that expenses such as depreciation and the valuation of assets are treated alike by all divisions.

One particular problem arises when products are transferred between divisions and that is the price set (transfer price).

Transfer pricing

Goods or services transferred between divisions of a business have to be priced so that the supplying division gets the credit – which then becomes a cost to the buying division. The price used for this purpose is known as a transfer price. A transfer price may take the form of a cost of some kind or a price which includes a profit; examples are variable cost, incremental cost, full cost, cost plus a percentage for profit, market price and negotiated price.

Cost centre v profit centre

Transfers between cost centres – as compared with divisions – also involve the use of transfer prices but these will only take some form of cost. Incremental or variable cost is the best transfer price that enables the manager who ultimately sells outside the business to make the best decision for the business; he knows the total variable cost of the work sold and can maximize contribution from the sale.

Transfers between cost centres present no problem as managerial performance is likely to be based on traditional cost control techniques which may include standard costing.

Two requirements of a transfer price may therefore be satisfied with a transfer price at cost:

(a) If a variable cost transfer price is used then decision making is facilitated, and
(b) Managerial performance may be measured by cost variances.

If a department supplying the work inside the company also sells outside then the business will be regarded as a profit centre because it makes a profit on its outside sales. To transfer some work inside at variable cost would not please the supplying profit centre manager as this would not contribute to his profit centre profit (although the buying profit centre would gain by it). Transferring at a price which includes a profit, such as cost plus a percentage, may not lead the buying profit centre manager to act in the best interest of the company.

Profit centres may be better than cost centres for motivating managers to be profit conscious, but where work is transferred between profit centres there can be problems in agreeing what is the best transfer pricing system.

The amount of work transferred inside relative to work sold outside the business by profit centres has a significant effect on the importance attached to a transfer price. A very small quantity of work transferred inside would mean that the method of establishing the transfer price would not be important and vice versa. Further discussion therefore concerns transfer pricing between profit centres where the value of work transferred is significant.

Market price

A market price is the best transfer price, if one is available and the supplying division is working to capacity. This price leads to the best make or buy decision for the buying division. If the receiving (buying) division were to obtain its work from outside, the outside buying price would be its variable cost. If the same work were transferred inside, the supplying division, if working to capacity, would lose an outside sale, the loss being the contribution (sales price minus variable cost). The product would be made in any case, and its variable cost incurred. There would therefore be no difference to company profit if the work required by the buying division were bought out or transferred inside by the supplying division so long as a common market price ruled. If however the buying price (e.g. £350) were higher than the first division's own market price (£325) then the buying division would prefer to buy from the inside division to make more profit. This would be best for the company too:

Total Company Cash flows

		Make and sell outside £	Make and sell inside £
Selling division	{ Variable cost	(200)	(200)
	{ Revenue	325	—
Buying division	{ Variable cost	(350)	—
Net cost to the company		(225)	(200)

The real cost of buying from the selling division – inside the company – is the variable cost of making plus any lost contribution. In this latter case the market transfer price of £325 is the variable cost of £200 plus the lost contribution – opportunity cost – of £125, together equal to the market price. If the selling division were working below capacity the cost to the company of buying inside would be simply the variable cost of £200 as there would be no lost contribution.

Variable or incremental cost

An incremental cost is the additional cost of each unit produced and if this is a constant variable cost then there is no difference between them. If, however, the total fixed cost increases after a particular level of activity, then variable cost per unit is not a meaningful term and the term incremental should then be used. Both terms mean the additional cost to the company associated with some decision or between two levels of activity.

It has already been mentioned that variable (or incremental) cost is a good transfer price for decision making for it is similar in concept to marginal/contribution pricing.

Nevertheless, for profit centres there remains the problem that it does not provide a profit for the selling division and it is therefore unsuitable for helping to measure divisional performance.

Cost plus a percentage profit

Cost plus a percentage for profit is the most popular method of setting a transfer price because it is simple to operate and provides the selling division with a profit. If actual cost is used as a base for the transfer price then the selling division's profit increases with increases in cost per unit. This does not encourage financial control of a division. A transfer price based on standard cost does overcome this disadvantage, however, because the inefficiencies of the selling division are not passed on to the buying division as the standard cost would be set for a given time period.

Negotiated price

A negotiated price is the result of the buying and selling division bargaining about the price. This method has the advantage of providing divisional managers with substantial control over their individual profits. Negotiating a price however may take a long time and top management may need to intervene if negotiations break down.

Conflict of transfer pricing requirements

A divisional transfer price is required to:

   (a) encourage good decision making, that is the making of decisions which will be best for the division and for the company. The achievement of this is called goal congruence;
   (b) enable divisional performance to be fairly measured; and
   (c) provide a vehicle for achieving divisional autonomy.

A single transfer price method however, rarely satisfies all these objectives and so some compromise is usual. The most common price in practice is the cost plus a percentage for profit, and the market price is used whenever one is available.

It has been shown that variable cost is a recommended transfer price for decision-making when the internal selling division is working below capacity. Such a price would not satisfy the divisional performance requirement if the selling division is a profit or investment centre, for the division would not even recover its full cost, let alone receive any profit. There would be no motivation for the selling division to supply the goods and the divisional manager might resort to a ruling from Head Office. Should the division be instructed to supply the goods at a particular price, then there would be a loss of divisional autonomy.

Resolving such a conflict of objectives is not easy, and a negotiated transfer price system helps. Another possible solution is to use two transfer prices for each transaction, known as a dual pricing system. The internal selling division is credited with a price which includes a profit if it has been earned, and the buying division is charged at variable or incremental cost to encourage it to make the best decision for itself and the company. This method clearly involves additional accounting work.

Within each division there are large numbers of profit centres. Whitbread Inns Division has 1,764 outlets which are either managed houses or pubs. The Managing Director's *Review of Operations* (1983/84) of this division states: 'Trading profits increased by 28%. . . . This has been achieved by better cost control, more effectively applied capital investment, and an increased range of facilities provided in our pubs.'

Questions and problems

8–1 Give examples of a cost centre, profit centre and investment centre in the hotel and catering industry.

8–2 Suggest the kind of catering operation which would give rise to the need for a system of transfer pricing.

8–3 Explain the relationship between divisional performance and transfer pricing.

8–4 Explain why a single method of transfer pricing is unlikely to prove satisfactory for all demands made upon it when associated with profit centres.

8–5 See pp. 122, 123

Wander Inn Hotels
Profit Statement for year ended 31st December, 1992

	Total Organization		Hotel No. 2			Hotel No. 2	
	Chairman	Director Operations	General Manager	Manager House	Manager Food and Beverage	House Dept. Head Rooms	Food and Beverage Dept. Head Food
	£	£	£	£	£	£	£
Revenue	1,000,000	1,000,000	400,000	250,000	150,000		35,000
Cost of sales	280,000	280,000	60,000		60,000		
Gross profit	720,000	720,000	340,000	250,000	90,000		
Other direct departmental expenses	350,000	350,000	140,000	90,000	50,000	25,000	20,000
Dept. operating profit	370,000	370,000	200,000	£160,000	£40,000		
Undistributed operating expenses	150,000	150,000	70,000				
Contribution to fixed costs	220,000	220,000	130,000				
Common fixed costs	130,000	100,000*	50,000				
Profit before tax	90,000	£120,000	£80,000				
Corporation tax	36,000						
Profit after tax	£54,000						

* Excluding £20,000 loan interest

Wander Inn Hotels
Balance Sheet at 31st December, 1992

	Total Orgn. £	Hotel No. 2 £
Current Assets:		
Cash at bank	28,000	11,000
Debtors	80,000	35,000
Stocks	25,000	10,000
Prepaid expenses	17,000	7,000
Total	150,000	63,000
Fixed Assets:		
Fixed assets	1,500,000	750,000
Less: Accumulated depreciation	(250,000)	(113,000)
Total	1,250,000	637,000
Total Assets	£1,400,000	£700,000

	Total Orgn. £	Hotel No. 2 £
Current liabilities:		
Creditors	65,000	24,000
Accrued expenses	35,000	6,000
Total	100,000	30,000
Long-term Liabilities:	300,000	170,000
Owners' Interest:		
Share capital	800,000	380,000
Retained profits	200,000	120,000
Total	1,000,000	500,000
Total Liabilities and Owners' Interest	£1,400,000	£700,000

123

Required:

(a) What are investment centres, profit centres and cost centres?

(b) From the information given which areas do you consider could be regarded as investment centres, profit centres and cost centres?

(c) As far as you can determine from the information provided calculate the following ratios:

Chairman
1. Return on total assets
2. Return on owners' interest

Director, Operations
1. Return on total assets
2. Profit related to sales revenue

General Manager, Hotel No. 2
1. Return on hotel assets
2. Profit on hotel sales revenue
3. Hotel controllable profit
4. Revenue/cost relationships

Manager, Hotel No. 2
1. Departmental operating profit related to sales revenue
2. Departmental gross profit related to revenue

Department Heads, Hotel No. 2
1. Food and beverage costs and/or other direct department costs related to revenue

(d) Consider the rationale for treating the various areas as investment centres, profit centres and cost centres.

Chapter Nine
Cost–Volume–Profit Analysis

Before finalizing a business plan, account should be taken of feasible opportunities so that the best use is made of available resources. Alternative plans might consider factors such as volume of business, pricing policy, advertising, food supply and prices, and standards for portion control.

Where *additional capital resources* are included in a forecast then a number of techniques are used to assess the profitability of the investment. These range from traditional average rate of return measures to the more elaborate net present value method using discounted cash flow techniques. This chapter, however, focuses on cost and profit planning using *existing resources*, leaving the subject of appraising plans that require additional capital to be dealt with separately in Chapter 17.

The mathematical equation method

In order to undertake the task of profit planning consideration should be given to the interaction between sales revenue, total costs and volume of activity. The interrelationship of these three elements of profit under different conditions will determine the outcome of the opportunities available to management. As a first step, it is useful to express the relationship in the form of a simple equation:

Profit = Total sales revenue − Total costs

The equation shows that profit is dependent upon revenue and cost. However, to arrive at a particular revenue and cost position for a given profit, details of the estimated unit selling price and costs together with volume of sales must be determined. To analyse these components the basic equation is expanded into what can appropriately be termed the 'cost–volume–profit (CVP) equation', as follows:

Net profit = (Unit selling price × Units sold) − [Fixed cost + (Unit variable cost × Units sold)]

125

For simplicity, the CVP equation can be written in mathematical form, as below:

$$\pi = px - (a + bx)$$

where
- π = net profit for the period;
- p = unit selling price;
- x = units sold;
- a = fixed cost for the period;
- b = unit variable cost.

The CVP equation can now be used to provide answers to a number of important managerial questions which are repeatedly raised during the financial planning stage of business operations. Examples of these are:

(a) How many products need to be sold during the period for the business to break-even, i.e. sales revenue to equal total costs?
(b) How many products are required to be sold during the period to achieve a given profit?
(c) What selling price per product should be charged to achieve a given profit at different levels of activity?

These fundamental questions to which a business should address itself can be answered by applying modified forms of the CVP equation, as illustrated using the assumed data for the Hospitality Restaurant Ltd presented in Exhibit 9–1.

Exhibit 9–1

Hospitality Restaurant Ltd

Relevant range of activity	15,000–30,000 units (meals)
Selling price per unit	£10
Variable cost per unit	£4
Fixed costs per annum	£120,000

(a) Break-even point (BEP) in number of units:
To achieve BEP (zero profit) total revenue must equal total costs:

$$\therefore px = a + bx$$

By substitution in the CVP equation the position is:

$$10x = 120,000 + 4x$$
$$\therefore x = 20,000 \text{ units (meals)}$$

(b) Unit sales to achieve a given profit of (say) £15,000:

By substitution in the CVP equation the position is:

$$15,000 = 10x - (120,000 + 4x)$$
$$\therefore 6x = 135,000$$
$$\therefore x = 22,500 \text{ units (meals)}$$

(c) Selling price to achieve £15,000 profit on sales of 25,000 units:

By substitution in the CVP equation the position is:

$$
\begin{aligned}
15{,}000 &= p(25{,}000) - [120{,}000 + 4(25{,}000)] \\
\therefore\ 15{,}000 &= 25{,}000p - 220{,}000 \\
\therefore\ 25{,}000p &= 235{,}000 \\
\therefore\ p &= £9.40 \text{ (i.e. a decrease of £0.60 per unit (meal))}
\end{aligned}
$$

The contribution margin method

An alternative approach to examining CVP relationships is known as the 'contribution margin method'. The difference is, however, merely one of emphasis. The mathematical equation method concentrates more upon the underlying mathematics whereas the contribution margin approach offers an accounting emphasis. The contribution margin is determined as follows:

Contribution margin = Sales revenues − Variable costs

The term contribution margin is an apt description as it represents the margin from sales revenue minus variable cost which is available to 'contribute' towards covering fixed costs and providing a profit.

In order to discuss the contribution margin approach the assumed data of the Hospitality Restaurant Ltd is presented in Exhibit 9–2 in the form of two profit statements which show the contribution margin.

Exhibit 9–2

Hospitality Restaurant Ltd

Relevant range (meals)	15,000	Unit	30,000	Unit
	£	£	£	£
Sales revenue	150,000	10	300,000	10
Less: Variable costs	60,000	4	120,000	4
Contribution margin	90,000	6	180,000	6
Less: Fixed costs	120,000		120,000	
Net profit(loss)	(30,000)		60,000	

Remember the 15,000–30,000 relevant range of activity simply reflects the restaurant's normal limits of operation.

From Exhibit 9–2 it can be seen that total contribution margin varies according to the level of activity, i.e. £90,000 at 15,000 units and £180,000 at 30,000 units. However, note that because unit selling price and variable cost are assumed to be constant at £10 and £4, *the contribution margin per unit* is also assumed to remain constant at £6. (Fixed costs are also assumed to remain constant at £120,000 per annum.)

The restaurant data shows that over the relevant range each unit sold generates a contribution margin of £6 towards fixed costs and profit. Therefore, the number of units required to be sold to break-even can be determined from the following contribution margin formula:

$$\text{BEP in units} = \frac{\text{Fixed costs}}{\text{Contribution margin per unit}}$$

$$= \frac{£120,000}{£6}$$

$$= 20,000 \text{ units (meals)}$$

The basic CVP equation of $\pi = px - (a + bx)$ can be adapted to show the contribution margin as follows:

$$\pi = (p - b)\,x - a$$

i.e. profit is equal to total contribution minus fixed costs where, $(p - b)x = $ total contribution. However, if profit is to be equal to zero then the equation will appear as:

$$a = (p - b)x$$

Therefore, to determine the break-even point in number of units the equation will be:

$$x = \frac{a}{(p - b)} = \frac{£120,000}{(£10 - £4)} = 20,000 \text{ units (meals)}$$

where $(p - b) = $ contribution margin per unit.

If management wish to achieve a profit of £15,000 during the year then, in addition to selling 20,000 units to make sufficient contribution margin to cover the £120,000 worth of fixed costs, the restaurant will need to generate a further contribution margin to attain the required profit. The contribution margin formula will thus appear as:

$$\text{Units sold for required profit} = \frac{\text{Fixed costs} + \text{Required profit}}{\text{Contribution margin per unit}}$$

$$= \frac{£120,000 + £15,000}{£6}$$

$$= 22,500 \text{ units (meals)}$$

Again, the basic CVP equation can be adapted to include a profit target and will appear as:

$$\pi + a = (p - b)x$$

Therefore, to determine the level of unit sales which will cover fixed costs and provide the desired profit the equation will be:

$$x = \frac{a + \pi}{(p - b)} = \frac{£120{,}000 + £15{,}000}{(£10 - £4)} = 22{,}500 \text{ units (meals)}$$

From the foregoing examples it becomes apparent that the contribution margin method amounts to a variation in presentation of the more mathematical CVP equation method. Both approaches are equally acceptable and it is a matter of personal choice as to which method is implemented.

The contribution margin to sales ratio

Attention has focused upon the determination of *unit sales* for a business to break even or achieve a particular profit target. However, in certain circumstances it may be necessary to directly compute the *sales value* required to attain break-even point or a given profit level. One way to obtain this is by use of the 'contribution margin to sales ratio' (C/S ratio) sometimes referred to as the 'profit-volume ratio' (P/V ratio). The contribution margin to sales ratio is calculated in the following manner:

$$\text{C/S ratio} = \frac{\text{Contribution margin} \times 100}{\text{Sales revenue}}$$

or

$$\frac{\text{Contribution margin per unit} \times 100}{\text{Selling price per unit}}$$

Referring to the Hospitality Restaurant Ltd data the contribution to sales ratio is:

$$\frac{£90{,}000 \times 100}{£150{,}000} = 60\%$$

or

$$\frac{£6 \times 100}{£10} = 60\%$$

To calculate break-even point in terms of sales value the contribution margin formula is adapted to give:

$$\text{BEP in sales value} = \frac{\text{Fixed costs}}{\text{C/S ratio}}$$

$$= \frac{£120,000}{60\%}$$

$$= £200,000$$

Using the basic CVP equation the formula is expressed as:

$$px = \frac{a}{\left(\dfrac{p-b}{p}\right)} = \frac{£120,000}{0.6} = £200,000$$

To achieve a given profit of £15,000 in the period the contribution margin formula will appear as:

$$\text{Sales value for required profit} = \frac{\text{Fixed costs} + \text{Required profit}}{\text{C/S ratio}}$$

$$= \frac{£120,000 + £15,000}{60\%}$$

$$= £225,000$$

Again the basic CVP equation can be adapted to include a profit target and will appear as:

$$px = \frac{a + \pi}{\left(\dfrac{p-b}{p}\right)} = \frac{£120,000 + £15,000}{0.6} = £225,000$$

Margin of safety

The margin of safety is the amount by which sales may decrease before a business sustains a loss. In other words it represents the difference between budgeted sales and the break-even point of a business. The margin of safety may be calculated in terms of number of units sold or sales value. For example, the break-even point of the Hospitality Restaurant Ltd is 20,000 meals (£200,000). Assuming the restaurant budgeted 30,000 meal sales (£300,000) for a coming period, then the margin of safety will be 10,000 meals (30,000 − 20,000) or £100,000 sales value (£300,000 − £200,000). Alternatively, the margin of safety can be expressed as a percentage based on the following ratio:

$$\frac{\text{Budgeted sales} - \text{Break-even sales}}{\text{Budgeted sales}} = \frac{£300,000 - £200,000}{£300,000} = 33\frac{1}{3}\%$$

The break-even chart

In addition to determining the CVP relationship by computation, it is frequently useful to present the information in the form of a break-even chart. A break-even chart is illustrated in Exhibit 9–3 using data drawn from the Hospitality Restaurant Ltd.

Exhibit 9–3   Break-even chart: Hospitality Restaurant Ltd

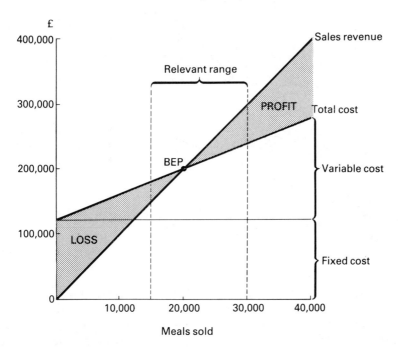

The basic information provided by the break-even chart is the point at which sales revenue equals total costs. Using the relevant range concept it is also possible to read off profit and loss estimates at different levels of activity. An estimate is determined by ascertaining the vertical distance between the sales revenue line and the total cost line directly above a given number of meals. However, perhaps the most important attribute of the break-even chart is that it provides management with a visual insight into the overall cost–volume–profit relationship of their particular business. (The procedure for drawing a break-even chart is given on page 138 at the end of the chapter.)

The contribution chart

By taking the information presented in the break-even chart in

131

Exhibit 9–3 a contribution chart can be prepared by reversing the order of the fixed and variable costs, as illustrated in Exhibit 9–4.

Exhibit 9–4   Contribution chart: Hospitality Restaurant Ltd

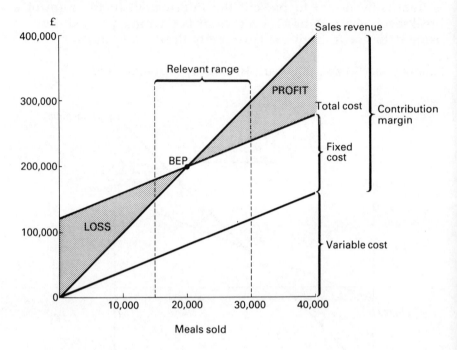

Meals sold

The main advantage of this form of presentation is that the contribution margin is highlighted on the chart. It is identified by ascertaining the vertical distance between the sales revenue line and the variable cost line. The other elements of the chart are similar to the break-even chart.

The profit–volume chart

While the break-even and contribution charts are useful in determining the approximate break-even point and visual overview of a business, they are less useful as a means of indicating profits and losses at various activity levels. A more effective chart for showing the impact on profit of different activity levels is the 'profit–volume chart' (P/V chart). A profit volume chart is illustrated in Exhibit 9–5, again using the data from the Hospitality Restaurant Ltd.

The ease with which profits and losses may be read off the chart can readily be seen. For instance, if the restaurant was to sell zero meals during a period, then no contribution margin would be

Exhibit 9–5   Profit–volume chart: Hospitality Restaurant Ltd

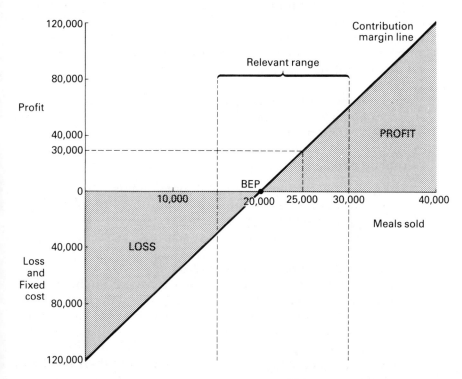

generated and the maximum loss it would sustain would be the £120,000 fixed costs. However, as the restaurant does sell meals a contribution margin of £6 per meal sold will be made towards fixed costs and profit. If 20,000 meals are sold then £120,000 contribution margin will be generated, i.e. 20,000 × £6, and the restaurant will break-even; this is the point at which the contribution margin line cuts the horizontal axis. Above 20,000 meals each meal sold will generate £6 profit for the restaurant. For example, assume the restaurant sold 25,000 meals during a period. The profit–volume chart shows that a profit of £30,000 will be earned, i.e. 25,000 × £6 contribution margin per meal = £150,000, minus fixed costs of £120,000. Hence, any number of profit and loss results can be determined by simply estimating the likely meal sales along the horizontal axis, then moving vertically, up or down, to the contribution margin line, and reading the figure off the scale on the vertical axis. The procedure for drawing a profit–volume chart is given on page 139 at the end of the chapter.

Underlying assumptions of CVP analysis

As already demonstrated, CVP analysis can be used to answer

several types of question and assist in management decision making. However, a number of assumptions underlie the use of CVP information and it is essential for managers to recognize them and attempt to assess their influence in a practical situation. If these assumptions are not considered then serious errors of judgement may ensue, resulting in incorrect conclusions being drawn from the analysis.

The more important assumptions of CVP analysis are:

(a) Revenue and cost behaviour are linear, i.e. take the form of a straight line on a chart, over the relevant range.

(b) All variables, other than those which are under consideration, remain constant throughout the analysis:

(i) selling prices per unit will not change;
(ii) variable costs are directly proportional to sales;
(iii) fixed costs remain constant;
(iv) cost prices remain unchanged, e.g. food prices, wage rates;
(v) productivity remains unchanged;
(vi) methods of production and service are unchanged;
(vii) the analysis covers a single product/service. Where this is not so then it is assumed that the given sales mix remains constant as sales change (discussed later in the chapter).

(c) All costs (and revenue) can be segregated into their fixed and variable components.

(d) Revenue and costs are related to a single independent variable which is normally based on some levels of activity, i.e. number of units sold or sales value of units sold.

(e) Volume of activity is the only relevant variable that determines cost behaviour. Clearly, there are many factors other than volume which affect revenue and costs, e.g. the quality of management and staff, working methods, industrial relations, the economic situation, training policies, climatic conditions. These and other variables are widely acknowledged as being relevant to cost and revenue behaviour. However, their lack of inclusion in CVP analysis is mainly due to the difficulties encountered when trying to quantify the extent of their influence.

Economist's versus accountant's CVP model

Although the accounting model of CVP analysis is criticized for the number of simplifying assumptions it makes, there are reasonable grounds for arguing that the approach is valid in many practical situations. This can best be discussed by comparing the economist's and the account's break-even charts, illustrated in Exhibit 9–6.

Exhibit 9–6   Graph showing accountant's and economist's break-even model

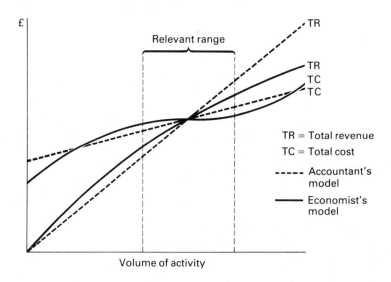

Of the assumptions listed earlier, a major criticism levelled at the accountant's model is that it assumes constant selling prices and variable cost per unit, i.e. linearity. The economic argument is clear. Referring to Exhibit 9–6, from the demand point of view, in order to expand market share selling prices frequently require to be reduced. From the cost standpoint, as demand for products and services grows, variable cost per unit declines in response to the benefits gained from the economies of scale. However, if demand persists and rises towards full capacity, variable cost per unit will normally increase as a result of diminishing returns.

The economic argument is undoubtedly valid, but the accounting model is not intended to provide a precise representation of total revenue and cost functions throughout all levels of activity. The objective is to represent the revenue and cost behaviour over the relevant range of activity which a firm expects to experience in the future. Accountants suggest that since most routine business decisions fall within the relevant range, which is a relatively narrow band of activity, the linearity assumption as depicted in Exhibit 9–6 is likely to hold. Furthermore, they argue that the benefits which might be gained from more accurate information are likely to be outweighed by the costs of obtaining the data.

Sales mix

Until now the discussion has assumed that a firm produces only

135

one product. Many firms produce a range of products and this is particularly so in the hotel and catering industry. In the case of multiproduct firms it is still useful to employ CVP analysis. Here the additional assumption present is that sales mix, i.e. the proportion each product represents of total sales, remains constant at all levels of sales in the relevant range.

Products can be analysed in a number of ways. Some of the more sophisticated approaches take the form of some kind of individual product arrangement, e.g. menu analysis. Others are based on departmental point of sale analysis, e.g. restaurant, coffee shop, banqueting room. However, for practical purposes hotel and catering firms usually collect cost and revenue data in a departmental form based on the services offered, i.e. rooms, food and beverage. The reasons for this are twofold. First, it is normally possible to match and relate cost and revenue data under the general headings of the services offered, and this assists in management control of profitability. Secondly, compared with their size, hotel and catering firms offer a wide variety of modestly priced products for a relatively low and erratic level of demand. Because of this it is usually uneconomic to develop the more detailed forms of product or departmental analyses.

Exhibit 9–7 shows the assumed data of the Armada Hotel presented in the form of services offered.

Exhibit 9–7

Armada Hotel – Projected Profit Statement

Department	Rooms	Food	Beverage	Total
Sales mix	50%	30%	20%	100%
Contribution margin to sales ratio	80%	60%	50%	68%*
	£	£	£	£
Sales revenue	150,000	90,000	60,000	300,000
Less: Variable costs	30,000	36,000	30,000	96,000
Contribution margin	120,000	54,000	30,000	204,000
Less: Fixed costs				153,000
Net profit				51,000

* Weighted average C/S ratio

From the details given in Exhibit 9–7, the Armada Hotel break-even point and net profit can be computed in terms of sales value, using the contribution margin to sales ratio, as follows:

$$\text{BEP} = \frac{\text{Fixed costs}}{\text{C/S ratio}}$$

$$= \frac{£153,000}{68\%} = £225,000$$

$$\text{Projected NP in sales value} = \frac{\text{Fixed costs + Required net profit}}{\text{C/S ratio}}$$

$$= \frac{£153,000 + £51,000}{68\%}$$

$$= £300,000$$

The hotel data is presented on a profit–volume chart, as shown in Exhibit 9–8.

Exhibit 9–8   Profit–volume chart: Armada Hotel

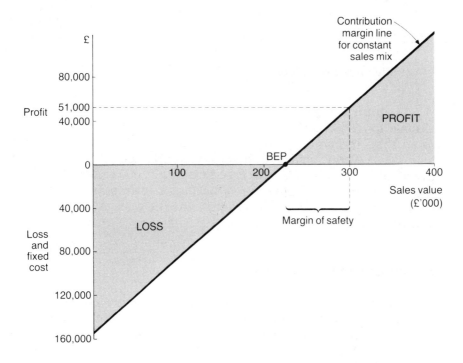

Notice that the contribution margin line is based on the assumption that the hotel sales mix remains constant. In other words, for each £100 of total revenue, room sales generated should be £50, food sales £30, and beverage sales £20. If the sales mix proportions do not hold, then even in the event of total sales revenue being the projected £300,000, net profit is likely to result in a figure other than £51,000. For example, assume the actual results of the Armada Hotel were as presented in Exhibit 9–7, with the exception of the projected sales mix which changed to room sales of 30%, food sales 50%, and beverage sales 20%, i.e. a reverse in the proportions of rooms and food sales. The outcome is presented in Exhibit 9–9.

Exhibit 9–9   The Armada Hotel – actual profit statement

Department	Rooms	Food	Beverage	Total
Sales mix	30%	50%	20%	100%
Contribution margin to sales ratio	80%	60%	50%	64%*
	£	£	£	£
Sales revenue	90,000	150,000	60,000	300,000
Less: Variable costs	18,000	60,000	30,000	108,000
Contribution margin	72,000	90,000	30,000	192,000
Less: Fixed costs				153,000
Net profit				39,000

* Weighted average C/S ratio: $\text{BEP} = \dfrac{£153,000}{64\%} = £239,063$

As Exhibit 9–9 shows, the projected net profit has dropped from £51,000 to £39,000. This is due to a decline in the more profitable room sales in favour of the less profitable food sales even though total sales revenue achieved the projected £300,000. Correspondingly, the break-even point has increased from £225,000 to £239,063. Thus, it can be seen from these figures that break-even points and profits are not unique numbers; they depend on the sales mix composition and indeed, many other factors.

Drawing a break-even chart:

1. Calculate values of maximum sales revenue and maximum activity, activity being measured in units, covers, hours, etc.
2. Determine X (horizontal) and Y (vertical) scales taking into account:
   (a) Y scale represents £s
   (b) X scale represents activity
   (c) maximum sales and activity
   (d) the larger the scale the more accurate will be results
   (e) wherever possible multiples of 5 or 2 in the scale
   (f) a chart may cover 1 month, 3 months or 1 year according to the problem.

3. Draw in X line and two Y lines, one from 0 and one from maximum X value, inserting scales, bottom left being 0.
4. Mark off maximum sales value on right hand Y line and join up to 0 with a straight line. This represents sales revenue.
5. On left and right hand Y mark off fixed cost and join points with a line parallel to base line.
6. Inserting variable costs above the fixed cost will give a line representing total cost. Two points needed for total cost line are the fixed cost point on left hand Y and total cost point at maximum activity (a calculation is needed here).
7. Break-even point is where total cost line cuts sales revenue.
8. A vertical dotted line from break-even point (BEP) touches X at activity BEP.
9. A horizontal dotted line from BEP to left hand Y shows sales turnover at BEP.

Drawing a profit–volume chart

1. Calculate profit at maximum sales level. This added to the fixed cost is the maximum value of the vertical (Y) line.
2. Draw the vertical line to scale and insert 0 value so that above it represents profit and below it fixed cost.
3. Draw in the horizontal (X) line to a scale to represent sales units or value.
4. The 'contribution' line starts at the fixed cost point on the vertical line and needs one more point to fix its position. This point can be either the break-even point or the profit at any particular sales level, and each involves calculation.
5. The fixed cost is joined to, say, the BEP and the profit graph is completed.

Questions and problems

9–1 Explain the following terms:
    (a) contribution margin
    (b) break-even point
    (c) margin of safety.

9–2 What is the 'contribution margin to sales ratio'?

9–3 Below is an outline break-even chart:

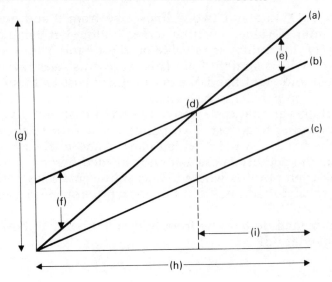

Name the various points indicated by the letters. What is the name of the area taken in by the 'origin', (a) and (c)?

9–4 Below is the outline of a profit–volume break-even chart.

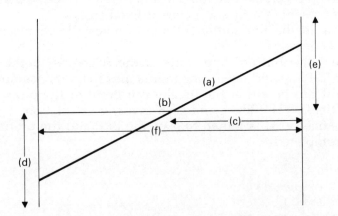

Name the various points indicated by the letters.

9–5 Accounting and economics break-even charts differ. Describe the principal differences between the charts and indicate the extent to which one is justified in using the accounting kind of chart.

9–6 Complete the following tabulation:

Annual fixed costs £	Contribution per unit £	Break-even point Units
10,000	0.50	*
*	0.85	9,000
30,000	*	20,000

9–7 The budgeted sales of three companies are as follows:

	Company 1	Company 2	Company 3
Budgeted sales in units	10,000	10,000	10,000
Budgeted selling price per unit	£2.00	£2.00	£2.00
Budgeted variable costs per unit	£1.50	£1.25	£1.00
Budgeted fixed expenses total	£3,000	£5,500	£8,000

From the above information you are required to compute for each company:
(a) budgeted profit;
(b) the budgeted break-even point in unit sales;
(c) the impact on profits of a ± 10% deviation in sales.
Comment briefly on the effect of this in relation to the distribution between the company's fixed and variable expenses.

9–8 A hotel company plans to open a new theme restaurant adjacent to one of its existing properties which it intends to operate as a separate entity.

Equipment and furniture is to be purchased for the restaurant at a cost of £144,000 and working capital of £6,000 is to be provided for operations. The restaurant is expected to generate a return on capital employed of 15% per annum, before taxation.

Budgeted annual costs for the first year of operation are: rent and rates £35,000; salaries £47,500; insurance £2,500; equipment and furniture is to be depreciated at the rate of 10% per annum on the original cost; and administration £6,350. Variable costs of the restaurant, other than the cost of food are estimated to be 13% of sales revenue.

It is the policy of management to add a mark-up of 150% to the food cost to give an average spend of £25 per cover.

You are required to:
(a) calculate the number of covers per annum for the restaurant to break-even;
(b) calculate the number of covers per annum for the restaurant to achieve the return on capital employed expected by management;
(c) prepare a break-even chart for the restaurant and indicate the break-even point and margin of safety

9-9 Silvermere Developments Ltd has the opportunity of opening a restaurant in Brightsea which would be called 'Silversea Chef'. Silvermere Developments Ltd would have to pay £36,000 for the fixed assets and provide £4,000 working capital. A feasibility study has been completed and the results indicate annual costs (exclusive of VAT) as follows:
  (i) food costs of between 35% and 45% of sales
  (ii) wages £14,000, and
  (iii) other costs £16,000.

Although the 'Silversea Chef' would be able to cater for 30,000 customers per annum, the feasibility study forecasts a demand of between 20,000 to 25,000 customers per annum with an average spending power of £2.70 (inclusive of VAT at 15 per cent) per customer. The wages and other costs will cover the range of demand forecasted.

You are to prepare a report for the Board of Directors of Silvermere Developments Ltd (which expects a return on capital of 15%) on the viability of financing the opening of the 'Silversea Chef' to include a statement of the forecast of the range of profit or loss per annum and a break-even (or contribution) chart.   (HCIMA)

9-10 The following information relates to three alternative forecasts A, B and C, each of which has the same price and the same potential level of sales but only one can be included in the next period's budget. Present this information in a suitable graphical form and comment on it in respect of the particular problem under consideration.

	A	B	C
Selling price	£1	£1	£1
Contribution to sales ratio	20%	15%	10%
Fixed costs	£9,500	£6,000	£3,750
Estimated sales	60,000 (covers)	60,000 (covers)	60,000 (covers)

9-11 The following information is taken from the accounts of the Linda Restaurant.

	Sales £	Total costs £
Year 1	60,000	54,000
Year 2	64,000	56,400
Year 3	70,000	60,000

(a) From this information calculate the net profit to be achieved in Year 4 if sales are £80,000 as estimated and fixed costs increase by £4,000.
(b) Calculate also the break-even point when sales are £80,000.

9–12 A food processing job is done manually by employees who can each carry out 1,500 jobs in a week, and whose wages are £90 each per week. The cost of food supplies required in this task is £500 per 1,000 jobs.

As a result of a work study investigation it is found that the task can be undertaken by a piece of equipment costing £32,500 with a capacity of up to 9,000 jobs per week. The operator would be paid £120 per week but would not be available for other work as he is a specialist operator. The present employees on this work are moved to other work should the need arise.

Costs associated with the equipment are:

Maintenance per week £30
Operating costs £20 per 1,000 jobs
Food supplies £500 per 1,000 jobs
The machine would be depreciated over 5 years of 50 weeks on a straight line basis with no residual value

You are required to ascertain the weekly level of activity beyond which there would be a cost saving to the company by having the work mechanized.

Your answer should be arrived at by each of the following methods:
(a) tabulation;
(b) calculation;
(c) break-even chart.

9–13 The wash-up section of the Atlas Hotel currently deals manually with washing-up for 15,000 covers per month. However, demand forecasts prepared by the food and beverage department indicate that this is likely to increase to 18,000 covers per month and could possibly rise to a monthly maximum of 20,000 covers or more. In the light of this, management are contemplating whether or not to introduce either a semi-automatic or fully automatic washing-up system.

The operating costs associated with the existing and proposed systems are detailed below:

	Manual £	Semi-auto £	Fully auto £
Wages per 1,000 covers	240	120	—
Salaries per month	—	1,200	2,100
Detergents per 1,000 covers	20	20	70
Power usage per month	—	400	600
Maintenance per month	—	100	300
Towels etc. per 1,000 covers	10	5	—
Depreciation per month	—	300	500

Note: The monthly costs are fixed.

You are required to:
(a) Prepare a graph of the cost curves representing the washing-up alternatives which reflects the current and forecast demands on the hotel's wash-up section for the existing and proposed systems.
(b) Evaluate the relative cost effectiveness of the wash-up systems and advise management on the results.

(BAHA)

9–14 The owners of Today's Speciality, a successful medium-priced wine bar, are contemplating moving up-market in the coming year in order to sell fewer, but more expensive dishes. The anticipated sales and costs for this proposal are:

	£
Budgeted sales revenue	1,000,000
Fixed costs	500,000

Menu category	Sales mix	Variable costs
	%	£
Seasonal	12	60,000
Speciality	60	150,000
Vegetarian	28	140,000

However, if the above proposal is not implemented then the current medium-priced market will be maintained. The expected annual sales and costs for this are:

	£
Budgeted sales revenue	1,000,000
Fixed costs	210,000

Menu category	Sales mix	Variable costs
	%	£
Salads	50	300,000
Hot	30	200,000
Cold	20	150,000

Annual fluctuations in demand are not expected to exceed 10% for either proposal.

Required:
(a) Present the anticipated results for the two proposals on a profit–volume graph, showing workings clearly.
(b) Draw attention to the factors that should be considered by the owners of Today's Speciality prior to their making a decision on whether or not to develop the up-market proposal.

9–15 Go-Ahead Hotels Ltd offer a package holiday which during the current year has sold for £40, the variable cost being £25. The company's accountant has estimated the profit for the year at £150,000 after allowing for fixed costs of £120,000.

During discussion on the 1988 budget the hotels' controller said he anticipated a unit variable cost rise of £1 following a recent wage award. The accountant expects fixed costs to rise by £5,000 this being due, in the main, to increased rental payable under the company's leases which are currently being re-negotiated. The marketing manager thought the market was buoyant but also owing to rising costs, competitors would increase the prices of their holidays in 1988. He expressed the views that:

    (i) with the price remaining at £40, the number of holidays sold next year would increase by 10%; and

    (ii) if the price could be reduced by £1, increase in sales of 25% could be expected.

You are required to:

    (a) present a statement to show which of the marketing manager's proposals provide the greater amount of profit;

    (b) calculate in respect of each alternative the break-even point in terms of sales volume; and

    (c) under alternative (ii) how many holidays would the company need to sell to earn a profit of £160,000?

9–16 By way of experiment the Northern Area Health Board set up a central kitchen which produces, using traditional catering methods, 60,000 portions of food per month for a number of its hospitals. The costs of one month's production are as follows:

	per month £
Variable costs:	
Food	45,000
Direct labour	24,000
Fixed costs	40,000

The Board is now planning to expand production by 50% and is also considering the installation of a cook–chill system to replace the traditional system. The estimated costs of the

145

cook–chill system per 10,000 portions per month are detailed below:

	per month £
Variable costs:	
Food and foil containers	8,000
Direct labour	1,300
Semi-variable costs (historical data reveal the following relationship applicable to various levels of production):	

Portions	£
50,000	17,000
70,000	19,000
80,000	20,000

Fixed costs	37,600

You are required to:
  (a) prepare a statement showing the costs per month of the two systems at the planned level of production;
  (b) determine the number of portions per month at which:
      (i) the costs of the two systems equate;
      (ii) there is a cost saving of £2,400 from the cook–chill system; and
  (c) assuming the Board does expand production, briefly state, with reasons, whether or not the cook–chill system should be adopted.

(HCIMA)

9–17 Feasts Ltd own and operate the Elizabethan Rooms which specialize in medieval-style banquets.
   The average cost and profit structure per cover for the current year, based on 50,000 covers, has been prepared:

	£
Food	2.00
Direct labour	0.60
Variable overhead	0.40
Fixed overhead	1.20
Profit	0.80
Average spending	5.00

At present the directors are considering alternative courses of action for the coming year:

Alternative 1
To continue with the existing method of operation. If this alternative is adopted, then it is anticipated that the current year's costs will increase as follows:

	%
Food	11.5
Direct labour	15.0
Variable overhead	20.0
Fixed overhead	10.0

Alternative 2
To modernize the system of food production and service by introducing convenience foods and a limited degree of self-service. An analysis has been carried out and, if this alternative is adopted, the new system will have the following effect on the current year's costs:

Decrease in total variable cost per cover £0.20

Increase in fixed cost per annum £45,000

Irrespective of which alternative is selected, the directors estimate that:
(i) the volume of business will increase during the coming year to 70,000 covers;
(ii) a 6% price rise, effective from the beginning of the coming year, is unlikely to affect the estimated level of demand.

You are requested to:
(a) calculate, for each alternative, the number of covers that would have to be sold in order to maintain the current year's profits at their present level;
(b) calculate (or determine graphically) the number of covers beyond which it would prove more profitable to introduce the modernized system; and
(c) comment briefly on the financial implications of the alternatives and recommend to the directors which alternative should be adopted. (HCIMA)

9–18 Set out on page 148 is the rooms department profit statement of the 260-room Osaka International Hotel for the month ended 31st March, 1992. The Osaka consistently achieves an average room rate of £100.

Rooms Department Profit Statement

	£	£
Sales revenue		504,000
Less: Allowances		4,000
Net sales revenue		500,000
Less: Department expenses		
Payroll and related	100,000	
Travel agent commissions	16,500	
Laundry and cleaning	10,000	
Operating supplies	12,500	
Other expenses	7,500	146,500
Departmental profit		£353,500

An analysis of past rooms department expenses indicates the following cost behaviour relationships:

1. Payroll and related: £60,000 is fixed and the balance is a variable expense.
2. Travel agent commissions: this is a variable expense.
3. Laundry and cleaning: £4,000 is fixed and the balance is a variable expense.
4. Operating supplies: this is a variable expenses.
5. Other expenses: £2,500 is fixed and the balance is a variable expense.

The hotel's marketing department anticipates that net room sales revenue will increase by 25% in April.

Required:
(a) Prepare a projected rooms department profit statement for April in a form which shows:
(i) departmental contribution margin;
(ii) departmental profit
(b) Calculate the rooms department contribution margin to sales ratio and determine the break-even point in terms of sales revenue and occupancy for April.
(c) Comment upon the fact that the rooms department expenses do not include a share of the hotel's undistributed operating expenses and fixed charges such as administration, energy and interest.

(BAHA)

9–19 The Cozy Restaurant has made a loss of £3,636 over the first six months of the year although it had been estimated that a profit of £10,000 would be made for the year.

Various proposals have been made to rectify the situation. You are required to evaluate and comment upon each of these proposals.

Figures for the six months show:

	£
Sales revenue	100,000
Cost of food used	60,000
Labour cost	25,000
Overheads	18,636

The average spending is exactly £2 per customer. The full capacity of the restaurant is twice the occupancy which has been achieved.

However, labour costs have been analysed and it has been ascertained that £5,000 is constant but the remainder is proportionate to the level of sales.

Of other overheads, £8,636 is fixed. This figure would be increased, however, if the restaurant was working above 75% capacity constantly, as additional plant would be required.

Proposal 1   Spend £1,000 on advertising to increase sales.

Proposal 2   Introduce a scheme for bulk buying of food used. It is estimated that this will reduce costs by 9% but fixed overheads will be increased by £1,000.

Proposal 3   To reduce prices by 15% to achieve 100% capacity utilization.

Proposal 4   For the foreseeable future to plan only to break even and to reduce variable costs other than cost of goods used to achieve this.

(HCIMA)

9–20 A company which produces two food products has annual fixed costs of £12,000.

	Food product A	Food product B
	£	£
Selling price	5	4
Less: Variable costs	2	2
Contribution	3	2

The desired product mix is two of A for every one of B. You are required to show by both calculation and break-even chart how many of each food product need to be sold to break even.

9–21 Precise Limited has prepared the following budget for the forthcoming year:

	Restaurant	Canteen	Total
No. of meals	40,000	120,000	160,000
	£	£	£
Sales	80,000	360,000	440,000
Expenses:			
Food	20,000	80,000	100,000
Direct labour	4,000	140,000	144,000
Overheads	40,000	90,000	130,000
	64,000	310,000	374,000
Profit	16,000	50,000	66,000

The overhead figures contain both fixed and variable overheads. The variable element is estimated to be 30% of the direct labour expense.

You are required to:
  (a) ascertain by calculation the break-even point assuming sales remain constant; and
  (b) draw a profit–volume chart and read off the profit if sales revenue increases to a level of £200,000 in the budgeted proportions.

9–22 The Oxford Leisure Centre showed the following financial results for the year:

	£		£
Admission sales (fees)	14,000	Expenses:	40,000
Coffee shop sales	60,000	Payroll (variable)	56,000
		Payroll (fixed)	90,000
Total sales	200,000	Other (fixed)	
			186,000
Food Cost	24,000		
Gross profit	176,000	Net profit/(loss)	£(10,000)

You are required to:

  (a) Determine the variable cost percentage and contribution margin percentage for each of the following items (round all percentages to the nearest whole number):
    (i) admission;
    (ii) coffee shop;
    (iii) admission and coffee shop combined.

Answer the additional questions below, independent of each other.

(b) What increase in sales volume is necessary to break-even assuming that admission and coffee shop sales remain in their present mix?

(c) What increase in sales volume is required to achieve a net profit of £15,000 assuming that admission and coffee shop sales remain in their present mix?

(d) What overall percentage increase in prices is necessary to attain break-even point?

(e) If all prices are reduced by 10%, what overall increases in sales volume would be necessary to break-even assuming that admission and coffee shop sales remain in their present mix?

(f) How much additional sales volume is required to generate a net profit of £15,000 assuming that these sales will be in a 60% admission and 40% coffee shop mix?

(g) If an additional swimming attendant was employed at a cost of £8,000 per annum, what increase in admission sales would be necessary to make the decision worthwhile?

(h) If coffee shop sales could be increased by 20% as a result of increasing the sales promotion budget by £1,200 per annum and increasing overall food cost to 45%, should the project be undertaken?

Chapter Ten

Approaches to Decision Making

Decision making in business has a special meaning when accounting is being considered, for in general all business activities are involved in the making of decisions. Decisions are needed first to establish an annual business plan and then to maintain control so that planned objectives are met. There are many ways of classifying decisions and one is to take account of the kind of cost involved.

Classification of decisions

Three classes of decision may be identified:

(a) *Decisions involving clear-cut fixed and variable costs* or where costs can be placed into these categories by calculation. Cost behaviour here is paramount so that the contribution margin may be manipulated. This is useful when considering different strategies for the budget period. Maximizing profit from limiting factors is an example of this kind of decision. Linear programming is a technique to use when more than one limiting factor is present.

(b) *Decisions involving semi-variable costs* which cannot be placed into fixed and variable categories. Profit from different levels of activity is best determined by using flexible budgets. Mathematical calculation is difficult.

(c) *Decisions involving relevant costs* where behaviour plays a minor role.

Decisions involving fixed and variable costs

Contribution margin per unit of limiting factor

In circumstances where there is opportunity to change the limits of operating departments it may be advisable to enlarge the most profitable department at the expense of another department. Accordingly the floor space may be regarded as the limiting factor and a calculation made to discover which department has the highest contribution per sq. metre of floor space.

Listing departments in order of contribution per sq. metre is the start-point in a profitability study.

Forecast Profit Statement year ended . . . . .

	Dept. A	Dept. B	Dept. C	Total
1 Contribution	£2,000	£4,000	£5,000	£11,000
2 Square metres	1,000	1,000	2,000	4,000
(1 ÷ 2) Contribution per sq. metre	£2	£4	£2.5	
Order of profitability	3	1	2	

On the face of it, if say 500 square metres of Dept. A were to be used to expand Dept. B and B's sales increased by ½ without dropping selling prices total contribution would be:

	Dept. A	Dept. B	Dept. C	Total £
1 Contribution per sq. m.	£2	£4	£2.5	
2 Square metres	500	1,500	2,000	
(1 × 2) New total contribution	£1,000	£6,000	£5,000	12,000
Former contribution				11,000
Increased annual contribution				1,000

This change in contribution takes account of changes in the total cost of food and drink caused by new sales levels. If no additional fixed costs such as salaries, equipment and advertising were involved then the additional contribution of £1,000 would become the additional profit. If equipment costing £3,000 were required, depreciation of £600 per annum over 5 years would mean the increase in profit was only £400 p.a.

Other factors to be considered would be the effect on profit if any sales in Dept. A influenced sales in Dept. B. A very small contribution by one department might be the cause of a large contribution in another department, a state of affairs which might be acceptable because in the final analysis it is *total* contribution and *total* profit that counts.

A restaurant in a department store may show only a small contribution, but may attract customers to sales departments where good contributions are being made.

Clearly the contribution per unit of limiting factor is a useful start for a plan to increase profitability; indeed it should precede the preparation of the sales budget.

Linear programming

If there are two different products, services or departments competing for two or more limited resources then the linear programming 'graphical technique' will provide the answer in terms of the optimal activity mix which maximizes profits. An example will illustrate the technique.

A speciality restaurant offers two groups of dishes known as 'frieds' and 'grills', which have average contributions of £1 per dish.

	'frieds'	*'grills'*
Average labour times per dish:		
Kitchen staff	2 mins	3 mins
Restaurant service	5 mins	2 mins

Total food production and service available per day:
Kitchen staff   30 hours
Restaurant staff 40 hours
Current ingredient scarcity allows only 500 'grills' to be available per day.
Determine graphically the dish mix which maximizes contributions.
The solution is best commenced by laying out the relevant facts in mathematical form:

(a) Kitchen limiting factor $2f + 3g \leqslant 1800$ minutes*
(b) Restaurant limiting factor $5f + 2g \leqslant 2400$ minutes
(c) Food scarcity factor $g \leqslant 500$ dishes
(d) Maximize contributions   £1f + £1g
     As negative production is not possible f and g must be each $\geqslant$ zero.

The first three expressions may now be graphed as illustrated in Exhibit 10–1.
For example, with the kitchen limiting factor the maximum number of dishes which could be produced is:

$$\text{'frieds'} \quad \frac{1800 \text{ mins}}{2 \text{ mins}} = 900$$

or

$$\text{'grills'} \quad \frac{1800 \text{ mins}}{3 \text{ mins}} = 600$$

* f = 'frieds' and g = 'grills'.

Exhibit 10–1 Graphical solution to linear programming problem

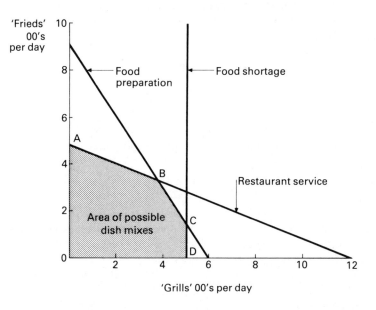

Similarly either 480 'frieds' or 1,200 'grills' could be served in 40 hours. These alternatives may be plotted on the graph together with the 500 'grills' food shortage. Points A, B, C, and D become the possible combinations of dishes. A ruler joining 200 'frieds' with 200 'grills' will represent all combinations of dishes to give a total contribution of £200, e.g. 200 'frieds' or 200 'grills' or 100 'frieds' and 100 'grills' etc. Keeping the slope constant and moving the ruler outwards from O, which represents increasing the total contribution, point B is the last to be reached. This point is where 327 'frieds' and 382 'grills' are produced. Maximum contribution is therefore at point B:

$$
\begin{array}{lr}
 & £ \\
\text{'frieds' } 327 @ £1 = & 327 \\
\text{'grills' } 382 @ £1 = & 382 \\
\hline
 & 709 \\
\hline
\end{array}
$$

This is better than point C which gives:

$$
\begin{array}{lr}
 & £ \\
\text{'frieds' } 150 @ £1 = & 150 \\
\text{'grills' } 500 @ £1 = & 500 \\
\hline
 & 650 \\
\hline
\end{array}
$$

155

It will be noted that the food shortage is not a constraint on the optimum mix. However, if the contribution were 'frieds' . . . £1 and 'grills' @ £1.60, then C would represent the best mix and the food shortage factor would become an effective constraint.

	Point B		Point C	
	£		£	
'frieds'	327	327	150	150
'grills'	382	611	500	800
		938		950

More complex planning problems involving more than two outputs, e.g. dishes, require much tedious calculation necessitating the use of a computer.

Decisions involving semi-variable costs

The flexible budget

The first class of decision mentioned on p. 152 – clear cut fixed and variable costs – is dealt with in Chapter 9 and there are clear mathematical rules for solving problems. The second class requires a detailed consideration of each cost item so as to determine how it should be treated for decision making. The flexible budget is designed to change with changing levels of activity. The approach is to show total costs and revenues associated with the different options involved. There may be several different levels of activity or just two courses of action. The financial consequences of each option or course of action is built up from a study of each cost item, as illustrated in Exhibit 10–2.

Exhibit 10–2

The Park Hotel's owner/manager is considering closing for the period October to March because the accounts show a small loss during the winter half. You have been asked to advise him of the real financial consequences of closing based on last year's accounts and estimated future costs should he decide to close for six months.
Recorded accounts for last year:

Profit statement 19X6/X7

	April/Sept. £	Oct./March £	
Sales	90,000	40,000	
Cost of sales	33,300	14,800	
	56,700	25,200	
Wages and salaries	26,000	14,000	
Rates	2,250	2,250	
Depreciation	3,000	3,000	
Light and heat	2,200	3,000	
Cleaning	1,500	1,000	
Laundry	1,100	600	
Advertising	900	900	
Sundries	1,600	1,100	
	38,550	25,850	
Profit/(loss)	£18,150	£(650)	Total £17,500

You decide to prepare a flexible budget which shows the profit or loss at two levels of activity for the twelve month period, covering 12 month opening and covering 6 month opening:

Profit statement showing effect of opening for 6 or 12 months

	12 months £	6 months (April/Sept.) £
Sales	130,000	90,000
Cost of sales	48,100	33,300
	81,900	56,700
Wages and salaries	40,000	26,000
Rates	4,500	4,500
Depreciation	6,000	4,500
Light and heat	5,200	2,200
Cleaning	2,500	1,500
Laundry	1,700	1,100
Advertising	1,800	1,200
Sundries	2,700	1,600
	64,400	42,600
Profit/(loss)	£17,500	£14,100

The statement shows £14,100 profit made from April to September and £17,500 when open all the year. A further £3,400 profit is made when open all the year – this is the financial consequence.

Two points need to be emphasized. If rates cover the whole year with no refund for the period closed, the cost is truly a fixed cost for the year and must appear in total for any level of flexible budget activity. The depreciation is based on £6,000 for the full year. Because it is reckoned the equipment will last longer if not used for six months, some depreciation will be saved. Full depreciation is £3,000 for operating for six months but only half this amount for six months when not used.

The lesson to be learned from this illustration is that where possible it is best to look at the *total* cost and profit from each alternative course of action and ignore any apportionment of costs between departments, products or, as in this case, between periods.

Decisions involving relevant costs

A number of principles may be considered in this class of decision making, mainly to assist in presenting the financial information clearly.

(a) Only future costs are relevant to decision making. This applied to Exhibit 10–2 because the past figures were assumed to be similar to ones expected in the future.

(b) Past costs not expected to be repeated in the future are not relevant to a decision. These are known as sunk costs.

(c) Relevant costs are costs which will differ for each alternative course of action. Therefore if any costs are truly fixed in behavioural terms, they may be ignored. The only fixed cost in the illustration is the rates expense. This could have been ignored and the difference between the profit from opening twelve as compared with six months would have been unchanged. It is not wrong to include fixed costs for all options, but it does add time and makes for complexity when large numbers of fixed costs are included unnecessarily.

(d) Opportunity cost is the highest alternative benefit foregone in selecting a course of action. It is an economic term rather than an accounting term and does not appear in the books of account. Its use may be avoided by using accounting cash flow in its place. It is a particular way of presenting financial information for decision making (see Exhibit 10–3).

Exhibit 10–3

A large showcase in an hotel is reckoned to provide an annual gross profit of £2,500 less expenses of £500, a net £2,000. A local firm has offered to take over the position for £5,000 per annum in cash for a period of five years. In presenting this situation the accountant might show in the books:

	Present annual profit	Future profit
	£	£
Sales	4,500	5,000
cost of sales	2,000	—
Gross profit	2,500	5,000
Expenses	500	—
Net profit	2,000	5,000

Increase in annual profit of £3,000.

Presented in an opportunity cost manner, the present profit is shown as the cost of the proposed contract:

	£
Annual revenue from letting the space	5,000
Opportunity cost	2,000
Net annual benefit of letting the space	3,000

Should management be planning changes which would remove the space in its present earning capacity, the £5,000 per annum would be the opportunity cost of giving up the space.

Questions and problems

10–1 Explain the term 'contribution per unit of limiting factor'.

10–2 How does linear programming assist management in maximizing profit?

10–3 Why are past costs regarded as not relevant in decision making?

10–4 The monthly sales budget of IMHI Fish House, an upmarket speciality restaurant, which offers four menus A, B, C, and D is £214,000 made up as follows:

	£
Menu A	60,000
Menu B	56,000
Menu C	48,000
Menu D	50,000

Data relating to each menu is set out below:

	A	B	C	D
	£	£	£	£
Food cost (mainly fish)	8	20	15	10
Variable labour	3	6	3	4
Fixed overhead	1	4	3	2
Profit	8	10	9	9
Selling price	£20	£40	£30	£25

Food suppliers have warned the company that owing to world shortages, they will be unable to deliver more than £80,000 worth of fish per month until conditions improve. Management realise that this will result in curtailment of production and sales but with a view to keeping the company's menus in the minds of the public they wish, if possible, to produce a minimum of 1,000 of each per month, and to use any fish which remain in the most profitable manner.

You are required to prepare statements showing:

(a) the contribution per unit of limiting (scarce) factor for each fish menu;

(b) the quantities of each product which the company should produce each month;

(c) the original and revised budgeted profit.

10–5 As the recently appointed catering manager in a leisure complex you have been asked to evaluate the performance of the three catering departments which are situated in a separate building:

A. Banqueting
B. Restaurant
C. Self-service

You are required to:

(a) prepare a statement for the year ended 30th April, 1987, showing the departmental contributions and total profit for the catering departments;

(b) comment on the relative effectiveness of the departments; and

(c) recommend any changes you feel would improve total profitability. For this purpose you are to assume that the sales of each department can be expanded.

The information given below relates to the year ended 30th April 19X9.

Departments		A	B	C
Sales	£000	290	120	300
Gross profit margin added to cost of goods sold	%	45	100	50
Floor area occupied	sq. ft.	4,000	3,000	5,000

Staff: One supervisor is employed in each department at an inclusive cost of £3,000 per year.
One assistant is employed for each 500 square feet of floor space at an inclusive cost of £2,000 per year.

	£	Bases of Apportionment
Rent and rates	36,000	Floor space
Heat and light	19,000	Floor space with a weighting:
		Department A 1.5
		B 1.0
		C 2.0

			%
Advertising	20,000	Department A	45
		B	25
		C	30

Other expenses not allocated departmentally, amount to £56,000 per annum.

(HCIMA)

10–6 A large hotel has 500 rooms divided into 200 suites and 300 double bedrooms. The hotel is full for nine months of each year but from January to March business is fairly quiet. Room tariffs, costs etc., are as follows:

	Suite	Double room
Selling price	£20	£12
Variable costs (including room servicing)	£9	£5
Room servicing times	1 hour	½ hour

Experience has shown that during the three-month period the maximum number of room lets that can be made are 4,000 suite room nights and 9,000 double room nights. The total number of room servicing hours available is estimated to be 7,000 hours.

Using the linear programming graphical technique determine the combination of suite/room lets which will yield the greatest profit.

10-7 Your company is considering the purchase of an hotel in Torquay. On the basis of past years' trading results, the estimated figures for future years' trading results are as follows:

	1st April to 30th September £	1st October to 31st March £
Sales	43,000	15,000
Other income	4,000	700
Cost of sales	23,000	8,000
Wages	14,000	4,000
Heat and light	600	700
Repairs and maintenance	500	250
Rates	1,000	1,000
Other expenses	400	50
Depreciation:		
Premises	2,000	2,000
Fittings	900	900
China, cutlery etc.	300	100

If the hotel closed during the off season, then the depreciation on fittings would be reduced to £500 and China, cutlery, etc., £Nil.

You are required to:

(a) prepare financial statement(s) to illustrate the advisability of remaining open (or closing) during the off season periods; and

(b) if it is the company's policy to achieve a return on investment of 12%, what is the maximum price it could offer for the hotel?

10-8 In April 1985, the budget committee of The Lawrence Hotel Ltd, formulated the master budget for the year ended 31st May 1986, on the basis of information then available. A summary of the master venue accounts follows:

The Lawrence Hotel Limited
Master trading, profit and loss account for the year ended 31st May 1986

		Total		Season		Off-season
	£	£	£	£	£	£
Sales		100,000		80,000		20,000
Variable costs	44,000		32,000		12,000	
Fixed costs	40,000		33,000		7,000	
Total costs		84,000		65,000		19,000
Net profit		16,000		15,000		1,000

Additional information:

(a) Normally the hotel opens all the year. The season is regarded as June to September inclusive.

(b) Variable costs are:
  (i) 40% of sales in the season; and
  (ii) 60% of sales in the off-season.

(c) The actual results for the 3 months June to August 19X5 inclusive show:

	£	£
Sales		50,000
Variable costs	20,000	
Fixed costs	24,750	
Total costs		44,750
Net profit		5,250

(d) Bookings for the rest of the year are down and the forecast sales for September is £10,000, and for the off-season is £12,000.

(e) The marketing director recommends an advertising campaign to the board of directors which can only be launched for both September and the off-season. This offers a reduction in charges which will increase the sales forecasts in (d) by 50% and effectively increase the variable costs in September to 50% of sales and in the off-season to 65% of sales.

(f) Other hotels in the area are in a similar position. The Grand Hotel has offered to take over all the off-season business of The Lawrence Hotel at the current rates charged by the Lawrence Hotel and to give it agents commission of 15% of sales. The September bookings will have to be honoured.

You are required to prepare:

   (i) the forecasted trading, profit and loss accounts for September and the off-season assuming the company makes no changes at all;

  (ii) the revised forecast, for the same periods if the marketing director's proposal *is* accepted; and

 (iii) the revised forecast, for the same periods, if the offer from the Grand Hotel is accepted; and

 (iv) a report for the board of directors indicating, *with reasons*, which of the alternatives it should accept.

(HCIMA)

Chapter Eleven

Price Determination

Pricing decisions form one of management's most important tasks. The success or failure of an undertaking may depend on the ability of management to develop acceptable prices for goods and services. Formulating an effective price policy is a complex and delicate matter and one which calls for a knowledge of economic, market, financial and psychological factors. However, the subsequent discussion is concerned with the more practical financial aspects of pricing in relation to hotel, catering and institutional activities.

There are two cost-based approaches to pricing with numerous variations of each.

Traditional cost-plus pricing

In essence, this approach consists of adding a predetermined amount, termed 'mark-up', to an estimated product or service cost to arrive at a selling price. Normally mark-up is applied in the form of a percentage and this may be expressed as a simple equation:

$$\text{Cost} + \text{Mark-up} = \text{Selling price}$$

The composition, in terms of the proportion of cost to mark-up, gives rise to the cost-plus pricing variations.

The basic approach, known as 'full' or 'total' cost pricing, entails establishing the total cost of individual products to which is added an anticipated amount for net profit. Thus, referring to the basic cost-plus equation the cost component represents total cost, and mark-up depicts net profit.

A variation, termed 'direct cost pricing', requires the ascertainment of product prime costs, i.e. direct material, direct labour and direct expenses, to which is added a margin sufficient to cover indirect costs (overhead) and provide an adequate net profit. Reference to the cost-plus equation indicates that the cost element represents total direct costs whilst mark-up comprises overheads plus net profit.

Another variation, referred to as 'gross margin pricing' calls for an expected amount for gross profit to be added to the direct material cost, i.e. food and beverages. This should normally be sufficient to cover all remaining costs plus an acceptable net profit. Again, referring to the cost-plus equation, it will be seen that the cost component consists solely of direct material while the mark-up element embraces all other costs plus net profit. An example of gross margin pricing follows.

Market research indicates that a proposed new restaurant has an annual sales volume potential of 80,000 covers at a selling price between £1.50 and £2.50 per cover. Estimated annual costs are food £64,000, labour £55,000, and all expenses £21,000. The directors expect the restaurant to achieve a net profit of £20,000 per annum. Determine a pricing policy, in terms of the average mark-up percentage to be added to the food cost per cover, which will realize the directors' objective:

	£
Net profit required	20,000
Labour	55,000
Expenses	21,000
Gross profit	96,000
Food cost	64,000
Total sales revenue	160,000

$$\therefore \text{Mark-up pricing policy} = \frac{£96,000}{£64,000} \times \frac{100}{1} = 150\%$$

This establishes that an average mark-up being 150% of cost requires to be added to the food cost in order that the £76,000 labour and expense costs are recovered and the net profit of £20,000 achieved. This will result in a selling price of £2 per cover.

It is worth mentioning that in absolute terms mark-up and gross profit are the same figure. However, gross profit becomes gross profit percentage when related to selling price, but mark-up when related to cost. Therefore, if the pricing policy of the previous example had been expressed in terms of an average gross margin (profit) percentage then the result would have appeared as follows:

$$\text{Gross margin pricing policy} = \frac{£96,000}{£160,000} \times \frac{100}{1} = 60\%$$

This in turn indicates that an average of 60% of the selling price must be added to the food cost so as to cover other costs and provide the desired net profit. The traditional cost-plus pricing variations are summarized in Exhibit 11–1.

Exhibit 11–1 Traditional cost-plus pricing variations

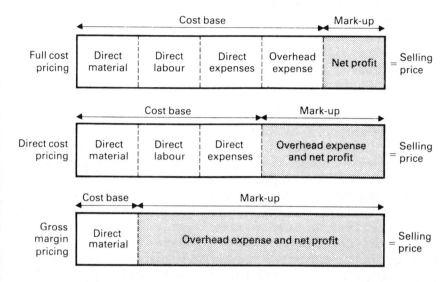

A further variation of cost-plus pricing is 'rate of return pricing'. In this case net profit is established from the rate of return on capital employed laid down by top management. Having ascertained the net profit figure any of the preceding methods may then be adopted to apply to the average dish cost. An example of pricing using the rate of return approach follows.

A catering company is investigating the possibility of investing £200,000 in a new restaurant venture from which the directors would require a return of at least 15% per annum. The average spending per customer is anticipated to be £5. Activity is estimated to be in the region of 40,000 covers per annum and associated labour and overhead costs of £100,000. Determine the gross margin pricing policy which will give the return required by the directors.

Net profit to achieve
desired return on investment $= £200,000 \times \dfrac{15}{100} = £30,000$

Estimated gross profit:

	£
Net profit	30,000
Labour and overheads	100,000
Gross profit	130,000

Anticipated sales turnover $=$ $40,000 \times £5$ $= £200,000$

$\therefore$ Gross margin pricing policy $= \dfrac{£130,000}{£200,000} \times 100 = 65\%$

Providing the sales and cost levels occur as planned then the gross profit percentage of 65% will ensure that the required net profit, and therefore return on investment, is achieved.

In practice it is the gross margin variation (with or without the rate of return element) which is normally adopted and this is usually applied to food and beverages. The reason stems from the nature of catering activities. In contrast to those of manufacturing, catering undertakings experience what may be described as 'short-run' or 'erratic' activity cycles. For instance, take the case of a table d'hôte restaurant in an hotel. In order to provide meals for breakfast, luncheon and dinner services the restaurant has to engage in three distinct production cycles per day, each of which comprises a relatively small number of different dishes. It therefore becomes impractical to build up full or total product (dish) costs by allocating and apportioning associated costs, and as a result the gross margin pricing variation is employed to facilitate the recovery of wages and other indirect costs and provide a net profit. A similar kind of situation occurs with beverages in that, although there is no production activity and the length of the service cycle is not so significant, the wide variety of low value drink items available also renders total cost ascertainment impractical.

As total and even prime cost ascertainment often proves an uneconomic exercise it becomes apparent that the material cost of food and beverages provide the only suitable base on which mark-up or gross profit percentage may be applied. This means that by comparison with manufacturing undertakings the link between cost and price is relatively tenuous. Moreover, the further upmarket the undertaking the weaker the link becomes, as the tendency is for the material cost to pale into insignificance.

In larger catering organizations where centralized food production may be employed it sometimes becomes possible to ascertain a higher proportion of total unit cost. This normally occurs through specialization derived from the division of labour and this permits, in addition to food cost, the identification of direct labour cost. The use of convenience food provides a similar example. In this case the price paid for the food will include the processor's material, labour and expense costs plus an element of net profit. Therefore, in both instances, the amount of unit cost that may be identified increases and subsequently has a stronger bearing on selling price.

Turning to accommodation, the case for traditional cost-plus pricing is even less convincing than for food and beverages. Room sales effectively constitute a rental or hire charge and by their nature do not involve material cost. This, coupled with the fact that other identifiable costs are normally insignificant in relation to selling price, stretches the already tenuous link between cost and price to a point where for practical purposes the relationship becomes meaningless.

Contribution margin pricing*

Whereas traditional cost-plus pricing aims to cover total cost and a target profit, contribution pricing seeks to achieve a target contribution towards fixed costs and profit. This necessitates the identification of fixed and variable cost behaviour patterns and is based on the premise that prices are set using variable cost as the floor and what the market will bear as the ceiling. The general philosophy behind this approach is that although individual sales may not achieve a net profit the sum total of contributions from all sales will be sufficient to cover fixed costs and provide an adequate net profit.

Where this approach is implemented fixed costs are treated as 'period costs' and subsequently written off against profit at the end of the accounting period. They may be allocated to products and services or departments for planning purposes, but this should be in total for an anticipated volume and sales mix and not per unit, the reason being that unit costs are valid only at a given sales volume and mix.

Contribution margin pricing can serve as a particularly useful approach in service industries such as hotel and catering where a relatively high proportion of fixed cost to total cost is apparent. For instance, assume the variable costs and selling price of an hotel room night is as indicated below:

	Room	
	£	£
Selling price		50
Less: Variable costs		
Direct labour	5	
Variable overhead	3	8
Contribution margin		42

Providing the room sale achieves a price in excess of the amount of the variable cost, i.e. £8, then a contribution will be generated towards fixed cost and net profit for the period as a whole. The extent of the price latitude, what economists call price discretion, is equal to the difference between the variable cost and the normal selling price, or viewed another way, equal to the contribution which in either case is £42. This provides the high fixed cost undertaking with considerable scope in which to develop an imaginative (flexible) pricing policy that will increase capacity utilization and net profit. This is illustrated in Exhibit 11–2.

* Sometimes referred to as 'marginal cost pricing'.

Exhibit 11–2 Cost structure and pricing decisions

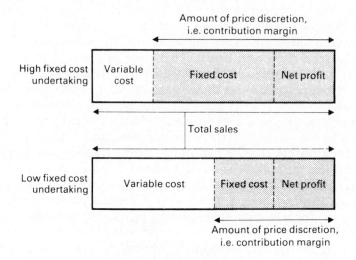

Cost-plus v. contribution margin pricing

A considerable amount of controversy surrounds the issue of the most suitable pricing approach to adopt.

Arguments for cost-plus pricing:

– it forms a logical basis on which to recover total costs;
– compared with other approaches, which require the separation of fixed and variable costs, it is simple to understand and 'safe' to use;
– it provides what businessmen describe as a 'fair' profit;
– it encourages price stability, whereas constant short-term price changes may prejudice long-term objectives.

Criticisms of cost-plus pricing:

– demand is ignored in terms of what the customer is prepared to pay, and it erroneously suggests that the correct price is the sum of all costs plus an assumed mark-up;
– it involves circular reasoning in that cost depends on volume, but volume is influenced by price;
– as the combination of cost and mark-up in respect of competitors is unlikely to result in a similar price, sales will normally go to the lower priced product or service;
– it is misleading in that it exaggerates the precision by which costs may be allocated.

Arguments for contribution margin pricing:

- it provides the scope for an imaginative (even aggressive) pricing policy;
- in cases where demand is elastic the price that maximizes contribution, and therefore profit, may be more or less than total cost plus mark-up;
- the presence of multi-product/service undertakings renders the allocation of fixed cost meaningless and therefore cost-plus pricing unreliable;
- as opposed to current costs marginal costs are said to reflect more accurately the future.

Disadvantages of contribution margin pricing:

- the practical difficulties encountered in locating the demand curve of a particular undertaking;
- the problems associated with the determination of fixed and variable costs;
- the fact that many businessmen are not familiar with cost–volume–profit techniques and therefore, are unable to make full use of such aids;
- the fear that if prices are set at a level which will maximize contribution, constant price changes could adversely affect price stability;
- in certain situations competition may prove so severe as to reach a climax where no individual undertaking is able to generate sufficient contribution to cover fixed costs and achieve a reasonable profit.

Where the traditional cost-plus pricing approach is operated in respect of normal business, contribution pricing can still be used to good effect for what Sizer* describes as 'secondary pricing decisions'. Examples of these include low season holidays, special weekends, prestige functions and so on. In fact the support role is particularly useful in those establishments which experience marked demand fluctuations, a characteristic that is inherent in many sections of the industry.

Pricing hotel accommodation

A time-honoured rule of thumb method of pricing rooms is known as the 'rule of a thousand'. This provides for an average room rate of an hotel to be ascertained on the basis of £1 for each £1,000 of capital cost. Initially, capital cost included only the cost of construction but this now appears to embrace the total investment per room.

* John Sizer, *An Insight into Management Accounting*, Penguin Books

The rule was established a number of years ago and founded on prevailing occupancies, operating costs, interest rates and acceptable profit margins. Since then, however, the variables and their relationships have changed and although for practical purposes it remains a broad guide, this rule of thumb must be used with full knowledge of its severe limitations.

An additional method of accommodation pricing is based on the rate of return variation of the cost-plus pricing approach. This yields a minimum average room rate sufficient to earn a stated rate of return on capital employed. Essentially this requires an estimate of total unallocated costs and costs of the accommodation department together with the desired return on investment, less contributions/ profits from other operating departments. The amount is divided by the estimated number of rooms sold for the year to obtain the average room rate. As for all cost based pricing computations this has a number of deficiencies. Cost allocation is an accounting technique used mainly for internal management control purposes and since the allocations cannot be measured in a true economic sense, such substitutions for real economic value subsequently lead to inaccuracies in the result.

This method has been used in various forms in this country for some years but in the United States the procedure has been formalized for the American Hotel and Motel Association and is known as the 'Hubbart Formula' (see Exhibit 11–3). It should be noted that as the formula results in an average, an accommodation price structure will need to be developed for different kinds of rooms.

Exhibit 11–3
Average Room Rate Computation (100 Room Hotel)

	£
Net assets:	
Hotel fixed assets	1,450,000
Working capital	50,000
	1,500,000
Capital employed:	£
Ordinary share capital	1,000,000
12% Debentures	500,000
	1,500,000
Required return on capital employed at 10%	150,000
UK corporation tax at 50%	150,000
Required profit before tax	300,000
12% Debenture interest	60,000

Required profit before interest and tax	360,000
Rates, depreciation and insurance	160,000
Required profit before fixed charges	520,000
Undistributed operating expenses:	
Administration	50,000
Marketing	30,000
Energy costs	40,000
Property operation	20,000
Total	140,000
Required total department operating profit	660,000
Estimated department operating profit (excluding rooms):	
Food	150,000
Beverage	100,000
Other	10,000
	260,000
Required rooms department operating profit	400,000
Estimated rooms department expenses	110,000
Required rooms department revenue	510,000
Number of room nights per annum at an average occupancy of (say) 70%	25,500
Required average room rate (£510,000 ÷ 25,550) = £19.96 or	£20

Pricing food and beverages

Earlier it was stated that food and beverage selling prices are normally based on the cost-plus approach using either the gross margin or rate of return variations. Where this is so a general procedure should be adopted in order to evolve individual prices for dishes, meals and drinks. One way is to develop what may be described as a 'multi-stage approach' that comprises a number of distinct steps commencing with the estimated sales for a period and ending with individual food and beverage selling prices, as illustrated in Exhibit 11–4.

In the initial stage it is necessary to determine the annual sales and average gross margin percentage that will provide a desired return on capital employed. For example, the details of a proposed catering undertaking are as follows:

173

Exhibit 11–4   Food and beverages multi-stage approach to cost-plus pricing

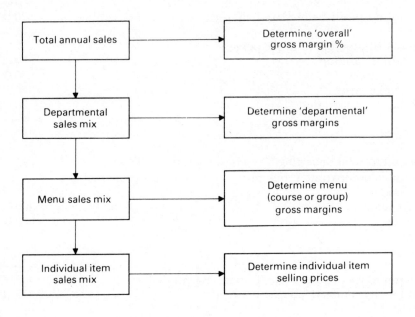

Capital employed	£175,000
Desired return	20%
	£
Target net profit	35,000
Plus: Fixed costs	27,000
Estimated gross profit	62,000

Average gross margin 62%

$$\therefore \text{Estimated sales} = \frac{£62,000}{62} \times \frac{100}{1} = £100,000$$

The second stage requires the estimation of departmental sales mix together with the anticipated gross margin percentages. On the assumption that the proposed catering establishment will contain four departments: à la carte restaurant, buttery, cocktail bar, and shop, the analysis might appear as follows:

Estimated departmental analysis

	Sales mix		Gross margin	
	£	%	£	%
Restaurant	50,000	50	35,000	70
Buttery	25,000	25	15,000	60
Bar	20,000	20	11,000	55
Shop	5,000	5	1,000	20
	100,000	100	62,000	62

The departmental gross margin percentages are a matter of policy and may be checked against the overall percentage. This is carried out by weighting each gross margin percentage by the sales mix percentage, as follows:

Sales mix		Gross margin		
%		%		%
50	×	70	=	35
25	×	60	=	15
20	×	55	=	11
5	×	20	=	1
100				62

Stage three comprises the departmental menu sales mix estimates, i.e. starters, main course, etc., for food, and wine, spirits, beers, etc. for beverages, again with the respective gross margin percentages. For example, take the à la carte restaurant:

Estimated menu analysis

	Sales mix		Gross margin	
	£	%	£	%
Starters	9,000	18	7,650	85
Main course	25,000	50	16,250	65
Vegetables	5,000	10	3,750	75
Sweets	8,000	16	4,800	60
Coffee	3,000	6	2,550	85
	50,000	100	35,000	70

The final stage consists of estimating individual food and drink items and determining the selling prices which will ultimately appear on the menus, wine lists and bar tariffs. In the final stage it is also necessary to take into account minor adjustments in respect of operational factors, market influences and price roundings.

Where appropriate the procedure may be reversed. Thus, selling prices are set for each dish or drink whilst the overall gross margin for the department and business becomes a residual matter.

Total pricing

In developing a pricing policy an important aspect to consider is the relationship, if any, that exists between products and/or services produced by an undertaking. Firms in some industries manufacture or process products that from the consumer point of view are self-contained items, independent of each other. Where this is evident pricing structures must be aimed at maximizing profit from the individual products themselves. However, due to its nature, the hotel and catering industry experiences a relatively high degree of product and service interrelationship. In many undertakings, such as hotels, the interdependence of facilities is two dimensional. For instance, an à la carte menu contains a number of courses which are interdependent in so much as they constitute a complete meal. The meal cannot, however, be seen in isolation, as the restaurant in which it is served is itself an interdependent component of the hotel in that it forms part of the total service offered to a guest. Therefore, as far as a customer is concerned the facilities provided are regarded as a 'composite' product. Where this is so then on no account should departmental price structures be determined independently, but prepared as a 'total' pricing effort. In this way departmental gains will not be made at the cost of overall results. This is based on the synergy doctrine which suggests that the outcome of combined effort is greater than the sum of individual action.

Mark-up and gross profit

The percentage added to food or drink cost for determining selling price is known sometimes as mark-up. The figure added is gross profit and becomes gross profit percentage when it is related to the selling price. The mark-up and gross profit are the same figure in absolute terms, but are different percentages because the figure is related to different bases, viz. mark-up percentage relates to cost and gross profit percentage relates to selling price.

If food costs 50p and the customer is charged 75p then there has been a mark-up of 25p. If 25p is expressed as a percentage of cost (50p) the result is a 50% mark-up. However, if the mark-up of 25p is expressed as a percentage of selling price there results a gross profit percentage of 33⅓%. To establish the mark-up when the cost and gross profit percentage are known:

$$\frac{\text{Gross profit}}{\text{\% required}} = \text{Mark-up of}$$

$$50\% = \frac{50}{(100-50)} \times 100 = 100\%$$

$$33\tfrac{1}{3}\% = \frac{33\tfrac{1}{3}}{(100-33\tfrac{1}{3})} \times 100 = 50\%$$

$$25\% = \frac{25}{(100-25)} \times 100 = 33\tfrac{1}{3}\%$$

Questions and problems

11–1 Compare 'full cost-plus pricing' with 'gross margin pricing'.

11–2 Is the 'rate of return' method of pricing a variation of cost-plus pricing? Explain.

11–3 'Gross margin pricing is frequently used in the hotel and catering industry for pricing food and beverages.' Discuss.

11–4 What reasons can you advance for and against having a pricing policy in a restaurant based on a fixed percentage mark-up on the food cost of each dish? Explain briefly two other methods of establishing the menu price of a dish.

11–5 Distinguish between 'cost-plus pricing' and 'contribution margin pricing'.

11–6 'Contribution margin pricing can serve as a particularly useful approach in service industries . . .' Do you agree? Explain.

11–7 Distinguish between the 'rule of a thousand' and the 'Hubbart Formula' methods of pricing hotel room rates.

11–8 Explain briefly how you would approach a total pricing policy for either an hotel or a university hall of residence.

11–9 'Rule of thumb cost-orientated procedures are much utilized in the industry. For accommodation, rate of return procedures (e.g. the Hubbart Formula widely used in the USA) are often used. . . . Food and beverage pricing is generally based on a cost-plus procedure to permit given gross profit margins.' H. Anthea Rogers, 'Price Formation in Hotels', *HCIMA Review*, Spring 1976

Discuss the general arguments for and against the adoption of a cost-plus pricing procedure, with reference to those aspects of hotel accommodation, food and beverages you consider relevant.

(HCIMA)

11–10 The management of The Estuary Restaurant has been reviewing its pricing policy for the Table d'hôte menu, bearing in mind a £43,500 net profit is required to be achieved in the coming year.

The restaurant, which is open for 50 weeks per year, is expected to serve 200 covers per week. Labour and overhead costs are anticipated to be £1,200 per week.

Management proposes the food cost and·sales mix structure to be as follows:

	Food cost % of SP per dish	Sales mix % of total sales revenue
Starters	40	15
Main courses	45	50
Selection of vegetables	33⅓	9
Sweet trolley	40	10
Cheese and biscuits	50	12
Coffee or tea	25	4
		100

Required:
   (a) From the above figures, estimate the overall gross profit percentage that will be achieved.
   (b) Set selling prices for the whole meal and the individual courses based on the expected number of covers and the required net profit (assume all covers take coffee or tea).
   (c) Calculate the restaurant's break-even point in terms of sales revenue.
   (d) In what circumstances will gross profit be found to be equivalent to contribution margin?

(BAHA)

11–11 Pharmaceuticals Ltd operates a staff dining hall for the provision of meals to its employees and provides 900 meals per day, 5 days a week for 50 weeks of the year. The current year's costs with respect to employee feeding are expected to be:

	£
Food	87,750
Labour	80,000
Overheads	47,250

In future the directors would like to provide meals at an average price of £0.60 each and are prepared to subsidize the eating facilities to a limit of £50,000 per annum.

Surgical Ltd, which occupies an adjoining factory, has recently approached Pharmaceuticals Ltd to inquire if they would be willing to provide similar meals each day to their 500 employees at the same price. They have offered to take their meals at a different time, thus avoiding capacity problems and are prepared to pay £16,000 per annum for the use of the facilities. Pharmaceuticals Ltd has estimated that the additional labour and overhead costs of providing the extra meals would be £8,000 and £3,250 per annum respectively.

Required:

(a) Bearing in mind the above information you have been asked to recommend to the directors of Pharmaceuticals Ltd whether they should, on financial grounds, provide meals to the employees of Surgical Ltd.

(b) Based on your recommendation in (a) above, you are further requested to suggest a pricing policy in terms of the average percentage to be added to the cost of each dish in order to recover the associated costs.

(c) List factors, other than financial aspects, that should be considered prior to making a final decision in this kind of circumstance.

(HCIMA)

11-12 The banqueting manager of the Sismat Hotel Group Ltd is issued with the following procedure for calculating net profit arising from functions held in the banqueting facilities of the Group:

(i) establish food cost,

(ii) charge £2 per person, to recover the head office fixed cost,

(iii) charge £50 per function, to recover wages of permanent banqueting staff and banqueting fixed overheads,

(iv) calculate the charge for casual labour (basis, 40p per customer, for every customer in excess of 40),

(v) wines are charged for separately. Charge based on gross profit of 66⅔% on sales.

Three requests have been received to use the banqueting facilities available, only one of which can be accepted. Details of these requests are:

Request from:	Westley	Worthington	*Wilson
Number of customers	140	80	40
Total food cost	£90	£30	—
Estimated demand for wine	50 to 70 bottles	40 to 60 bottles	—
Estimated cost for wines	70p	£1	—
Price per customer (excluding wines)	£2.50	£2.20	—

* Wilson just wishes to hire the banqueting facilities for £275 and will make his own arrangements to provide the meals and drinks.

You are required to prepare:
(a) statements showing the estimated range of net profit for each function, using the procedure laid down by the head office;
(b) statements showing the range of contribution estimated to arise from each function;
(c) statement ranking the requests in the order in which they should be accepted, giving the reason for your choice; and
(d) a brief comment on the procedure laid down by head office for calculating net profit on banqueting facilities.
(HCIMA)

11–13 Construction of The Eurotel, a 300 room hotel, is nearing completion. The owners have raised £19,900,000 to fund the property with an additional cash injection of £100,000 for working capital purposes. Of the £20,000,000 investment, £15,000,000 has been obtained in the form of a 12% loan with the owners providing the remainder in cash from which they expect an initial annual return of 6% after tax. The current rate of tax is 40%

Additional data for the first year of operation are estimated as follows:

	£
Fixed charges (excluding loan interest)	712,500
Undistributed operating expenses	1,693,750

£

Departmental profits and losses:
Food and beverages 450,000
Telephone (50,000) loss
Rentals and other income 200,000

Rooms department expenses are £10 per room sold.
Occupancy rate of 75%
The hotel will be open 365 days of the year.

Required:
(a) Determine the average room rate using the Hubbart Formula required to achieve the after tax profit target
(b) If the double rooms are sold at a premium of £12 above single rooms, what are the prices of the single and double rooms? Assume a double occupancy rate of 60%.
(c) Suggest other factors that should be taken into account before finalising the room rates for the coming year.

11–14 Construction of Natureland, a wildlife centre and tourist attraction with a maximum annual capacity of 185,000 visitors, is almost complete. The developers have raised £2,500,000 for the project of which £2,000,000 has to be borrowed from banks at a rate of interest of 14%. The developers are supplying the remaining £500,000 from which they expect an initial annual return of 5% after tax. The current rate of tax is 30%.

Additional data relating to the first year of operation are anticipated to occur as follows:

	£
Fixed charges (excluding loan interest)	120,000
Undistributed operating expenses	350,000
Profits from non-wildlife activities:	
Souvenir shops	130,000
Cafes and burger bar	175,000
Adventure railway	40,000
Wildlife feeding and care expenses	100,000
Number of visitors (including adults and children)	40% of maximum annual capacity

You are required to:
(a) Determine the average admission fee, based on cost-plus rate of return pricing, required to achieve the developer's after tax profit target.

(b) If a family admission fee (two adults and two children) were to be charged at £20, what should the single visitor admission fee need to be in order to achieve the profit target? Assume 60% of visitors would be in families of four.

(c) Suggest other factors that should be taken into account prior to finalising admission fees for the coming year.

11–15 A group of investors has raised £12,000,000 to buy The Country Club Hotel with 240 double bedrooms and extensive function and leisure facilities. They expect a return (after tax at a rate of 50%) of 10%.

They estimate unallocated costs of overhead departments as follows:

	£000
General administration	125
Marketing	75
Energy	100
Property operation maintenance	150
Depreciation and insurances	275

For the operated departments the estimates are:

	Variable cost % of sales	Payroll and related costs £000	Departmental target profit £000
Rooms	12½	250	(see (a))
Food & beverage	40	650	550
Income from leisure facilities	33⅓	300	200

Assume the accounting profit is also the taxable profit.

There is a season of twenty weeks when the room occupancy is expected to be 100%. For the other thirty weeks an average occupancy of 48.81% is expected. The daily room rate in the season is to be one and a half times that during the off-season.

You are required to:

(a) calculate the departmental target profit for the rooms department;

(b) calculate the daily room rate for the on and off seasons;

(c) calculate the daily room rate, including VAT;

(d) prepare a detailed budget for the first year's activities of The Country Club Hotel;

(e) comment on the method of pricing rooms.

(HCIMA)

11–16 The Serenity Club intends to hold a dinner which will be attended by an estimated number of 200 members. The Grand Hotel has been approached with a possible menu and is in process of calculating costs, bearing in mind the club's hope that the charge could be kept down to £1.75 per head. The costs of the function have been apportioned as follows:

Food cost (exclusive of meat)	£80	
Other direct costs:		
Trio with soloist	£40	
Sundries (menu cards, flowers)	£20	
Extra labour		20% of sales
Extra overheads		10% of sales

Fixed cost per day of the function suite is £40.

Meat weighing 60 kg (exclusive of bone and waste) has been purchased by the piece costing £75. The comparative cost of the meat bought retail by the separate cuts would work out at £90. Roasting meat which is to be used from the piece has a retail cost of £1.80 per kg. It is estimated that there will be a 40% cooking loss. It is intended to serve a meat portion of 120 g.

(a) Calculate the charge per head necessary to make a 10% net profit on sales.

(b) Taking into account the fact that no other function has been booked for that day, consider, with calculations, the advisability of offering the dinner at the club's price of £1.75 per head.

11–17 The Heathrow International, a hotel located at London Airport, is temporarily operating at a low occupancy level due to a general economic recession. Each month for the coming year the costs of the accommodation department (excluding meals), based on normal activity of 3,000 sleeper-nights, are predicted to be:

	Per month £
Variable wages	25,200
Variable expenses (laundry, etc.)	6,300
Variable overhead	12,600
Fixed overhead	48,000

The tariff per sleeper-night will normally be £60, exclusive of breakfast.

183

A foreign national airline has invited the hotel to tender for the provision of accommodation, exclusive of meals, for their flying crews during the coming year. There will be 21 crew members who will each stay an average of 10 nights per month. In addition, a specific safe-deposit facility would be required for the crew members' exclusive use when they stay at the hotel.

With a view to submitting a tender you ascertain the following information:

1. The fixed accommodation overhead of £576,000 per annum is applicable to occupancy levels up to a full house.
2. The particular safe-deposit facility can be hired by the hotel at a cost of £7,056, for the year.
3. The price bid to the airline is in no way expected to influence the hotel guests who pay the normal full sleeper-night tariff.
4. If the airline rejects the bid the hotel is unlikely to sell the rooms during the coming year.

You are required to:
  (a) calculate the bidding price per sleeper-night which will yield a 30% profit thereon;
  (b) determine the number of sleeper-nights for the tender to break even;
  (c) prepare a statement showing the effect on the coming year's profit if the hotel's tender is accepted;
  (d) explain briefly the principle(s) you have applied in answering this question and draw attention to possible dangers inherent therein.

11–18 Haddo Abbey, the stately home of the Duke of Cumberland, is suffering from the effects of a general turndown in the number of tourists visiting Britain.

The commercial manager of the Abbey has been approached by a Japanese tour operator who has requested a quotation for an inclusive price per head for his tours to visit the home. It would involve three forty-seater coach loads of Japanese tourists arriving daily for twenty weekdays per month for six months of the coming year.

The price per head quoted is to include admission and a guided tour of the house followed by a cultural talk with tea and biscuits. The guided tours and talks are to be conducted exclusively in the Japanese language.

With a view to submitting a quotation the following is available:

1. The costs of running the house based on 9,000 admissions in a normal month are estimated as follows:

	£
Variable payroll (inc. English speaking guides only)	4,500
Variable expenses (free literature, etc.)	1,800
Fixed payroll	16,700
Other fixed expenses	18,300

The normal admission fee has been fixed at £5.50 per head.

2. The total cost of engaging sufficient Japanese speaking guides and lecturers will be £3,600 per month. The cost of providing tea and biscuits is estimated to be £0.60 per head.
3. The price quoted to the tour operator is not expected to affect visitors who pay the normal admission fee.
4. The fixed payroll and other costs which amount to £420,000 per annum is applicable to the maximum capacity of 15,000 visitors per month.
5. If the tour operator rejects the quotation the stately home is unlikely to attract additional visitors during the months in question for the coming year.

Required:
   (a) Calculate the price to be quoted on a per head basis which will return a 20% profit thereon.
   (b) Calculate the total number of Japanese tourists required to arrive during the six months for the proposed arrangement to break-even.
   (c) Prepare a financial statement which shows the additional revenue, costs and profit that will result if the price quoted is accepted.
   (d) Explain briefly the principle(s) you have applied in answering this question and suggest the possible ripple effects which may follow if the price quoted is accepted.

11–19 The South Down University offers various 'Educational Holidays' on a normal commercial basis during the vacations.
   Each holiday was sold at the price of £30 per person last year and a total of 5,000 guests were accommodated. The costs incurred in producing the various holidays offered are the same.
   The variable cost of producing a holiday last year was:

	£
Food	10.00
Direct labour	9.00
Variable overheads	2.00
	21.00

The fixed overhead relevant to the holidays during the year was £20,000.

During the coming year, the costs of the holidays are expected to increase by the following:

	%
Food	10.00
Direct labour	16.67
Variable overheads	25.00
Fixed overhead	5.00

Market research carried out by a firm of hotel and catering consultants has shown that when the university increases the price of its holidays to its guests, so long as the increase is kept below 11%, this is unlikely to have an effect on the number of units sold. However, for every 1% prices are raised above an 11% increase, the number of holidays sold can be expected to fall by 2%.

The following is required for the coming year:

(a) the selling price of the holidays if the number sold and the annual profits are to remain the same as in the previous year;

(b) the number of holidays that the university would have to sell if it did not change the price charged for these, but maintained the profit level attained in the previous year; and

(c) a brief analysis of a situation where, when prices are changed, the number of units sold is affected. The data provided in the above example can be used to illustrate your analysis.

Further reading

1. Dean, J., *Managerial Economics*, Prentice-Hall Int. (1951).
2. Greer, H. C., 'Cost factors in price-making', *Harvard Business Review*, July–August 1952; pp 33–45.

3. Baxter, W. T., and Oxenfeldt, A. R., Costing and Pricing: The Cost Accountant versus the Economist, *Studies in Cost Analysis* (edited by Solomons, D.), Sweet and Maxwell, pp 293–312.
4. Rogers, H. A., 'Price formation in hotels,' *HCIMA Review*, Spring 1976.
5. Savage, C. I., and Small, J. R., *Introduction to Managerial Economics*, Stanley Thornes (1975), Chapter 6.
6. Sizer, J., *An Insight into Management Accounting* (3rd edn.), Penguin Books (1989), Chapter 9.
7. Tucker, S. A., *Pricing for Higher Profits*, McGraw-Hill (1966).

Chapter Twelve

The Impact of Cost Structure on Profitability

Most industries have characteristics which distinguish them from one another. For instance, the motor manufacturing industry has traditionally been associated with mass production, a large degree of standardization and, more recently, the introduction of automation. The data processing industry is characterized by high technology and rapid change. The hotel and catering industry also has distinguishing features. It is both capital and labour intensive, market centred, and comprises a large number of small solely owned establishments.

From an accounting standpoint a critical element common in all firms is the profile of their cost structure. Cost structure, also called operating leverage, is measured in terms of the proportions of fixed costs and variable costs present in the CVP equation of a firm. A firm which has a large proportion of fixed costs to total cost is said to have a high fixed cost structure; correspondingly, a firm which has a small proportion of fixed costs is referred to as having a low fixed cost structure. An understanding of the influence cost structure has on profits is a crucial element in management decision making.

In contrast with some industries, the hotel and catering industry is characterized by the wide variety of cost structures found in different kinds of firms. They range from the high proportion of fixed costs associated with luxury hotel firms to the markedly low proportion of fixed costs associated with outdoor catering businesses run from home. The purpose of this chapter is to examine the impact of cost structure in hotel and catering operations and assess its influence on profitability.

Sensitivity analysis

In order to measure the effect of cost structure on profitability a technique known as 'sensitivity analysis' can be employed. Sensitivity analysis is a technique used to determine whether a given factor is critical to a decision. In a CVP context, if a small change in a factor such as volume of activity causes a large change in profit, then it can be said that profit is sensitive to changes in volume and that volume is a critical factor. In broad terms, the critical factors are unit volume, selling price, variable costs and fixed costs, but these groups can be further divided as required.

To assist in assessing the extent to which cost structure can influence profitability, assumed data for two hotel and catering firms is presented in Exhibit 12–1.

Exhibit 12–1

Projected Profit Statements

	Firm A		Firm B	
Relevant range in units:	4,000–12,000		4,000–12,000	
Volume of activity in units:	10,000	Unit	10,000	Unit
	£	£	£	£
Sales revenue	20,000	2.00	20,000	2.00
Less: Variable costs	15,000	1.50	6,000	0.60
Contribution margin	5,000	0.50	14,000	1.40
Less: Fixed costs	3,000		12,000	
Net profit	2,000		2,000	

Note that in order to focus attention on cost structure, only the fixed and variable cost information differs between the two firms. All other items, i.e. relevant range, budgeted activity and selling price, are similar for both firms.

Before measuring the effects of particular critical factors on profits it is useful to gain a visual impression of the two firms' contrasting cost structures. This is shown in Exhibit 12–2.

Exhibit 12–2 Graphs showing cost structures

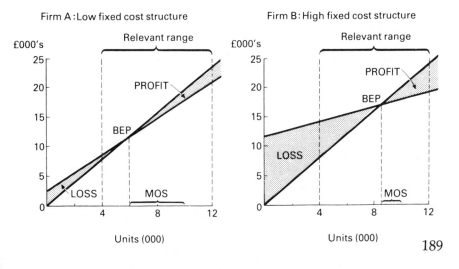

Observation of Exhibit 12–2 shows that Firm A has a low break-even point (6,000 units) and a high margin of safety (4,000 units). By contrast, Firm B has a relatively high break-even point (approximately 8,570 units) and low margin of safety (approximately 1,430 units), which means it needs to generate more revenue to cover its total costs. Beyond break-even point, however, Firm B derives a greater rate of profit, depicted by the shaded area, than Firm A; below break-even point Firm B sustains larger losses. In fact, assuming other factors remain constant, throughout the relevant range of activity the change in profits and losses will be greater for Firm B.

Thus having made some visual observations it is now appropriate to consider each critical factor separately and measure its impact on the position of the two firms. Reference to the data in Exhibit 12–1 shows that both firms expect to sell 10,000 units and achieve net profits of £2,000. Hence, if the anticipated projections occur as planned the firms will make similar profits. This is of course true, but what will be the effect on the profitability of each firm if there are changes in the critical factors? To answer the question, using the assumed data in Exhibit 12–1, each critical factor will be increased in turn by 10% whilst holding all other factors constant, and the effect on profits will be determined and evaluated.

Change in sales volume

The impact of a 10% increase in sales volume is as follows:

	Firm A	Firm B
Volume of activity in units:	1,000	1,000
	£	£
Sales revenue	2,000	2,000
Less: Variable costs	1,500	600
Contribution margin	500	1.400
Less: Fixed costs (unchanged)	—	—
Additional net profits	500	1,400
Projected net profits	2,000	2,000
Total	2,500	3,400

The 10% increase in demand will provide an extra 1,000 (10,000 × 10%) units sold, which will generate additional sales revenue of £2,000 (1,000 × £2) for both firms. Variable costs will rise by £1,500 (1,000 × £1.50) and £600 (1,000 × £0.60) giving contribution margins of £500 and £1,400 respectively. Fixed costs will be unaffected by the sales increase and, therefore, additional net profits will be £500 and £1,400. It is worth noting that additional sales volume can be derived from either an increase in the number of units sold, as in this case, or an increase in the average spending of customers.

An interpretation of the results reveals that Firm A profit will increase by 25% (£500/£2,000), whilst Firm B profit will increase by 70% (£1,400/£2,000), i.e. almost triple that of Firm A. The reason for such a dramatic difference lies in the profile of the two cost structures. Firm A has a low proportion of fixed costs and, therefore, a high proportion of variable costs, giving a contribution margin per unit of £0.50. Conversely, Firm B has a high proportion of fixed costs and thus a low level of variable costs, giving a contribution margin per unit of £1.40, i.e. nearly three times that of Firm A. Hence, for each additional unit sold the firms generate an extra £0.50 and £1.40 contribution margin respectively.

From this example it can be seen that a change in sales volume in a firm which has a high percentage of fixed costs has a greater impact on profits than a firm which has a low percentage of fixed costs. Thus, demand changes do affect relative profitability in firms with different cost structures.

Change in selling price

The impact of a 10% increase in selling price will be as follows:

	Firm A	Firm B
Volume of activity in units (unchanged)	—	—
	£	£
Sales revenue	2,000	2,000
Less: Variable costs (unchanged	—	—
Contribution margin	2,000	2,000
Less: Fixed costs (unchanged)	—	—
Additional net profit	2,000	2,000
Projected profits	2,000	2,000
Total	4,000	4,000

The increase in selling price will not change the volume of sales, but will provide an extra £2,000 (10,000 × £0.20) sales revenue for each firm. Variable and fixed costs will remain unchanged resulting in additional net profits of £2,000. Thus, additional revenue brought about by a price level change increases profit by a similar amount.

The results reveal that the increase in the profit of both firms is 100% (£2,000/£2,000) and, therefore, price level changes do not affect the relative profitability of firms with different cost structures.

Change in variable costs

The impact of a 10% increase in variable costs will be as follows:

	Firm A	Firm B
Volume of activity in units (unchanged)	—	—
	£	£
Sales revenue (unchanged)	—	—
Less: Variable costs	1,500	600
Contribution margin	(1,500)	(600)
Less: Fixed costs (unchanged)	—	—
Additional net loss	(1,500)	(600)
Projected profits	2,000	2,000
Total	500	1,400

The 10% increase in variable costs will have no effect on revenue. Variable costs will rise by £1,500 (£15,000 × 10%) and £600 (£6,000 × 10%) respectively for each firm. This in turn will result in negative (decline) contribution margins of £(1,500) and £(600) and, as fixed costs will be unchanged, a net loss will be incurred of a similar amount.

The results reveal that Firm B's profit will decrease by 30% [£(600)/£2,000] and Firm A's profit will decrease by 75% [£(1,500)/ £2,000], i.e. two and a half times more than Firm B. From this it will be appreciated that a change in variable costs in a firm with a low percentage of fixed costs has a greater impact on profit than in a firm which has a high level of fixed costs. Thus, variable cost changes do affect relative profitability in firms with different cost structures.

Change in fixed costs

The impact of a 10% increase in fixed costs will be as follows:

	Firm A	Firm B
Volume of activity in units (unchanged)	—	—
	£	£
Sales revenue (unchanged)	—	—
Less: Variable costs (unchanged)	—	—
Contribution margin (unchanged)	—	—
Less: Fixed costs	300	1,200
Additional net loss	(300)	(1,200)
Projected profits	2,000	2,000
	1,700	800

The 10% increase in fixed costs will have no effect on sales revenue and contribution margin. Fixed cost will rise by £300 (£3,000 × 10%) and £1,200 (£12,000 × 10%) respectively for each firm giving net losses of similar amounts.

The results reveal that Firm A's profit will decrease by 15% [£(300)/£2,000] and Firm B's profit will decrease by 60% [£(1,200/£2,000], i.e. precisely four times that of Firm A. This shows that a change in fixed costs in a firm with a high proportion of fixed costs has a greater impact on profit than in a firm with a low proportion of fixed costs. Hence, fixed cost changes do have an effect on the relative profitability of firms with different cost structures.

Evaluation of critical factors

Having determined the individual effect of each critical factor on profitability, it is useful to provide a summary of the results highlighting the relative importance of the different factors. In order to do this it is possible to compute profit multipliers* as follows:

$$\frac{\% \text{ change in net profit}}{\% \text{ change in critical factor}}$$

For example, the percentage change in the net profit of the two catering firms due to a 10% increase in sales volume is 25% and 70% respectively. Therefore, the profit multipliers are computed as:

Firm A $\qquad$ Firm B

$$\frac{25\%}{10\%} = 2.5 \qquad \frac{70\%}{10\%} = 7.0$$

* Kotas, R., 'The ABC of PSA', HCIMA Journal, February 1978, pp. 15, 17, 19.

The profit multipliers indicate that, in this case, for every 1% increase in sales volume net profits will increase by 2.5% and 7.0% respectively.

The profit multipliers for all the critical factors are presented in Exhibit 12–3.

Exhibit 12–3

Critical factors	Profit multipliers	
	Firm A (low prop. fixed costs)	Firm B (high prop. fixed costs)
Sales volume	2.5	7.0
Selling price	10.0	10.0
Variable costs	7.5	3.0
Fixed costs	1.5	6.0

Care should be taken when interpreting profit multipliers as their magnitude can vary substantially from firm to firm, i.e. their values are determined by the relationships present in the CVP equations of particular firms.

Interpretation of the computed results in Exhibit 12–3 reveal the following points:

(a) both firms' profits are highly sensitive to price changes;
(b) Firm A's profit is sensitive to changes in variable cost changes;
(c) Firm B's profit is sensitive to fixed cost changes;
(d) Firm B's profit is sensitive to changes in sales volume;
(e) Firm B's profits are more sensitive to demand fluctuations, that is sales volume, and changes in fixed costs, whereas Firm A profits are more sensitive to changes in variable costs.

A general conclusion that can be drawn from the sensitivity analysis is that profits in firms that have high fixed cost structures are relatively more sensitive to changes in critical factors. This in turn would suggest that their profits are potentially more at risk than for firms with low fixed cost structures.

As mentioned earlier, the hotel and catering industry contains firms with varying cost structures. Hotel and catering firms which have a relatively low proportion of fixed costs are usually associated with higher volumes of lower priced and/or subsidized products and services, e.g. institutional catering and employee feeding. On the other hand, firms with high proportions of fixed costs are associated with lower volumes of more expensive and commercially targeted products, e.g. hotels and restaurants.

The relatively low proportions of fixed costs incurred by the welfare and lower priced concerns is related to the more modest facilities, service and product range offered together with the larger volumes of products consumed. However, with regard to the commercially based undertakings the opposite is true. The more costly environment, service and production facilities attract a high level of fixed costs, whilst the smaller volumes of sales result in a lower proportion of variable costs. In fact, across the vast range of products provided by the industry, the more upmarket the products are, the higher the proportion of fixed costs, leaving the variable cost component to become insignificant.

Apart from the more explicit consequences on a firm's profitability, cost structure has implications on management decision making. Welfare catering concerns, with their relatively low proportions of fixed costs are said to be 'cost oriented', whereas commercial concerns with their high proportions of fixed costs are referred to as 'market oriented'.* Briefly, the significance of this is that in the case of a cost oriented firm, where demand may be less critical, the large variable cost presence provides management with the opportunity to improve profits by placing greater emphasis on cost control technique than would otherwise be justified. This does not imply that marketing should be disregarded, but simply suggests that it may be more profitable to concentrate additional resources on cost reduction and control procedures.

In contrast to this, in the market oriented commercial firm, the emphasis should be different. The lower levels of variable costs experienced by this type of firm means there is less latitude to improve profits by cost control techniques. Instead, profitability may be better served by emphasizing the market in order to generate additional revenue. Again, it is not a case of disregarding cost control procedures, but merely diverting more resources into the marketing effort.

Questions and problems

12–1 Discuss the implications of cost structure on pricing decisions and profitability in the hotel and catering industry.

12–2 The summarized income statements for two seasonal restaurants for the year ended 31 December 1985 are as follows:

	Restaurant A £	Restaurant A £	Restaurant B £	Restaurant B £
Sales		160,000		160,000
Less: Variable costs	50,000		100,000	
Fixed costs	100,000	150,000	50,000	150,000
Profit		10,000		10,000

* Kotas, R., 'Market orientation', HCIMA Journal, July 1973, pp. 5–7.

195

The forecast for the year ending 31 December 1986 is:

Average spend per customer	£4	£2
Covers	30,000–50,000	60,000–100,000

Fixed costs are to remain the same and the proportion of variable costs to sales is to be the same.

You are required to explain and illustrate the role of the cost structure in determining the:

(a) profitability;
(b) pricing policy; and
(c) closure policy during the off-season;

for both restaurants for year ending 31 December 1986.

12–3 (a) Sketch *either* a break-even chart, *or* a profit–volume chart to illustrate each of the following (five charts are required in all):

(i) a highly profitable luxury hotel;
(ii) an unprofitable fast food unit;
(iii) a highly profitable public house;
(iv) a student refectory aiming to break even;
(v) an unprofitable high-class restaurant.

(b) Discuss the limitations of using break-even and profit–volume charts for decision making.
(c) Explain why an understanding of cost behaviour is essential in financial decision making.

(HCIMA)

12–4 From the following charts select one break-even and one profit–volume chart which illustrate each of the five listed businesses.
1. An industrial canteen which breaks even.
2. A successful luxury restaurant.
3. A successful fast food unit.
4. An unsuccessful luxury hotel.
5. An unsuccessful sandwich bar.

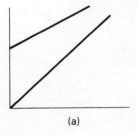

(a)

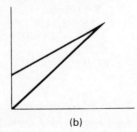

(b)

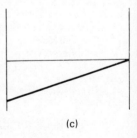

(c)

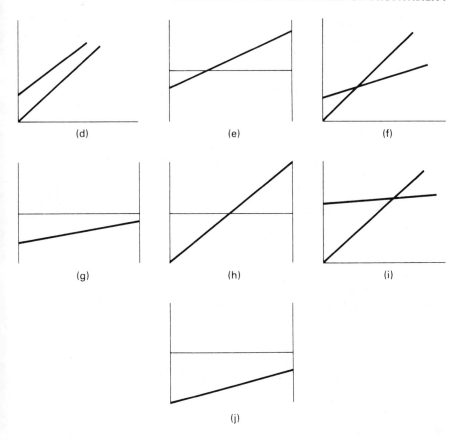

(d)   (e)   (f)

(g)   (h)   (i)

(j)

12–5 A small company, operating several restaurants, is looking for a location to open another. Two opportunities have been identified, one in Oldtown and the other in Newtown. The directors have examined these alternatives, and the following estimates have been made:

	Oldtown	Newtown
Total cost of investment	£350,000	£450,000
Estimated annual demand	20,000 covers	40,000 covers
Estimated average spend per cover	£11.96	£9.20
Cost of sales	38%	42%
Variable labour costs	20%	18%
Overheads (excluding interest)	£17,360	£36,000

Notes:

1. The average spend includes VAT at 15%.

2. The company has £200,000 of its own funds available. A further sum of £150,000 may be borrowed at 12% interest, and whatever may be needed beyond that will be available at 16%.

You are required to:

(a) Calculate the forecast net profit for each alternative.
(b) Explain which alternative is the more profitable.
(c) Calculate the break-even point and margin of safety for each proposal.
(d) Discuss briefly the relative risk of each investment, and whether this consideration might affect your choice.

(HCIMA)

12–6 Below are the cost–volume–profit graphs of two restaurant businesses:

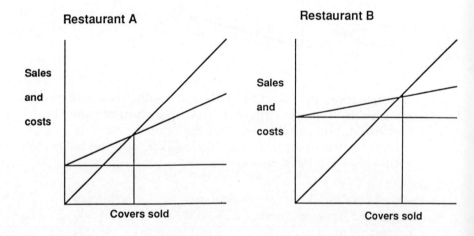

Restaurant A

Restaurant B

Sales and costs

Covers sold

You are required to:

(a) Compare the CVP graphs of the two restaurants in terms of sales, costs and profitability.
(b) Suggest, giving reasons, the kind of restaurant that each graph could represent.
(c) Suggest the business orientation of each restaurant you have identified in (b) above, and explain the influence this has on managing the restaurants.

12–7 The summarized year end results of two restaurants are as follows:

	Restaurant 1		Restaurant 2	
Meals sold:	10,000		10,000	
	£	£	£	£
Sales revenue		50,000		50,000
Less: Variable costs	10,000		30,000	
Fixed costs	30,000	40,000	10,000	40,000
Net profit		10,000		10,000

Assume that the change in key factors is 10%.

Required:

(a) Calculate the following profit multipliers for the two restaurants:

    (i) price level;
    (ii) sales volume;
    (iii) variable costs;
    (iv) fixed costs.

(b) Rank the profit multipliers in order of size.
(c) Comment on the profit multiplier profile of the two restaurants.

12–8 Below is the profit statement of the Nicosia International Hotel for the year ended 31st December:

	Net revenue £000	Cost of sales £000	Payroll and other £000	Profit (Loss) £000
Department				
Rooms	2,400	—	690	1,710
Food	1,000	400	410	190
Beverage	600	300	240	60
	4,000	700	1,340	1,960

Undistributed operating expenses:

Administration and general	400	
Marketing	200	
Energy	140	
Property operation and maintenance	160	900
Profit before fixed charges		1,060

Fixed charges	730
Net profit	330

Assume that:
1. Payroll and other expenses contain a fixed element of £1,040,000 and the balance is a variable expense.
2. Undistributed operating expenses contain a fixed element of £800,000 and the remainder is a variable expense.

You are required to:
   (a) calculate the profit multipliers for the hotel based on a 10% change in the key factors.
   (b) rank the profit multiplier values and comment briefly on the accounting and control strategy that should be adopted by management.

12–9 Below is a summary of the trading results of a restaurant business for the current year:

Number of covers sold		10,000
Average spend		£5

	£	£
Sales revenue		50,000
Less: Expenses		
Food and beverage costs	20,000	
Labour – fixed	10,000	
Labour – variable	2,000	
Other expenses – fixed	13,000	45,000
Net profit		5,000

At a budget committee meeting the following comments were made:

Managing Director: 'Our target for next year is to raise net profit by 10 per cent.'

Financial Controller: 'One way of increasing net profit by 10 per cent is to raise prices by 10 per cent.'

Manager: 'I disagree, in my view we need to increase sales volume by 10 per cent.'

Food and Beverage Manager: 'Surely, the easiest way to increase net profit is to decrease all expenditure by 10 per cent.'

Required:
  (a) Calculate separately the percentage increase in net profit which will result from a 10 per cent change in each of the restaurant's key factors.
  (b) Using your results in (a) above, calculate the restaurant's profit multipliers and determine the percentage change in each key factor which will achieve the target increase in net profit set by the managing director.
  (c) Explain why the effect on net profit based upon the managers' suggestions differ from the results obtained by using profit sensitivity analysis.

12–10 Given below is the profit and loss statement of the York City Hotel in respect of the year ended 31st March 1986.

Profit and Loss Account

Department	Sales	Cost of sales	Dept'l payroll	Dept'l expenses	Dept'l profit
	£000	£000	£000	£000	£000
Rooms	1,420	—	270	110	1,040
Food & beverage	1,280	450	570	120	140
M.O.D.	300	150	60	10	80
	3,000	600	900	240	1,260

Less: Undistributed operating expenses:

Administrative and general	330	
Marketing	105	
Energy	95	
Property operation and maintenance	180	
Depreciation and fixed charges	310	1,020

Net profit   240

Assume that:
  1. All undistributed operating expenses are fixed costs.
  2. The change in key factors is 10%.
  3. Of the total departmental payroll and departmental expenses (£1,140,000), £890,000 is the fixed element and the balance is wholly variable.

You are required to:

(a) Calculate the profit multipliers for:

    (i) price level;
    (ii) sales volume;
    (iii) cost of sales;
    (iv) departmental payroll;
    (v) departmental expenses;
    (vi) undistributed operating expenses.

(b) Calculate price level profit multipliers for the three revenue producing departments and suggest three alternative price level adjustments which, other things being equal, will raise the overall net profit by approximately 25 per cent, i.e. to £300,000.

(c) Comment on the effectiveness of profit multipliers as a tool for planning and controlling hotel operations.

(BAHA)

Chapter Thirteen
Analysis of Financial Statements

Financial statements provide a summary of a firm's activities, in monetary terms, over a given period, most commonly one year. Essentially, the statements take the form of a profit and loss statement, which highlights the revenue accrued during a period together with the associated expenses, and the balance sheet, which indicates the assets, liabilities and owner's interest at the close of the period. Modified forms of these statements provide perhaps the single most important base on which to examine and assess the economic health of a business.

Interested parties

All those interested in a particular firm will usually want to scrutinize the statements at some stage. However, before discussing the ways of analysing financial statements it is worthwhile to identify briefly the various parties who have an interest in reviewing the financial position of a business.

Owners

Whether sole proprietors or shareholders, owners are primarily concerned with the rate of return on their investment in the form of profits or dividends and capital appreciation in terms of asset or share valuation. Owners are usually the parties at most risk and will therefore tend to focus attention on the 'bottom line' financial figure, i.e. net profit after taxes, and share valuation.

Management

Management are responsible for the effective planning, organization and control of resources and are as such concerned with all aspects of a firm's financial position, right through to the overall return on investment. They require a more detailed breakdown of financial and related information than other interested parties. Without adequate reports management are not able to monitor performance and take appropriate action to improve areas which are in need of attention.

Creditors

Creditors fall into two main groups, long-term and short-term. Long-term creditors, which include banks which grant overdraft facilities on a permanent basis, are interested in the value of a firm's assets, e.g. freehold land and property, on which to secure their loans. They are also concerned that there is sufficient pre-tax profit to service the debt interest.

Short-term creditors, such as suppliers of goods and services, are more concerned with a firm's immediate liquidity position; i.e. its cash and near cash assets, in order that they can receive payment of amounts due. Secured creditors are less at risk than other parties as, after the Crown, they have first claim on a firm's assets for debt repayment.

Employees

Trade unions and employees are also interested in the financial position of a firm. Knowledge of the health of a business is critical for pay bargaining and negotiations appertaining to employee benefits and conditions of service. Union leaders are aware that although the best possible deal should be struck for their members, unrealistic demands placed upon a firm may well jeopardize its very existence and thus the future employment prospects of the membership they represent.

Inland Revenue

The Inland Revenue require details of financial results such as annual operating revenue and associated expenses together with information relating to the purchase and sale of capital assets. These details are necessary in order to agree allowances and assess the level of taxable profits.

Prospective investors

These include potential financial investors wishing to acquire holdings in a firm or enter into negotiations regarding mergers or takeovers. Some are interested in complementing and strengthening their own firms whilst others are seeking to obtain businesses whose balance sheets are undervalued, not with a view to maintaining operations, but to sell off the assets in order to make a capital profit, i.e. asset strippers. These interested parties are concerned with all the information obtainable on the financial position of a firm, ranging from share values and dividend policies to profits and asset valuations.

Other interested parties

In addition to those mentioned above, other interested parties include financial journalists and commentators, stockbroker and consultancy firms, market and financial analysts, university and polytechnic research units, government agencies, students studying for hotel management and general business qualifications – the list is endless!

It therefore should be apparent that numerous individuals and organizations with a wide variety of motives are interested in the financial results of firms. Each party is concerned with all or some aspects of the financial position of particular firms. However, no party has, or requires, the same degree of access to the financial and related information of a firm as the management entrusted with the firm. The current and following chapters, therefore, aim to examine the more important approaches to analysing financial statements and measuring financial performance with particular emphasis on the needs of managers.

Financial statement analysis

A fundamental approach to financial analysis is to measure performance against some base (or yardstick). The main bases available for comparison purposes are:

(a) past performance;
(b) budgeted performance;
(c) inter-company results;
(d) industry studies.

The most common base used to compare current results is past performance, and this is used in the examples that follow. Even in cases where businesses do not operate some form of budgetary control system, or are unable to take advantage of inter-company or industry statistics, they will usually have their previous period results against which they may compare current performance.

Essentially, there are two ways of carrying out a comparison of financial results. One approach is to compare the differences between current results and past results on an absolute and relative (percentage) basis. This is known as 'comparative statement analysis'. The alternative approach is to convert the current and past results to a common basis and then compare the differences in absolute and relative terms. This alternative approach is known as 'comparative common size statement analysis'. The two approaches are discussed and illustrated below using assumed data of the Sloane Restaurant (see Exhibits 13–1 and 13–2 later).

Before comparative computations are undertaken it is important to select an appropriate base against which current results are to be measured. As mentioned earlier, the bases available for comparison purposes are past performance, budgets, inter-company results and industry statistics. Once a base has been chosen then the absolute difference is determined by subtracting the base figure from the current figure. Where the difference is larger than the base figure the value is given a plus sign (+) and where the difference is smaller than the base figure the value is given a minus sign (−).

Comparative statement analysis

Exhibits 13–1 and 13–2 show the financial results of the Sloane Restaurant for Year 5 and Year 6. Each exhibit also shows two additional columns. The first column indicates the absolute increase or decrease from the previous year. The second column shows the relative increase or decrease from the previous year. The relative change is determined by expressing the absolute difference between the two years as a percentage of the base figure. For example, take the case of the first items in Exhibit 13–1, sales revenue for food and beverage:

	Current result	−	Previous result (base)	=	Absolute difference
	£		£		£
Food revenue	562,500	−	455,000	=	+ 107,500
Beverage revenue	187,500	−	230,000	=	− 42,500

$$\frac{\text{Absolute difference} \times 100}{\text{Previous period (base)}} = \text{Relative difference}$$

Food revenue:
$$\frac{+ £107,500 \times 100}{£455,000} = + 23.6\%$$

Beverage revenue:
$$\frac{- £42,500 \times 100}{£230,000} = - 18.5\%$$

Exhibit 13–1

Sloane Restaurant
Comparative Profit Statements for years ended 31st December

	Year 5 £	Year 6 £	Absolute diff. £	Relative diff. %
Sales revenue:				
Food	455,000	562,500	+ 107,500	+ 23.6
Beverage	230,000	187,500	− 42,500	− 18.5
Total	685,000	750,000	+ 65,000	+ 9.5
Less: Cost of sales:				
Food	158,500	212,625	+ 54,125	+ 34.2
Beverage	92,000	73,125	− 18,875	− 20.5
Total	250,500	285,750	+ 35,250	+ 14.1
Gross profit	434,500	464,250	+ 29,750	+ 6.9
Less: Controllable expenses:				
Payroll and related expenses	191,800	195,000	+ 3,200	+ 1.7
Other direct expenses	47,950	54,750	+ 6,800	+ 14.2
Administration	63,020	69,000	+ 5,980	+ 9.5
Marketing	17,125	21,000	+ 3,875	+ 22.6
Energy	23,290	23,250	− 40	− 0.2
Property operation	22,605	24,000	+ 1,395	+ 6.2
Total	365,790	387,000	+ 21,210	+ 5.8
Profit before fixed charges	68,710	77,250	+ 8,540	+ 12.4

The increases and decreases shown in the balance sheets in Exhibit 13–2 are determined in the same way as for the profit statements.

Profit statement interpretation

Observation of the profit statement results shows that food revenue has increased by 23.6% and beverage revenue has decreased by 18.5%. The combined effect on total restaurant revenue is a rise of 9.5%. Thus, the overall revenue results have been constrained by the drop in beverage revenue. This should prompt management to raise questions, examples of which are:

(a) Are beverages being adequately promoted, i.e. merchandising, staff trained to sell?

207

Exhibit 13–2

Sloane Restaurant
Comparative Balance Sheets as at 31st December

	Year 5 £	Year 6 £	Absolute diff. £	Relative diff %
Current assets:				
Cash at bank	2,700	5,000	+ 2,300	+ 85.2
Debtors	25,200	22,500	− 2,700	− 10.7
Stocks	12,400	15,600	+ 3,200	+ 25.8
Prepaid expenses	4,700	4,200	− 500	− 10.6
Total current assets	45,000	47,300	+ 2,300	+ 5.1
Fixed assets:				
Land and buildings	650,000	650,000	0	0
Furniture and equipment	235,000	235,000	0	0
China, cutlery, etc.	64,000	64,000	0	0
	949,000	949,000	0	0
Less: Aggregate depn.	(294,000)	+ (329,000)	+ (35,000)	+ (11.9)
Total fixed assets (net)	655,000	620,000	− 35,000	− 5.3
Total assets	700,000	667,300	− 32,700	− 4.7
Current liabilities:				
Creditors	17,300	18,400	+ 1,100	+ 6.4
Accrued expenses	5,100	6,000	+ 900	+ 17.7
Advance deposits	1,600	2,300	+ 700	+ 43.8
Total current liabilities	24,000	26,700	+ 2,700	+ 11.3
Long-term liability:				
Bank loan	100,000	100,000	0	0
Owners' interest:				
Share capital	400,000	400,000	0	0
Retained profits	176,000	140,600	− 35,400	− 20.1
Total owners' interest	576,000	540,600	− 35,400	− 6.2
Total liabilities and owners' interest	700,000	667,300	− 32,700	− 4.7

(b) Are beverage prices too high or out of line with menu prices?
(c) Has there been a change in customer profile towards those who drink less?
(d) Are the right beverage products being offered?

Further observation reveals that total restaurant revenue has risen by 9.5%, but that overall gross profit has only increased by 6.9%. The reason for this is that although beverage cost of sales has decreased by more than beverage revenue, i.e. 20.5% compared to 18.5%, food costs of sales has increased proportionately at a greater rate resulting in a larger overall rise in total cost of sales compared to total revenue. This in turn should raise questions about food operations such as:

(a) Is the food production department being operated efficiently, i.e. production methods, pilferage, supervision?
(b) Is food purchasing being carried out effectively, i.e. shopping around, taking advantage of discounts?
(c) Are food stocks too high, resulting in deterioration and wastage?

Finally, observation of the controllable expenses shows that overall they have risen by only 5.8%. Apart from other direct expenses, which have increased by 14.2%, only marketing has risen at a greater rate than total revenue. Administration has increased at the same rate as revenue whilst the remaining items have risen at a lower rate. Therefore, as would normally be expected, the combined result of the controllable expenses is that they have increased at a lower rate than revenue. The overall outcome of the results is that profit before fixed charges, i.e. controllable profit, has increased at a greater rate than revenue.

Where comparative statement analysis is used to analyse profit statements it is important to note that changes in expenses should be compared with changes in revenue. If taken in isolation the increase or decrease in expenses is of little value. The main factor that normally influences expenses is the level of revenue.

Balance sheet interpretation

Unlike the interpretation of the profit statement where changes in costs can be compared and related to changes in revenue, there is not normally the same kind of proportional relationship between balance sheet items. However, a comparative analysis is useful in highlighting significant changes in assets and liabilities.

For instance, take the 'stocks' item under current assets in Exhibit 13–2. Depending on the size of a business an increase in stocks of £3,200 may or may not be large in absolute terms, but in the case of the Sloane Restaurant this represents a relative increase of 25.8%. This would seem to be a significant increase from the previous year and should, therefore, prompt management to question whether the rise in stock holding is justified. Bearing in mind the fact that stock levels are to some extent associated with the level of business, then the increase of 9.5% shown in the profit statement analysis (Exhibit 12–1) would appear to justify some degree of rise in stocks held. However, as the stock value has more than doubled in relative terms it would seem appropriate for management to investigate the reasons why the increase is so pronounced.

Other relatively significant changes in the balance sheets are increases in cash at bank of 85.2% and advance deposits of 43.8%. If there is no specific reason for holding the additional cash it might be appropriate to use part of it to reduce accrued expenses and creditors which combined have increased by £2,000 over the year. Finally, assuming that advance deposits have risen due to an increase in future business then there should be no cause for concern.

Comparative common size statement analysis

Exhibits 13–3 and 13–4 show the same financial results of the Sloane Restaurant (given in Exhibits 13–1 and 13–2), but presented in common size format. The common size format is obtained by expressing profit statement items as a percentage of total revenue and balance sheet items as a percentage of total assets. For example, consider food revenue in Year 5:

$$\frac{£455,000 \times 100}{£685,000} = 66.4\%$$

The exception to this is the food and beverage cost of sales. As food cost of sales relates to food revenue and beverage cost of sales relate to beverage revenue it is more helpful to management to express these costs as a percentage of their respective revenues. Thus, the sum of these two percentages does not equal the total cost of sales percentage. However, the total cost of sales is expressed as a percentage of total revenue, as are all the other items for the two years results in the profit statements (minor differences are due to roundings).

Exhibits 13–3 and 13–4 also show two additional columns. The first column indicates the absolute percentage points increase or decrease from the previous year. The second column shows the relative increase or decrease from the previous year by expressing the absolute difference between the two periods as a percentage of the base figure. For example, take the case of the first item in Exhibit 13–3, sales revenue for food:

$$\frac{\text{Current}}{\text{result}} - \frac{\text{Previous}}{\text{result (base)}} = \frac{\text{Absolute}}{\text{difference}}$$

$$75.0\% - 66.4\% = 8.6\%$$

$$\frac{\text{Absolute difference} \times 100}{\text{Previous period (base)}} = \frac{\text{Relative}}{\text{difference}}$$

$$\frac{0.086 \times 100}{0.664} = 13.0\%$$

The increases and decreases shown in the balance sheets in Exhibit 13–4 are computed in the same way as for the profit statements.

Observation of the comparative common size profit statement results shows that the comparisons highlight similar significant changes to the comparative statement analysis approach. For instance, consider the cost of sales category in Exhibit 13–1. Food cost of sales was highlighted for investigation because it increased 34.2% over the previous year whilst food revenue increased by only 23.6%. This item is also spotlighted in the common size analysis in Exhibit 13–3. Food cost of sales in Year 6 is 37.8% of food revenue. Compared with Year 5 when food cost of sales was 34.7% of food revenue this indicates that food cost of sales as a proportion of food revenue has risen by 3% in absolute terms which, relative to Year 5, is an increase of 8.6%. Most managers would wish to pursue the reasons for an increase in food consumption of this order.

The same goes for the comparisons in the common size balance sheets. For example, the common size balance sheet in Exhibit 13–4 highlights an increase in stocks over the year. In proportion to total assets stocks only increased by 0.5% points in absolute terms, i.e. one half of one percentage point, but in relation to the previous year this represents a 27.8% increase. Even when compared with the increase in total sales revenue of 9.5% (Exhibit 13–1), the rise is clearly open to question.

The choice as to whether comparative statements or comparative common size statements should be used in a given situation primarily depends upon how the base (yardstick) data is presented. In any event, it is only necessary to select one of the approaches as both draw attention to those items which require investigation, albeit in different ways.

Both approaches are suitable for a comparison of current results with past results or budgeted performance. However, if a firm has two or more similar kinds of business, e.g. restaurants, and wishes to compare their performance with one another then the financial results should be converted to common size statements. Allowances for particular differences in establishments can be made when the comparisons are being evaluated.

Exhibit 13–3

Sloane Restaurant
Comparative Common Size Profit Statements for year ended 31st December

	Year 5 %	Year 6 %	Absolute diff. % points	Relative diff. %
Sales revenue:				
Food	66.4	75.0	+ 8.6	+ 13.0
Beverage	33.6	25.0	− 8.6	− 25.6
Total	100.0	100.0	0	0
Less: Cost of sales:				
Food	34.8	37.8	+ 3.0	+ 8.6
Beverage	40.0	39.0	− 1.0	− 2.5
Total	36.6	38.1	+ 1.5	+ 4.1
Gross profit	63.4	61.9	− 1.5	− 2.4
Less: Controllable expenses				
Payroll and related expenses	28.0	26.0	− 2.0	− 7.1
Other direct expenses	7.0	7.3	+ 0.3	+ 4.3
Administration	9.2	9.2	0	0
Marketing	2.5	2.8	+ 0.3	+ 12.0
Energy	3.4	3.1	− 0.3	− 8.8
Property operation	3.3	3.2	− 0.1	− 3.0
Total	53.4	51.6	− 1.8	− 3.4
Profit before fixed charges	10.0	10.3	+ 0.3	+ 3.0

Note: *minor differences due to roundings.*

Assume for the sake of argument that the statements shown in Exhibit 13–3 are the current results of *two* establishments owned by Sloane Restaurants, the first being named 'Year 5' and the second named 'Year 6'. Further assume the restaurants are similar in all respects except that 'Year 6' restaurant is located in a remote area with high unemployment. From this it may be reasonable to find that, as per the comparative results, food is 3.0% more expensive to obtain, i.e. 37.8% of revenue compared with 34.8% for the 'Year 5' restaurant, and that labour is 2.0% cheaper, i.e. 26% of revenue compared with 28%.

Common size balance sheets can be used to compare the financial structures of different businesses, but they tend to be of greater value in highlighting the proportional changes in items between

Exhibit 13–4

Sloane Restaurant
Comparative Common Size Balance Sheets as at 31st December

	Year 5 %	Year 6 %	Absolute diff. % points	Relative diff. %
Current assets:				
Cash at bank	0.4	0.8	+ 0.4	+ 100.00
Debtors	3.6	3.4	− 0.2	− 5.6
Stocks	1.8	2.3	+ 0.5	+ 27.8
Prepaid expenses	0.7	0.6	− 0.1	− 14.3
Total current assets	6.4	7.1	+ 0.7	+ 10.9
Fixed assets:				
Land and buildings	92.9	97.4	+ 4.5	+ 4.8
Furniture and equipment	33.6	35.2	+ 1.6	+ 4.8
China, cutlery, etc.	9.1	9.6	+ 0.5	+ 5.5
	135.6	142.2	+ 6.6	+ 4.9
Less: Aggregate depn.	(42.0)	(49.3)	+ (7.3)	+ (17.4)
Total fixed assets (net)	93.6	92.9	− 0.7	− 0.8
Total assets	100.0	100.0	0	0
Current liabilities:				
Creditors	2.5	2.8	+ 0.3	+ 12.0
Accrued expenses	0.7	0.9	+ 0.2	+ 28.6
Advance deposits	0.2	0.4	+ 0.2	+ 100.0
Total current liabilities	3.4	4.0	+ 0.6	+ 17.7
Long-term liability:				
Bank loan	14.3	15.0	+ 0.7	+ 4.9
Owners' interest:				
Share capital	57.1	59.1	+ 2.0	+ 3.5
Retained profits	25.1	21.1	− 4.0	− 15.9
Total owners' interest	82.3	81.0	− 1.3	− 1.6
Total liabilities and owners' interest	100.0	100.0	0	0

Note: minor differences due to roundings.

periods. Common size statements are also necessary when comparing the results of a firm with industry statistics. Much of the data collected for industry studies is presented in common size format and therefore, in order to provide meaningful comparisons, financial statements must be converted to common size.

Absolute and relative differences

Care should be exercised in the evaluation of absolute and relative differences present in results. A small increase in absolute terms may represent a large increase in relative terms. For instance, consider cash at bank in Exhibit 13–4. The absolute increase of cash related to total assets of + 0.4% points (less than one half of one percentage point) represents an increase of + 100% relative to the previous year.

Conversely, a large increase in absolute terms may represent a small increase in relative terms. For instance, referring to total revenue in Exhibit 13–1, the absolute increase of £65,000 represents a rise of only + 9.5% relative to the previous year.

It, therefore, becomes apparent that a large or small difference in absolute terms may result in a large or small difference in relative (percentage) terms. The reason for a percentage not automatically reflecting the absolute difference between periods is that it is dependent upon the size of the base.

Questions and problems

13–1 Distinguish between comparative and comparative common size statements.

13–2 Below are the financial results of the Hanganara International Hotel Company for two years ended 31st May:

Balance Sheets as at 31st May

	1992	1993
	£	£
Current liabilities:		
Overdraft	8,000	23,000
Proposed dividend	50,000	60,000
Corporation tax due	76,000	121,000
Creditors	16,000	30,000
	150,000	234,000

Long-term liabilities:

20% loan (secured on property–1995)	240,000	240,000
Total liabilities	390,000	474,000

Owner's interest:

Common stock	380,000	511,000
Retained profits	180,000	249,000
	560,000	760,000
Total liabilities and owner's interest	950,000	1,234,000

Current assets:	£	£
Cash at bank	106,000	4,000
Debtors	24,000	100,000
Food and beverage stocks	40,000	150,000
	170,000	254,000

Fixed assets (net):		
Land and building	640,000	780,000
Equipment	60,000	80,000
Furniture	80,000	120,000
	780,000	980,00
Total assets	950,000	1,234,000

Profit Statements for year ended 31st May

	1992	1993
	£	£
Sales revenue	1,000,000	1,400,000
Less: Cost of sales	200,000	280,000
Payroll related expenses	280,000	400,000
Other expenses	320,000	430,000
Loan interest (20%)	48,000	48,000
	848,000	1,158,000
Net profit before tax	152,000	242,000
Less: Corporation tax (50%)	76,000	121,000
Net profit after tax	76,000	121,000
Less: Proposed dividend	38,000	52,000
Retained profits	38,000	69,000

Required:
- (a) Prepare comparative common size balance sheets and profit statements for the two year period.
- (b) Calculate the absolute and relative differences between the balance sheet and profit statement items.
- (c) Comment on the results revealed by the computations made in (a) and (b) above.

Chapter Fourteen

Measuring Financial
and Operating Performance

Most business results are presented essentially in the form of profit
and loss statements and balance sheets. These statements contain a
list of totals taken from the book-keeping and accounting system
which, although useful for an overview of the financial position of a
business, are limited in detail. If report totals alone are examined
their significance is not readily identified by the reader. In order to
gain a more informed understanding of results managers can introduce ratios to highlight meaningful relationships between specific
figures.

Ratio analysis

A ratio expresses the mathematical relationship between two values.
For example, if we wish to gain a better insight into beverage cost of
sales over a period, beverage cost of sales should be related to
beverage revenue as beverage cost is heavily influenced by the
volume of beverage sales. Similarly, if we wish to learn more about
rooms payroll during a period, rooms payroll can be related to room
sales revenue as this has a considerable effect on rooms payroll.

Although the ratios themselves are relatively straightforward to
calculate their interpretation requires a sound knowledge and understanding of the particular business under review. Ratios provide
managers with clues to the underlying operating conditions of a
business which might otherwise go undetected by examining their
separate components alone.

Kinds of ratio

Ratios are best classified into categories according to the information
required by management. A common grouping is as follows:

   (a)   liquidity management ratios;
   (b)   debt management ratios;

(c) asset management ratios;
(d) profitability ratios;
(e) operating ratios;
(f) investment ratios.

In practice ratios are often expressed as percentages or numbers as opposed to the traditional form of, say, 2:1. This is of little consequence as a ratio should be presented in a form that is most easily interpreted by managers.

Exhibit 14–1

Clarenden Hotel
Balance Sheet as at 31st December

	Year 1 £	Year 2 £
Fixed assets (net):		
Freehold land and buildings	350,000	350,000
Equipment and fittings	183,300	165,000
China, glass, cutlery	32,000	36,000
	565,300	551,000
Current assets:		
Food stocks	2,500	7,500
Beverage stocks	16,000	34,000
Debtors	90,400	149,600
Short-term investments	2,100	3,000
Cash at bank	3,700	4,900
	114,700	199,000
Total assets	£680,000	£750,000
	£	£
Owners' equity:		
Capital	250,000	250,000
Retained profits	50,000	115,000
	300,000	365,000
Long-term liabilities:		
13% Bank loan (repayable year 8)	188,000	188,000
Current Liabilities:		
Creditors	157,000	141,200
Accrued expenses	29,000	18,000
Bank overdraft	6,000	37,800
	192,000	197,000
Total liabilities and owners' equity	£680,000	£750,000

Exhibit 14–2

Clarenden Hotel
Profit and Loss Statement for year ended Year 2

	£
Rooms Department	
Sales revenue	500,000
Payroll and related expenses	75,000
Other expenses	35,000
Total expenses	110,000
Dept. profit	390,000
Food and Beverage Department	
Food revenue	300,000
Beverage revenue	200,000
Total revenue	500,000
Food cost of sales	150,000
Beverage cost of sales	80,000
Total cost of sales	230,000
Gross profit	270,000
Payroll and related expenses	135,000
Other expenses	20,000
Total expenses	155,000
Dept. profit	115,000
Total dept. profits	505,000
Undistributed operating expenses	
Admin. and general	145,000
Marketing	27,000
Energy	31,500
Property maintenance	26,500
Total UOE	230,000
Profit before fixed charges*	275,000
Fixed charges	
Occupation expenses	150,560
Loan interest	24,440
Total fixed charges	175,000
Net profit before tax	100,000
Tax (35%)	35,000
Net profit after tax	£65,000

* Sometimes referred to as Gross Operating Profit (GOP)

In order to assist the understanding of how the above ratios are computed we will use the assumed results of the Clarenden Hotel, given in Exhibits 14–1 and 14–2.

Liquidity management ratios

Liquidity management ratios give an indication of a firm's short-term solvency in terms of the ability to meet short-term obligations. If a business is unable to pay its short-term obligations such as suppliers, staff, taxes and dividends on a regular basis it will rapidly face a liquidity crisis.

Current ratio

The current ratio provides an overview of an undertaking's short-term liquidity position by indicating the relationship between current assets and current liabilities as follows:

$$\text{Current ratio} = \frac{\text{Current assets at end of year}}{\text{Current liabilities at end of year}}$$

$$= \frac{\pounds199,000}{\pounds197,000}$$

$$= 1.01 : 1$$

We can see that the Clarenden Hotel's current ratio at the end of Year 2 shows that it has £1.01 worth of current assets for each one pound of current liabilities. Thus, the hotel is able to fund its short-term debts out of short-term assets. However, does the hotel have sufficient liquid funds to repay its short-term debts?

Acid test ratio

A more effective indicator of an undertaking's ability to repay its short-term debts is the acid test ratio. This ratio, sometimes referred to as the quick assets ratio, shows the relationship between the quick assets, i.e. debtors, short-term investments and cash, and current liabilities as follows:

$$\text{Acid test ratio} = \frac{\text{Quick assets at end of year}}{\text{Current liabilities at end of year}}$$

$$= \frac{\pounds157,500}{\pounds197,000}$$

$$= 0.80 : 1$$

We can observe that the hotel's acid test ratio at the end of Year 2 shows £0.80 worth of quick, or liquid, assets for each one pound of current liabilities. Quick assets are so termed because they can readily be turned into liquid (cash) funds. The food and beverage stocks have yet to be sold and, therefore, take considerably longer to be liquidated.

In theory, a business should have one pound of quick assets to cover each pound of current liabilities. If, however, the Clarenden Hotel has a pre-arranged bank overdraft facility it could operate with an acid test ratio of less than 1 : 1. The problem with this is that as an overdraft can be called in at short notice it could cause the business to become insolvent through the inability to pay its immediate obligations.

Debt management ratios

As explained above, liquidity management ratios provide an indication of the short-term solvency of a business. In contrast, debt management ratios focus on the long-term solvency of an undertaking.

Solvency ratio

This ratio focuses on a firm's ability to meet its long-term obligations and, therefore, includes both short-term and long-term debts. The ratio is calculated as follows:

$$\text{Solvency ratio} = \frac{\text{Total assets at end of year}}{\text{Total liabilities at end of year}}$$

$$= \frac{£750,000}{£188,000 + £197,000}$$

$$= \frac{£750,000}{£385,000}$$

$$= 1.95 : 1$$

We can see that the Clarenden Hotel has a book value of 1.95 for each one pound of total liabilities. Thus, if the hotel was to liquidate its assets all creditors could be fairly sure of receiving most of their money. In fact, in this case all debts would be recovered if the hotel's assets were sold for a little over half of their book value.

Gearing ratio

The gearing ratio, sometimes known as the leverage ratio, is determined in order to show the relationship between fixed interest (and fixed dividend) capital, and owners' equity, as follows:

$$\text{Gearing ratio (a)} = \frac{\text{Fixed interest capital}}{\text{Owners' equity}}$$

$$= \frac{\pounds188,000}{\pounds365,000}$$

$$= 0.52 : 1 \text{ or } 52\%$$

The hotel has a gearing ratio which indicates that for each pound of owners' equity it has obtained fifty-two pence of borrowed capital. However, this ratio may be more easily understood if it is expressed as follows:

$$\text{Gearing ratio (b)} = \frac{\text{Fixed interest capital}}{\text{Total long-term capital}}$$

$$= \frac{\pounds188,000}{\pounds553,000}$$

$$= 0.34 : 1 \text{ or } 34\%$$

This indicates that the hotel has borrowed 34% of its long-term capital. Although there is no rigid rule for this ratio it is generally accepted that a business with a gearing ratio (b) of 40 percent or less is a low geared company, whereas a business with a ratio of above 40 percent would be regarded as highly geared.

Interest cover ratio

This ratio gives a reasonable indication of a company's ability to meet its interest repayment out of current profits and, therefore, is a broad indicator of long-term solvency. The ratio is calculated as follows:

$$\text{Interest cover ratio} = \frac{\text{Net profit before interest and taxation}}{\text{Annual interest repayments}}$$

$$= \frac{\pounds124,440}{\pounds24,440}$$

$$= 5 \text{ times}$$

Thus, after all other operating expenses have been recovered, the Clarenden Hotel has sufficient profits to repay annual interest charges five times over.

Asset management ratios

This group of ratios gives an indication of how well a business utilizes the assets at its disposal.

Stock turnover ratio

The fundamental stock turnover ratio is calculated in the following manner:

$$\text{Stock turnover ratio} = \frac{\text{Cost of sales}}{\text{Average stock}}$$

The average stock figure is determined by totalling the beginning and the end of year stock figures and dividing by two, as follows:

$$\text{Average stock} = \frac{\text{Opening stock} + \text{Closing stock}}{2}$$

In the hotel and catering industry the two most important stocks to be controlled are normally those relating to food and beverage:

$$\text{Food stock turnover ratio} = \frac{£150,000}{\dfrac{(£2,500 + £7,500)}{2}}$$

$$= \frac{£150,000}{£5,000}$$

$$= 30 \text{ times}$$

Thus, it can be seen that the Clarenden Hotel turned over its food stock 30 times during Year 2. This ratio is not very easy to interpret as it stands, so it is often considered easier to express the ratio as follows:

$$\begin{aligned}\text{Food stock ratio} \\ \text{(No. days supply)}\end{aligned} = \frac{\text{Days per year}}{\text{Stock turnover}}$$

$$= \frac{365}{30}$$

$$= 12.2 \text{ days}$$

This indicates that the hotel is holding a little under two week's food stocks. Depending on the type of restaurant this figure would normally be expected to be between one and two weeks, so the hotel seems to be controlling its food stocks fairly effectively. Although this ratio should be kept to a minimum to avoid excessive amounts of working capital being tied-up, if the figure is too low it may indicate that insufficient stocks are being held, resulting in restaurant menu items becoming unavailable to customers.

$$\begin{aligned}\text{Beverage stock} \\ \text{turnover ratio}\end{aligned} = \frac{£80,000}{\dfrac{(£16,000 + £34,000)}{2}}$$

$$= \frac{£80,000}{£25,000}$$

$$= 3.2 \text{ times}$$

Or expressed in terms of number of days supply, mentioned above:

$$\text{Beverage stock ratio (No. days supply)} = \frac{365}{3.2}$$

$$= 114.9 \text{ days}$$

The beverage stock ratio indicates that the hotel is holding an average of around four months supply of liquor stocks. Again, depending on the type of establishment, the amount of beverage stock held would normally be expected to be between one and three months. The hotel should, therefore, investigate the possibility of reducing its beverage stocks to a lower level as they appear to be getting out of control. This will in turn free cash resources and improve the hotel's acid test ratio. Beverage stocks are normally a great deal higher than food stocks due to the wide variety of liquor choice demanded by the consumer.

Whilst it is difficult to generalize about stock ratios it is generally expected that an up-market restaurant would have a lower stock turnover ratio (and thus a higher number of days supply) than a down-market establishment. The reason for this is that the higher average spend establishments tend to hold a wider variety of stocks, some of which comprise a considerable number of high cost items. This, together with the fact that numbers of covers are often relatively low, will result in beverage stocks in particular turning over at a slow rate.

Debtors ratios

These ratios, which are similar in principle to stock ratios, indicate how effectively credit control is managed. The debtor turnover ratio for Year 2 is determined in the following manner (assuming credit sales are 60 percent of sales revenue):

$$\text{Debtor turnover ratio} = \frac{\text{Credit sales}}{\text{Average debtors}}$$

$$= \frac{£500,000 \times 60\%}{\frac{(£90,400 + £149,600)}{2}}$$

$$= \frac{£300,000}{£120,000}$$

$$= 2.5 \text{ times}$$

The average debtors figure is obtained by totalling the beginning and end of year debtors and dividing by two. If the debtors turnover ratio is expressed in terms of the average debt collection period the result will be as follows:

Debtors ratio
Average collection period $= \dfrac{\text{Days per year}}{\text{Debtors turnover}}$

$$= \frac{365}{2.5}$$

$$= 146 \text{ days or approx. 5 months}$$

Thus, the hotel is taking around five months to collect its debts. The problem appears to be due to the significant increase in debtors in Year 2 and highlights the need for an immediate examination of credit control procedures. In practice the figure should be in the order of one to two months.

Fixed asset turnover ratio

This ratio indicates how effectively a business utilizes its fixed assets to generate sale revenue:

$$\text{Fixed asset turnover ratio} = \frac{\text{Sales revenue}}{\text{Average fixed assets}}$$

$$= \frac{\pounds500,000}{\dfrac{(\pounds565,300 + \pounds551,000)}{2}}$$

$$= \frac{\pounds500,000}{\pounds558,150}$$

$$= 0.9 \text{ times}$$

The average fixed assets figure is determined by totalling beginning and end of year figures and dividing by two. The ratio shows that the Clarenden Hotel has generated £0.9 over the year from each pound invested in fixed assets. This figure will generally range from around one to two times per year, so the hotel could be said to be slightly under-utilizing its fixed assets.

Total asset turnover ratio

This ratio gives an indication of how well a business is utilizing its fixed and current assets in the generation of sales revenue:

$$\text{Total asset turnover ratio} = \frac{\text{Sales revenue}}{\text{Average total assets}}$$

$$= \frac{\pounds500,000}{\dfrac{(\pounds680,000 + \pounds750,000)}{2}}$$

$$= \frac{£500,000}{£715,000}$$

$$= 0.7 \text{ times}$$

The average total assets figure is determined by totalling beginning and end of year total assets and dividing by two. The ratio indicates the hotel has generated £0.70 during the year for each one pound invested in total assets. In the hotel industry this ratio can vary between one-half to around two times per year, so the Clarenden Hotel does appear to be utilizing its total assets reasonably well, although there is room for some improvement.

Profitability ratios

The fact that a business generates a profit in a period does not necessarily mean that it is a profitable concern. The reason for this lies in the perceived relationship between profit generated from sales revenue, assets and owners investment. Thus, in order to determine the significance of a given profit it becomes necessary to relate the figure to the level of sales achieved or some other yardstick.

Profitability ratios provide the basis to evaluate profitability.

Net profit ratio

This ratio measures the profitability of a business in terms of the overall operating or trading efficiency of management and is in effect the net return on sales:

$$\text{Net profit ratio} = \frac{\text{Net profit before tax}}{\text{Total sales revenue}}$$

$$= \frac{£100,000}{£500,000}$$

$$= 20\%$$

The ratio in this case shows that the Clarenden Hotel is generating £0.20 net profit for each one pound sales revenue. Although fixed charges do not normally fall within the control of a hotel general manager they must be included in the measurement of overall trading profitability. This ratio tends to range between 10 and 20 per cent in hotel and catering concerns. Thus, the hotel's overall operating or trading activities appear to be being carried out effectively.

Profit before fixed charges ratio

This ratio, also known as the efficiency ratio, is another important measure of profitability because it gives an indication of the operating (trading) efficiency of unit management:

$$\text{Profit before fixed charges ratio} = \frac{\text{Profit before fixed charges*}}{\text{Total sales revenue}}$$

$$= \frac{£275,000}{£500,000}$$

$$= 55\%$$

*Sometimes referred to as Gross Operating Profit (GOP)

As mentioned above, fixed charges, i.e. rent, rates, loan interest, depreciation, etc., are not normally controllable by unit managers and therefore, the general manager would be accountable for this ratio. In hotels this figure should normally be around 30–40 per cent, so at 55 per cent the Clarenden Hotel can be said to be operating extremely efficiently at the unit level.

Return on total assets

This ratio gives an indication of how effectively total assets are managed in generating profits. It can also be used as a guide in assessing the advisability of obtaining more debt financing:

$$\text{Return on total assets ratio} = \frac{\text{Profit before interest and tax}}{\text{Average total assets}}$$

$$= \frac{£124,440}{\dfrac{(£680,000 + £750,000)}{2}}$$

$$= \frac{£124,440}{£715,000}$$

$$= 17.4\%$$

Average total assets are determined by totalling beginning and end of year total assets and dividing by two. The hotel is generating an annual return of £0.174, before deducting interest charges, for each pound invested in assets. Interest is omitted in order to determine the true profit earning achievement of senior management, without being influenced by the method of debt financing. This ratio can also be used as a rough guide when considering the purchase and funding of new assets. For instance, if an extension was being planned for the Clarenden Hotel and the current rate of interest for debt funding was 12 per cent it could reasonably be assumed that the new facilities

227

would generate a return (around the current 17.4%) which would cover interest repayments and leave a residual profit for distribution to owners.

Net return on total assets ratio

This ratio gives an indication of how total assets are managed in generating net profit after tax, i.e. the final profit figure after deducting all operating expenses (including tax). It can also be a useful guide in assessing the ability to obtain additional equity (ordinary share capital) funding:

$$\text{Net return on total assets ratio} = \frac{\text{Net profit after tax}}{\text{Average total assets}}$$

$$= \frac{£65,000}{\frac{(£680,000 + £750,000)}{2}}$$

$$= \frac{£65,000}{£715,000}$$

$$= 9.1\%$$

This indicates that the hotel is achieving an after tax profit of £0.091 for each one pound invested in total assets. It can also be used as a rough guide to assess the viability of equity funding for a proposed extension to the Clarenden Hotel. Owners are eligible for after tax profits so on the assumption that a new extension investment achieved a similar return after tax the owners could expect a reasonable return.

Return on owners' equity

This ratio indicates how effectively management generates profits from operations in terms of the owners' total investment, i.e. share capital + retained profits:

$$\text{Return on equity ratio} = \frac{\text{Net profit after tax}}{\text{Average owners' equity}}$$

$$= \frac{£65,000}{\frac{(£300,000 + £365,000)}{2}}$$

$$= \frac{£65,000}{£332,500}$$

$$= 19.6\%$$

Average owners' equity is determined by totalling beginning and end of year figures and dividing by two. The result indicates that the Clarenden Hotel is generating an annual return after tax (available to owners) of almost £0.20 for each one pound of owners' investment. In order to ascertain whether the hotel is a good investment the owners should compare their return with other alternative investment opportunities. This is examined later in more detail under investment ratios.

Operating ratios

The ratios discussed so far have focused on the performance of the Clarenden Hotel in terms of monetary results. Operating ratios include physical and monetary aspects of business performance. This enables management to gain a better understanding of the underlying operational symptoms of the financial results.

Sales mix

The sales mix of a business represents the proportion of sales revenue from different sources expressed as a percentage of total sales revenue. The Clarenden Hotel sales mix is as follows:

Department	£	%
Rooms	500,000	50
Food	300,000	30
Beverage	200,000	20
	£1,000,000	100%

This is a useful ratio as managers should not only be aware of the total sales trend but also the trend in the composition of total sales. For example, total sales may remain at a satisfactory level, but the proportion of rooms revenue may show a decline. As the rooms department of a hotel will normally generate the highest gross or contribution margin, management will want to reverse any downward trend in the proportion of room sales in order to maintain the overall profitability of the establishment.

Whether a restaurant is within a hotel operation or is a stand-alone establishment management should be aware of the trend in food and beverage sales to total food and beverage revenue. These ratios are calculated as follows:

$$\text{Food revenue to F and B revenue} = \frac{\text{Food revenue}}{\text{F and B revenue}}$$

$$= \frac{£300,000}{£500,000}$$

$$= 60\%$$

$$\text{Beverage revenue to F and B revenue} = \frac{\text{Beverage revenue}}{\text{F and B revenue}}$$

$$= \frac{£200,000}{£500,000}$$

$$= 40\%$$

Thus, management can monitor food and beverage sales mix. This is important because beverage sales tend to produce a higher gross profit than food sales, so the greater the portion of beverage sales the greater the potential profit. In order to determine whether a hotel or restaurant is optimising its sales mix a useful yardstick is to compare the results against budgeted sales mix or industry averages.

Other operating ratios and statistics can also be measured on a department basis. In order to illustrate these, additional assumed data from the Clarenden Hotel is given in Exhibit 14–3.

Exhibit 14–3

Clarenden Hotel
Additional Operating Data (Year 2)

Rack rate per room: Single		£55
Double		£65
Rooms available: Single	30	
Double	20	
	—	50
Rooms sold		11,000
Number of guests		14,500
Restaurant covers		20,000
Restaurant seating capacity		44

Rooms department

One of the most important and commonly monitored hotel operating indicators is the average achieved room rate. The ratio is calculated in the following manner:

$$\text{Average achieved room rate (AARR)} = \frac{\text{Rooms revenue}}{\text{Rooms sold}}$$

$$= \frac{£500,000}{11,000}$$

$$= £45.46$$

The trend of the average is important. The average achieved room rate can be influenced by increasing the selling effort of the higher priced rooms and by impróving the rate of double occupancy (explained below). The figure is normally determined on a daily basis and averaged weekly, monthly and annually. It is a useful statistic where hotels operate differential rates for different rooms and offers discounted rates. Notice at £45.46 the Clarenden Hotel's average achieved room rate falls well below the rack rates of £55 and £65.

$$\text{Room occupancy percentage} = \frac{\text{Rooms sold}}{\text{Rooms available}}$$

$$= \frac{11,000}{(50 \times 365 \text{ days})}$$

$$= \frac{11,000}{18,250}$$

$$= 60.1\%$$

Rooms which are temporarily unavailable because of repairs, redecoration or refurbishment are normally included in the rooms available figure, but rooms withdrawn for indefinite periods for staff occupation should not be included in the figure. Room occupancy percentage is an important indicator of room capacity utilization and this percentage is normally calculated daily and averaged for weekly, monthly and annual periods.

$$\text{Double occupancy percentage} = \frac{\text{Rooms double occupied}}{\text{Rooms sold}}$$

$$= \frac{14,500 - 11,000}{11,000}$$

$$= \frac{3,500}{11,000}$$

$$= 31.8\%$$

This ratio indicates that 31.8% of all rooms sold are occupied by two or more guests. It shows the extent to which a hotel is optimizing available bed capacity and, in cases where varying rates are changed for multiple occupancy, this will be reflected in the average achieved room rate.

$$\text{Yield management percentage} = \frac{\text{Room revenue}}{\text{Maximum potential rooms revenue}}$$

The maximum potential rooms revenue for the Clarenden Hotel is calculated as follows:

$$
\begin{aligned}
&\text{30 single rooms} \times \text{£55} \times \text{365 days} &=& \quad 602{,}250 \\
&\text{20 double rooms} \times \text{£65} \times \text{365 days} &=& \quad \underline{474{,}500} \\
&\text{Maximum potential rooms revenue} &=& \quad \text{£1{,}076{,}750}
\end{aligned}
$$

Thus, the yield management percentage $= \dfrac{\text{£500{,}000}}{\text{£1{,}076{,}750}}$

$$= 46.4\%$$

The yield management percentage is a more global and comprehensive ratio than other room statistics. It gives a measure of actual rooms revenue related to total potential room revenue. Potential room revenue is calculated on the basis of 100% room occupancy or 100% multiple occupancy according to how rooms are priced, i.e. per room or the number of guests per room, using the published rack rate (excluding breakfast), in other words the maximum attainable room revenue. Note that although the Clarenden Hotel has achieved 60.1% room occupancy, in terms of potential rooms revenue (yield) this represents a significantly lower figure of 46.4%. This ratio should be calculated daily and averaged for weekly, monthly and annual periods. Yield management is further considered later in this chapter and an alternative method of calculating the yield management percentage is given.

$$\text{Revenue per available room (annually)} = \frac{\text{Rooms revenue}}{\text{Rooms available}}$$

$$= \frac{\text{£500{,}00}}{50}$$

$$= \text{£10{,}000}$$

Annual revenue per available room is a useful ratio for comparing the revenue generating efficiency of similar establishments of different sizes (number of rooms) with industry averages.

$$\text{Cost per available room (annually)} = \frac{\text{Room expenses}}{\text{Rooms available}}$$

$$= \frac{\text{£110{,}000}}{50}$$

$$= \text{£2{,}200}$$

Annual cost per available room is useful in comparing the cost (operating) efficiency of similar establishments of different sizes in an organization and with industry averages. Where annual occupancy is known this ratio can be expressed as the average cost per 'occupied' room which is a more specific statistic for measuring rooms department expenses. So in the case of the Clarenden Hotel the ratio would be as follows:

$$\text{Cost per occupied room (annual)} = \frac{\text{Rooms expenses}}{\text{Rooms occupied}}$$

$$= \frac{£110,000}{11,000}$$

$$= £10$$

This ratio should be compared with previous periods and budget. It can also be useful as a guide to costs when deciding upon special room pricing offers.

$$\text{Labour cost percentage} = \frac{\text{Rooms payroll and related expenses}}{\text{Rooms revenue}}$$

$$= \frac{£75,000}{£500,000}$$

$$= 15\%$$

Rooms payroll and related expenses range from around 10–20 per cent so at 15 per cent the Clarenden Hotel is performing satisfactorily.

Labour is a significant expense in the hotel and catering industry and should be monitored weekly, monthly and annually.

Food and beverage department

$$\text{Average food spend per cover (restaurant)} = \frac{\text{Food revenue}}{\text{Covers sold}}$$

$$= \frac{£300,000}{20,000}$$

$$= £15$$

$$\text{Average beverage spend per cover (restaurant)} = \frac{\text{Beverage revenue}}{\text{Covers sold}}$$

$$= \frac{£200,000}{20,000}$$

$$= £10$$

Average spends should be calculated by per meal period, i.e. lunch, dinner, etc., and averaged weekly, monthly and annually. The trend of these ratios should be monitored closely in conjunction with food and beverage sales mix.

$$\text{Seat turnover} = \frac{\text{Covers sold}}{\text{Seats available}}$$

$$= \frac{20,000}{(44 \times 365 \text{ days})}$$

$$= 1.25 \text{ times}$$

Seat turnover ratio should also be determined by meal period, i.e. lunch, dinner, etc., and monitored regularly in conjunction with the average spend figures. A declining seat turnover may suggest high prices or poor quality or a combination of the two.

$$\text{Food cost percentage} = \frac{\text{Food cost of sales}}{\text{Food revenue}}$$

$$= \frac{£150,000}{£300,000}$$

$$= 50\%$$

$$\text{Beverage cost percentage} = \frac{\text{Beverage cost of sales}}{\text{Beverage revenue}}$$

$$= \frac{£80,000}{£200,000}$$

$$= 40\%$$

As food and beverage cost tends to range between 30–40 per cent (giving a GP of 60–70 per cent) the Clarenden Hotel food cost of sales percentage appears to be well above average and should be investigated.

Food and beverage costs are significant costs incurred by restaurants and as such should be closely controlled. Assuming sales mix remains relatively constant and selling prices are maintained, food and beverage cost percentages are an effective means of controlling purchasing efficiency, pilferage, wastage and supervision activities in restaurant operations. Sometimes managers prefer to express these percentages as gross profit percentages as they emphasize margins rather than costs, but essentially they convey similar information. Whichever percentages are used they should be monitored weekly, monthly and annually against budget.

$$\text{Labour cost percentage} = \frac{\text{F and B payroll and related expenses}}{\text{F and B revenue}}$$

$$= \frac{£135,000}{£500,000}$$

$$= 27\%$$

Again, labour is an important cost associated with operating a restaurant and should be controlled weekly, monthly and annually against budget. According to the market position of a restaurant labour cost can range between 15–50 per cent so the Clarenden Hotel appears to be maintaining a reasonable level.

Other operating ratios

$$\frac{\text{Rooms serviced}}{\text{per employee}} = \frac{\text{Number rooms serviced}}{\text{Average number of employees}}$$

$$\text{Covers served per employee} = \frac{\text{Number covers sold}}{\text{Average number of employees}}$$

$$\text{Revenue per employee} = \frac{\text{F and B revenue}}{\text{Average number of employees}}$$

$$\text{Profit per employee} = \frac{\text{Net profit}}{\text{Average number of employees}}$$

These ratios are basically calculated to assess productivity and should be compared by department and outlet against some pre-determined standard or yardstick on a daily/weekly/monthly/annual basis as appropriate.

Investment Ratios

Ordinary or equity shares tend to be sensitive to expected future company performance. Investors expecting good trading results will increase the demand for shares, pushing the price up until it reflects their anticipated results. Should profits fall short of investors' expectations share prices will tend to fall, even though the results were relatively high. Thus, changes in share price are not so much a reflection of past management performance as they are of future expected results. In order to explain investment ratios additional assumed data for the Clarenden Hotel is given in Exhibit 14–4.

Exhibit 14–4

Clarenden Hotel
Additional data relating to ordinary shares (Year 2)

Ordinary capital is made up of 250,000 shares of £1 each

Proposed dividend per ordinary share at end of Year 2 £0.07

Stock Exchange (market) share price at end of Year 2 £0.80

Earnings per share ratio

$$\frac{\text{Earnings per}}{\text{share ratio}} = \frac{\text{Net profit after tax} - \text{Preference share dividend}}{\text{Number of ordinary shares}}$$

$$= \frac{£65,000}{250,000}$$

$$= £0.26$$

It is generally considered that the market value of ordinary shares is closely related to the earnings per share. This ratio is therefore, a useful basis on which to predict the future value of ordinary shares. In order to evaluate the earnings per share investors should compare the ratio over past years' results or other investments. Note, the Clarenden Hotel has not issued any preference shares and therefore, it does not have a preference share dividend commitment.

Dividend yield percentage

This ratio relates the dividend per share to the market price of each ordinary share and indicates the current cash return to the investor in the form of dividend paid.

$$\text{Dividend yield percentage} = \frac{\text{Ordinary dividend per share}}{\text{Market price per ordinary share}}$$

$$= \frac{£0.07}{£0.80}$$

$$= 8.75\%$$

Investors interested in obtaining high-yielding shares are able to compare the dividend yield of various investments and purchase those offering the highest yield.

Earnings yield percentage

This ratio indicates the long-term return on shares as it takes into account earnings, i.e. profit after tax and preference dividends, if any:

$$\text{Earning yield percentage} = \frac{\text{After tax earnings per ordinary share}}{\text{Market price per ordinary share}}$$

$$= \frac{£0.26}{£0.80}$$

$$= 32.5\%$$

Again investors should compare this ratio with alternative investments in order to determine the relative return.

Price earnings ratio

This ratio is the reciprocal of the earnings yield percentage and is calculated as follows:

$$\text{Price earnings ratio} = \frac{\text{Market price per ordinary share}}{\text{After tax earnings per share}}$$

$$= \frac{£0.80}{£0.26}$$

$$= 3.1$$

The price earnings ratio is a way of emphasizing the relationship between earnings and the market price of an ordinary share. It indicates the market's evaluation of the share in terms of the number of years earnings necessary to equal the share price. In effect, the ratio is a capitalization factor.

Evaluation of results

Having carried out an analysis of results it is important to evaluate the findings. If ratio analysis is not used effectively the outcome will be a fragmented series of ratios and percentages which, whilst high-lighting individual aspects of performance, will fail to indicate the overall operating performance of a business. In other words we need to use ratios to assist in building up a total picture of business performance in order to assess the overall position.

With reference to the Clarenden Hotel the findings and con-clusions may be summarized as follows:

Short-term liquidity reflected by the negative acid test ratio is insufficient at 0.80 : 1 and should be improved. Remember, a bank overdraft is repayable on demand (within 24 hours) and this has grown from £6,000 to £37,800 in the last year. Long-term solvency is sound due mainly to the low level of debt capital, at 24 per cent of total long-term capital (equity + debt). Short-term assets in the form of beverage stocks at 115 days (almost 4 months) and debtors at 146 days (approx. 5 months) are rela-tively high and should be reduced by more effective stock control and credit control. Long-term asset management is satisfactory which suggests that management are utilizing assets adequately in generating sales revenue. Profitability ratios indicate that management are managing operations efficiently as they are also within expected norms. Of the operating ratios, room occupancy at 60 per cent, yield percentage at 46 per cent and food cost of sales at 50 per cent all appear to have scope for improvement. Investment ratios seem satisfactory overall.

Thus, if an effective system of stock and debtor control is implemented, the main problem of liquidity can be resolved. In addition, if room occupancy and particularly yield percentage can be increased and food cost of sales is reduced, the Clarenden Hotel will improve its already satisfactory return on sales and assets.

Yield management

Yield management is a technique which assists in the maximization of revenue in industries with the following characteristics:

(a) perishability over time;
(b) fixed capacity;
(c) fluctuating demand;
(d) minimal variable costs;
(e) ability to segment the market for a similar product or service.

In the hotel industry yield management, perhaps better referred to as rooms revenue management, assists in the maximization of revenue generated from the sale of rooms. Revenue is maximized by managing the reservation inventory (stock of rooms) in three main ways:

(a) room rate allocation (based on buying behaviour and needs);
(b) capacity management (overbooking levels);
(c) duration control (length of stay).

Yield management is a computer-based system in which historical room reservation data is collected and used to support future room booking decisions. Fundamentally, the system operates as follows:

(a) when demand exceeds supply the emphasis focuses on the maximization of room rate, and;
(b) when supply exceeds demand the emphasis focuses on the maximization of room occupancy.

Traditionally, hotel room sales have been measured in terms of occupancy and average rate. However, with yield management attention centres on the combined results of occupancy and rate in terms of the value of revenue generated. This can be illustrated by a simple example. Assume the recent results of a 400-room hotel, with a rack rate of £150 per room, are as follows:

	Room occupancy %	Average room rate £
Monday	55	136.36
Tuesday	73	102.74
Wednesday	95	78.95

Which results should be regarded as the most effective? At first sight Tuesday may seem to have the most balanced result compared to the other two days. Monday has a low occupancy but a high average rate. This could be interpreted as being more profitable because variable costs, i.e. room servicing cost for wages and laundry, are required for fewer rooms than the other two days. On the other hand Wednesday has a high occupancy, but a low room rate. This in turn could be argued to be more profitable because of the benefits to the food and beverage outlets of more guests staying in the hotel.

However, if we calculate room revenue per day we find that all three days generate approximately the same revenue, as follows:

	Rooms available	×	Room occupancy (%)	×	Average room rate	=	Rooms revenue
Monday	400	×	55	×	£136.36	=	£30,000
Tuesday	400	×	73	×	£102.74	=	£30,000
Wednesday	400	×	95	×	£78.95	=	£30,000

The arguments concerning profitability for each of the three days are quite varied, but for most hotels the final profit outcomes will be similar. What emerges from the discussion is that when rooms management is monitored only in terms of occupancy and rate it tends to divert attention away from the more global picture provided by the total revenue. The fact that a hotel has a fixed number of rooms and a published rack rate means that it is possible to determine the maximum potential rooms revenue at full capacity. Even though this may rarely be achievable it is by definition the ultimate yardstick against which actual rooms revenue should be measured. The measure is known as the 'yield percentage' which is basically calculated as follows:

$$\text{Yield percentage} = \frac{\text{Rooms sold}}{\text{Rooms available}} \times \frac{\text{Average room rate}}{\text{Maximum potential room rate}}$$

Thus, using Monday's figures, the result is as follows:

$$\text{Yield percentage} = \frac{220}{400} \times \frac{£136.36}{£150}$$
$$= 0.55 \times 0.91$$
$$= 50\%$$

All three days have achieved different occupancies and room rates, but they each achieved a 50 percent yield percentage. Thus, whilst the relative merits of each day's occupancy and rate can be argued there is little doubt that an improvement in the yield percentage would be welcomed by management. Occupancy and rate should not be disregarded. Room occupancy highlights physical capacity utilization and average room rate provides an indication of the typical room price achieved. Both these ratios should, however, be interpreted in conjunction with the yield percentage.

Working capital management

The primary object of management is to achieve profit targets – once set – over a number of years. Merely to ensure the firm continues in operation, an important short-term target has to be met continually without fail, and that is the ability of paying debts and other obligations as they fall due, otherwise the firm becomes insolvent. Herein lies the function of working capital management. A balance should be struck between having too much and too little working capital, an objective that can only be achieved with any degree of accuracy through regularly updated forecasts and budgets of each element of working capital. Too much working capital means that opportunity is being lost of using long-term investment inside or outside the business simply because the surplus is not recognized. Too little working capital endangers the very existence of the firm, so that it is clear that to err on the high side is the better course.

The major elements of working capital within the control of management are stocks, debtors, short-term investments, cash at bank and in hand, bank overdrafts and creditors. Ratios involving working capital items are useful in forecasting the working capital level, mention having been made already of current ratio, liquid ratio, stock ratio, debtors ratio, and creditors ratio. A policy decision is needed to determine target levels of ratios of each item, for instance the number of days' stock holding and the number of days' credit allowable to customers. Whilst past experience and comparison with similar firms may be the only way of assessing target cash and stock levels, debtor and creditor levels can be more clearly defined using ratios.

Estimating working capital

Whether in respect of a proposed new undertaking or the extension of existing activities, the necessary level of working capital that will be required to fund trading operations must be identified. Below is an example of estimating the average working capital for a proposed catering establishment:

Forecast annual sales £130,000
Average gross profit on sales 70%

It is estimated that:

(a) food and drink stocks held will amount to 5 weeks' supply;
(b) of the sales ¼ will be on credit and debtors will be allowed a payment period of 7 weeks;
(c) all purchases of stocks will be on credit and it is anticipated that suppliers will allow 4 weeks credit;
(d) advance booking deposits will amount to 5% of 1 week's sales;
(e) a cash balance equivalent to ½ of the other working capital requirements is to be maintained.

Estimated Working Capital Requirements

	£	£
Food and drink stocks:		
5/52 × 30/100 × £130,000		3,750
Debtors: 7/52 × ¼ × £130,000		4,375
		8,125
Less: Creditors		
4/52 × 30/100 × £130,000	3,000	
Advance booking deposits		
1/52 × 5/100 × £130,000	125	3,125
		5,000
Plus: Cash balance		
½ × £5,000		2,500
Total working capital required		7,500

At first sight the computation appears straightforward but it does conceal several deficiencies. These arise as a result of the fundamental assumption in the estimate that sales and costs accrue evenly throughout the period. However, many catering concerns experience some degree of seasonal fluctuation and therefore the increase in business that occurs during the on-season will require additional working capital funds, that is if the undertaking is to continue to pay its way. The additional amount of working capital may be established in a manner similar to that used in the example, thereby treating the on-season period as an extension, albeit temporary, of business activities.

Stock, debtor and creditor levels tend to follow the general pattern of sales activity and thus it is the cash balance that is probably the most suspect element within the estimate. This is due primarily to *ad hoc* payments in respect of such items as taxation, dividends and purchase of assets, in addition to the more regular payments to employees and creditors, which take place during a period. Even with the deficiencies outlined above the computation serves as a useful starting point from which the working capital level may be decided.

Overtrading

This is a shortage of liquid funds caused by expansion of sales without sufficient additional capital to back up the operation. Businesses which give credit to customers and hold large stocks are, however, more prone to overtrading than many hotel and restaurant concerns.

To expand sales usually demands a higher level of debtors and stocks, which if not completely offset by extra credit allowed from suppliers means holding more working capital investment. Where is this to be obtained? If overdraft facilities are fully stretched before expansion, difficulty is likely to arise in obtaining more cash with which to fund the difference.

A difficult situation usually arises in overtrading when, through lack of cash, creditors are kept waiting for their money and they become reluctant to supply goods on credit, debtors are chased for earlier settlement and offered attractive discounts, or cash customers are offered cut price sales to turn over the stocks faster. In any case profit is likely to suffer.

Undertrading is the opposite of overtrading in that sales are too low in relation to capital resulting in low profits. However, the cash position may be healthy unless too much is taken out of the business by shareholders.

Questions and problems

14-1 Compare and contrast 'profitability' and 'liquidity' ratios.

14-2 The gross profit percentage is one of the most closely controlled ratios within the hotel and catering industry. Why do you think this is so?

14-3 What factors should a manager be aware of when reading a financial performance report containing various accounting and operating ratios?

14–4

Firm	Sales	Net profit	Capital employed	Net profit ratio	Net turnover	Return on capital employed
	£	£	£	%	No. times	%
A	200,000	30,000	160,000	*	*	*
B	40,000	*	*	5	2	*
C	*	3,000	*	10	*	5
D	*	*	400,000	*	6	8
E	900,000	*	300,000	3	*	*

Compute the missing figures indicated by *.

14–5 The following are the financial results of the Bridge Hotel:

Trading, Profit and Loss Account
for year ended 31st December

	£	£
Sales		120,000
Opening stock	7,400	
Purchases	51,000	
	58,400	
Less:		
Closing stock	8,000	50,400
Gross Profit		69,600
Less:		
Wages and staff costs	30,000	
Expenses	22,800	52,800
Net profit		16,800

Balance Sheet
as at 31st December

	£
Freehold premises	71,000
Kitchen plant (net)	5,450
Fittings	7,050
Stocks	8,000
Debtors	17,700
Bank balance	8,400
Cash balance	600
	118,200
Capital	68,200
Profit	16,800
Loan	20,000
Creditors	11,600
Accrued expenses	1,000
Advance bookings	600
	118,200

Other information:

(a) Average daily cost of sales: food £60; liquor £80.
(b) Average daily credit sales £240 and credit purchases £150.
(c) Debtors and creditors at the beginning of the year were £13,500 and £8,400 respectively.
(d) Stocks at the beginning of the year: food £700; liquor £6,700.

(e) Stocks at the end of the year: food £1,100; liquor £6,900.

You are required to calculate the various profitability and liquidity ratios you consider to be relevant in assessing the financial performance of this hotel. Comment on your results.

14–6 The following relates to Wheelers Catering Company:

Trading, Profit and Loss Account for year ended 31st March		Balance Sheet as at 31st March	
	£		£
Sales (all on credit)	100,000	Fixed assets (net)	
Less: Cost of sales			
	─────		
		Stock	
Less: Labour and		Debtors	
expenses		Cash	Nil
	─────		─────
Net profit before tax			
			─────
Less: Corporation tax			£
	─────		
Less: Dividend paid		Share capital	50,000
	─────		
Retained profit c/f	Nil	Retained profit c/f	Nil
	─────	Creditors	
			─────
			─────

Given the following ratios you are required to fill in the missing figures in the outline final accounts:

Turnover to capital employed	2:1
Average collection period*	18 days
Acid test ratio	1:1
Stock turnover period*	36 days
Gross profit	60%
Net profit before tax	15%
Corporation tax	50%
Ordinary share dividend	15%

* Assume a 360 day year

14–7 From the following information prepare a trading, profit and loss account and balance sheet:

Issued share capital	£360,000
Working capital	£60,000
Rate of turnover of capital employed	2
Rate of stock turnover (times)	12
Current ratio	1.6 : 1
Debtors ratio	0.075 : 1
Acid test ratio	1.1 : 1
Labour and expenses in relation to sales	20%

Notes:
1. Capital employed is to be taken as issued share capital plus net profit.
2. Ignore depreciation and appropriation of profits.

14–8   (a) Given: 1. an annual sales figure of £400,000, of which 3% are credit sales, and
2. capital employed of £240,000,

show the figures you would expect to find in the annual profit and loss statement and balance sheet of an hotel proprietor, together with your method of calculation.
Base your figures on the average ratios and statistics of the industry.
(b) Choose any four of the figures you have produced above and explain how and why a different figure might occur.

Note: State all the assumptions you make.

(HCIMA)

14–9   The following information relates to the Chatsworth Restaurant, a sole owned establishment in a provincial city:

Balance Sheet as at 31st May 19X3

	Cost £	Total deprn. £	Net £
Fixed assets:			
Leasehold building	80,000	4,000	76,000
Kitchen equipment	15,000	1,500	13,500
Restaurant furniture	10,000	1,000	9,000
Loose equipment (china, etc.)	4,000	500	3,500
	109,000	7,000	102,000

Current assets:

Food and beverage stocks	3,000	
Trade debtors	2,500	
Prepaid expenses	500	
Cash at bank	1,700	
Cash in hand	300	8,000
		110,000

	£	£
Capital on 1 June 19X2	90,200	
Add: Net profit for year	19,000	
	109,200	
Less: Proprietor's drawings	3,500	105,700
Current liabilities:		
Trade creditors	2,800	
Advance reservation deposits	350	
Accrued expenses	1,150	4,300
		110,000

Additional information:

1. The owner/manager has been paid a salary of £7,000, which has already been charged against profits.
2. Sales for the year were:

	£
Cash	65,000
Credit	28,000
	93,000

3. Purchases for the year were all on credit and totalled £24,600.
4. On 1 June 19X2 food and beverage stocks, trade debtors and trade creditors were valued at £4,400, £3,100 and £3,600 respectively.
5. The restaurant is open 312 days per year.
6. This type of establishment is expected to achieve a 16% return on capital employed.

You are requested to examine the above data through the eyes of a prospective purchaser for profitability and liquidity and state, giving reasons supported by relevant calculations, if the restaurant would be a viable proposition at an asking price of £120,000.

(HCIMA)

14–10 Below are the financial results of the Classic International Hotel Company for two years ended 31st December:

Balance Sheets as at 31st December

	1991 £	1992 £
Current liabilities		
Overdraft	20,000	31,000
Proposed dividend	38,000	52,000
Tax due	76,000	121,000
Accounts payable	16,000	30,000
	150,000	234,000
Long-term liabilities 20% loan (secured on property – 1995)	240,000	240,000
Total liabilities	390,000	474,000
Equity interest		
Common stock	512,000	643,000
Retained profits	48,000	117,000
	560,000	760,000
Total liabilities and equity interest	£950,000	£1,234,000
	£	£
Current assets		
Cash at bank	106,000	4,000
Accounts receivable	24,000	100,000
Food and beverage inventories	40,000	150,000
	170,000	254,000
Fixed assets (net)		
Land and building	640,000	780,000
Equipment and furniture	140,000	200,000
	780,000	980,000
Total assets	£950,000	£1,234,000

Profit and Loss Statement for year ending 31st December

	1991 £	1992 £
Sales revenue	1,000,000	1,400,000
Less: Cost of sales	200,000	280,000
Payroll and related expenses	280,000	400,000
Other expenses	320,000	430,000
Loan interest (20%)	48,000	48,000
	848,000	1,158,000
Net income before tax	152,000	242,000
Less: Tax (50%)	76,000	121,000
Net income after tax	76,000	121,000
Unappropriated profits b/f	10,000	48,000
	86,000	169,000
Less: Proposed dividend	38,000	52,000
Retained profits c/f	£48,000	£117,000

Credit sales represent 30% of sales revenue and all purchases are made on credit.

During the year no fixed assets were sold; depreciation of £20,000 for equipment and furniture is included in 'Other expenses'. New equipment and furniture was purchased at a cost of £80,000.

Required:
(a) Compute the appropriate ratios for 1992.
(b) Comment on the financial position for 1992 revealed by the ratios and any other information you consider relevant.
(c) Be prepared to discuss the cash flow position for 1992.

14–11 A town centre department store operates two public eating areas: a self-service cafeteria, and a restaurant. The following information has been presented for three consecutive months:

	March Cafe	March Rest.	April Cafe	April Rest.	May Cafe	May Rest.
No. covers	3,750	1,667	4,667	2,128	5,714	3,043
	£	£	£	£	£	£
Sales (excluding VAT)	6,000	8,000	7,000	10,000	8,000	14,000
Food cost	3,000	3,200	3,780	4,200	4,560	6,020
Labour:						
Basic pay	3,500		3,910		3,000	
Overtime	300		350		1,400	

You are required to:

    (a) Analyse these results, highlighting the relevant operating ratios and statistics.

    (b) Comment on the performance of this catering operation.

(HCIMA)

14–12 The trading account of a licensed restaurant is shown below:

Trading Account for the year ending 31st May 1986

	Food £	Beverage £	Total £
Sales	110,000	50,000	160,000
Opening Stock	2,200	3,800	6,000
Purchases	45,600	18,000	63,600
Closing stock	(1,600)	(4,200)	(5,800)
Cost of sales	46,200	17,600	63,800
Gross profit	63,800	32,400	96,200

You are required to:

    (a) Calculate *both* the stock turnover rate, *and* the stockholding period in days for food and beverage.

    (b) Discuss the significance of the ratios you have calculated.

    (c) Explain why it is necessary to hold stock.

    (d) Describe the various costs involved in holding stock.

(HCIMA)

14–13   (a) Describe briefly what is meant by the term 'working capital cycle'.

    (b) The Glenfield Hotel has a traditional style à la carte restaurant which, due to a steadily growing demand, has recently been extended to increase the seating capacity.

        A summary of the current year results of the restaurant, prior to the extension, is outlined below:

	Food £	%	Beverages £	%
Sales revenue	100,000	100	60,000	100
Less: Cost of sales	35,000	35	27,000	45
Gross Profit	65,000	65	33,000	55

With the extension now completed the following is anticipated during the coming year:

1. Sales of food and beverages will rise to £150,000 and £100,000 respectively.

2. The amount of stocks held will be:

   Food   4 weeks' supply
   Beverages   8 weeks' supply

3. Of the total sales of food and beverages, 20% will be on credit and the debtors will take 6 weeks' credit.
4. Food suppliers will give 5 weeks' credit but will not offer any discount for prompt payment.
5. Beverage suppliers will give 8 weeks' credit, but will
   offer 3% cash discount for settlement within 4 weeks. (Assume that all the payments will be made within the discount period.)

7. Advance booking deposits, currently amounting to approximately 10% of 2 weeks' food sales, will continue at the same level.

You are required to prepare a statement analysing the estimated average working capital requirements necessary to fund the restaurant's anticipated business during the coming year.

Note: Amounts may be rounded up to the nearest whole pound and you may assume that sales and costs will accrue evenly throughout the year. A year comprises 52 weeks.

(HCIMA)

Chapter Fifteen

Sources of Finance

The two basic sources of long term finance are owners capital and long term loans. They enable a business to obtain tangible fixed assets such as land, buildings and equipment. Long term funds are needed to finance assets with fairly long lives.

There are ways however of having the use of buildings and other fixed assets without ownership, of which leasing is a good example. This tends to reduce the amount of long term funds needed.

Short term funds are needed to finance the investment in working capital that supports day to day operations. Levels of stocks and other items of working capital tend to vary with turnover and this means that cash requirements fluctuate.

Bank finance is suitable for financing these short term requirements.

Bank finance

Overdrafts

The bank overdraft is the cheapest and most flexible form of short-term business finance. An overdraft facility is agreed which states the maximum amount the business can overdraw on its current account. The period of the arrangement varies but the maximum term is usually 12 months when the facility is reviewed. It should be used to provide for fluctuating calls on working capital, not for the purchase of a fixed asset with a long life. Unless well established, a business may need to provide some form of security such as title deeds to property.

Banks charge between 2% and 5% above the base rate on over-drawn business accounts. The borrower may find the cost rising in times of Government restriction.

Loans

A loan account with the bank is an alternative facility to an overdraft. Loans with repayment up to five years are generally considered as short term. They are useful for purchasing assets with a short life, and as such are in competition with other sources of finance such as leases and hire purchase.

Medium term loans are generally of 5 to 10 years duration although short and medium term loans have much in common in relation to loan packages offered.

Long term loans are over 10 years duration and schemes for borrowing are available to suit individual circumstances.

Partnerships

Entering into a partnership agreement is a further way of obtaining more funds whereby an agreed sum will be contributed to the business as initial capital. A partnership is in a position to borrow from investment institutions on mortgage and in other ways although it is often difficult to raise substantial amounts of capital without offering a share of the business. A partner investing without taking part in management may limit his liability to the extent of his subscription and this constitutes a limited partnership. The cost of raising funds is relatively low, for others may be persuaded to join the partnership at a nominal charge.

The disadvantages to the sole trader of taking a partner in a business are:

(a) control of the management of the business is lost;
(b) profits must be shared;
(c) there is the risk that a partner may involve the firm in exceptional unbearable liabilities;
(d) private assets are put at stake;
(e) disposition of the share in the business is restricted.

As a partnership business grows and more cash is required consideration would be given to increasing the number of partners and possibly the formation of a limited company.

Companies

Private and public companies are owned by shareholders whose liability for the company's debts is limited to the amount, if any, unpaid on the shares taken up by them.

Private companies

A private company has at least two members. It is prohibited by law from offering its shares to the public. Most companies start as private companies because the risk of failure would deter the public from buying shares.

Public companies

A public company differs from a private company in the following ways: minimum issued share capital of £50,000 of which one quarter needs to be paid up; public limited company or p.l.c. is shown after its name; there is freedom to offer shares to the public. Advantages of 'going public' – making shares available to the public – include gaining capital at low cost as the majority of costs are one-off, and enhancement of the company profile.

Possible disadvantages include vulnerability to take-over bids, increased press scrutiny and the need to pay dividends regularly to maintain share price.

The largest of the markets for company shares is the Stock Exchange which is highly regulated; a 'full listing' is very onerous. The 'Unlisted Securities Market' (USM) provides a formal regulated market in the shares of smaller, young companies unable to apply for a full listing.

Ordinary shares (called equity capital)

Holders of ordinary shares accept the main risk involved in investing in a limited company but on the other hand stand to gain most when the company makes a high profit. To all intents and purposes ordinary shares are irredeemable and are treated as a permanent investment in the firm. Under conditions of inflation ordinary shareholders tend to keep in step with inflation and more particularly where hotel and restaurant premises are owned because of the significant rise in land and property values.

After all expenses, preference share dividend and taxation payments have been met, any surplus revenue benefits ordinary shareholders in the form of dividend distribution and share value appreciation following the ploughing back into the business of any residual surplus.

At the annual general meeting the board of directors declare a dividend per share after a consideration of the financial position. In many cases an interim dividend will have been paid in the middle of the financial year, a payment 'on account'.

The ordinary shareholders are entitled to share pro rata in the assets distributed after a forced or voluntary liquidation.

Preference shares

Although part of the company's share capital, these shares generally attract limited voting rights or no voting rights at all, and since dividends are at a fixed rate, preference shares have much in common with debentures.

These shares, however, are a relatively expensive source of capital compared with debentures because dividends are paid from after-tax earnings, whereas debenture interest is an expense which reduces taxable profit. With corporation tax at 35% it costs the company the same to pay interest on 10% debentures as it does to pay dividend on 6½% preference shares.

Rights issue

A company making a definite offer to its own shareholders to take up new shares is said to make a rights issue. The price is usually below market price as an attraction. Although an apparently attractive price may be asked of shareholders, they may benefit more from an alternative source of capital such as a debenture issue. Holders of shares to whom the offer is made may take up their rights or may sell them.

Bonus issue

Where a company's reserves are considerable and the market price of ordinary shares far above the nominal value, a bonus issue of new shares may be made to shareholders without a charge to them. The issue is in proportion to existing shares held such as an issue of one new share for every one held.

The total market share value, and similarly each shareholder's value of his holdings, will initially remain unchanged although the market price per share will tend to drop proportionately.

A lower declared dividend percentage will provide the shareholder with the same total dividend as before, which may be an advantage from a public relations viewpoint.

A script issue is another term for a bonus issue.

Retained profit

Profit not distributed to shareholders is one source of finance and goes by the name of retained profit, or ploughed back profits. When large profits are made, some need to be retained to offset the effects of inflation. Cash will be saved by not distributing all the profit that has been generated in a period, but it will not automatically be available for investment as it is likely to be represented by a range of existing assets.

Debentures

There are two main types of debenture, the mortgage debenture secured by the mortgage of particular property owned by the company, and the debenture with a floating charge. If the company goes into liquidation, mortgage debentures rank ahead of floating debentures up to the value of the secured property and floating debentures rank ahead of any unsecured creditors. All creditors rank ahead of any shareholder.

Most debenture issues are redeemable, that is repayable at or by a specified date, which may be effected:

(a) by annual drawings out of profit;
(b) by the company purchasing its own debentures in the open market when the price is favourable;
(c) in a lump sum at maturity provided by means of a sinking fund.

Debentures may be issued to named persons or made payable to bearer when they may be quoted on the Stock Exchange.

Convertible debentures

Loan stock holders who have the right to convert their stock to ordinary shares at a future date or series of dates hold convertible debentures, the final decision to convert resting with the debenture holder.

An advantage to the company compared with a redeemable debenture is that the debt is self-liquidating in that debentures are exchanged for ordinary shares and no funds are needed with which to redeem them.

Compared with an immediate ordinary share issue the convertible is cheaper in annual outgoings, which is helpful when required for a hotel development likely to take some time to build up to a profit earning stage.

Mortgage loans

A mortgage loan is one taken out against land or property and is similar in some ways to a secured debenture. However, differences between them include:

> (a) The interest rate of a mortgage cannot normally be fixed over the life of the agreement as is the interest on a debenture.
> (b) Regular payments of interest and principal are made to liquidate the loan which may be up to 30 years.
> (c) The mortgage holder has the first call on a company's assets in the event of a default in payment.

International loans

Borrowing by British hotel groups extends to the international money market, in particular the Eurodollar market which is the freest sector of this market. The market is so called because most of the banks accepting foreign currency deposits are in Europe, and such deposits are largely in US dollars although they may be for instance pound sterling, the Swiss franc and the German mark.

Venture capital

Venture capital is loan or share capital provided by institutions that share the risks as well as the rewards of investing in a business. Such institutions include clearing and merchant banks, pension funds, private and public investors.

Investment may be introduced at any stage of a company's life, even to financing management buy-outs.

Management buy-outs

A management buy-out is a transaction in which executive managers of a company, jointly with a financial institution, buy the company. It may take place when the future of the business is in doubt through for instance financial losses, possible take-over, or low share price. Knowing the business well, the managers can preserve their own jobs by improving business profitability.

Business Expansion Scheme (BES)

BES is a Government scheme to promote private investment in business by providing tax relief on the purchase of new ordinary shares from an unquoted company. Investment may be direct from the public or through a managed fund. In both instances the shares are held by the investor. The scheme offers entrepreneurs the chance of receiving relatively small amounts of equity which are otherwise difficult to obtain.

Franchises

A franchise is the granting of a licence by the franchisor entitling the franchisee to use its established trade name, such as Holiday Inn Worldwide, Sheraton Hotel Corporation, and Burger King, and to sell its products or services.

The franchisee's investment cost covers premises, equipment and stocks. There is also an initial fee and a fee based on turnover for management services and marketing/advertising.

The franchisor is thus able to expand whilst the franchisee benefits from a lower risk of failure than when setting up his own business.

Asset use without ownership

Financial arrangements of obtaining the use of capital facilities without ownership, open to the small and large firm alike, include leasing, hire purchase, rental and sale and lease back.

There is increasing awareness that two distinct decisions need to be made when obtaining long-term assets, one is to decide whether a particular asset is in fact required – an investment decision – and the other is the most appropriate means of financing the asset – a financial decision.

Leasing

This has been common for many years, for example internal telephones, and leasing companies provide virtually every industry with a convenient package deal if required. One lease can embrace complete furnishing of an hotel. The fundamental difference between leasing and other forms of finance is that title in the goods remains permanently vested in the 'lessor'. A lease comprises a primary period and a secondary period. During the primary period a rental commensurate with the cost of the equipment is paid by the lessee; the secondary period rentals are nominal. The total length of the lease is negotiated with the lessee but bears a relationship to the anticipated useful working life of the equipment; the normal primary periods are 3, 4 or 5 years' duration with 2, 6 or 5 year secondary periods respectively. The primary period rentals may be paid monthly, quarterly, half yearly or annually in advance.

Leasing offers a number of advantages to the lessee including:

(a) it is the use of equipment, not its ownership, which is vital for profitability;
(b) use of equipment is gained on payment of first rental;
(c) working capital is left free for more profitable employment;
(d) rentals are fully tax-deductible;

(e) budgeting is facilitated;
(f) managers are more easily able to face up to obsolescence of existing plant and equipment because of ease of renewal.

The main reason for buying rather than leasing assets is perhaps that the cost is often higher to lease, although this depends upon the interest cost of raising money to make the purchase, or if money is available, the earnings which would be sacrificed in making the purchase.

Contract hire

Contract hire is a form of leasing which is generally for shorter periods of time. Used for acquiring vehicles and special equipment. Shares some benefits of leasing.

Hire purchase

Hire purchase may be the only means of acquiring certain assets. The purchaser makes a down payment or deposit and enters into a contract to hire goods for a specific time, say two years, making regular periodic payments for the hire, and at once acquires possession but not ownership of the goods. At the end of the hire period the hirer may purchase the goods outright for a small cash consideration, or the ownership may pass on the last payment. Although the most expensive of all credit facilities hire purchase is particularly useful since no security is needed though the hirer may be required to provide private legal and financial information and offer a guarantee.

Sale and lease back

Sale and lease back of property is a popular source of finance for hotel companies. Companies owning freehold properties or long leaseholds and having good profit records may benefit from selling such properties or leases to a finance or life assurance company for full market value and then lease back for a long term, frequently 99–120 years, at a rental directly related to the sale price, including cost of purchase, and in the range of 8½–10%. Provision would be made during the course of the lease for upward rental review at intervals now normally of not more than 7 years. During the term of the lease the vendor would normally be responsible for maintaining and insuring the building.

Advantage to the vendor depends upon the use made of the money no longer tied up in the property. Inflation may add considerably to the rental and at the end of the long lease the vendor has no building as an asset. Many companies who have sold and leased back properties believe that with efficient management, monies released will earn a return which, having covered the rental, will provide a satisfactory dividend, allow for inflation, and still leave cash available for ploughing back. In short, many efficient managements consider this method of financing a profitable proposition.

A disadvantage might well be the effect on other sources of finance, for instance where property is secured. Too high a proportion of leased properties might inhibit the issue of debentures for lack of security.

Hotels are particularly suitable candidates for sale and lease back transactions because the appreciation in value of the land encourages property and other finance companies to obtain regular revenue and a hedge against inflation, while hotel managements are able to use the funds so freed to take advantage of expansion opportunities.

Takeovers and mergers

Expansion is designed to increase earnings per share of a business and buying hotels is a favourite means of achieving this growth. The blending of two or more existing undertakings into one goes under many names, the popular ones being takeovers and mergers. There is little difference between the two. The city code on takeovers and mergers aimed at protecting shareholders' interests never mentions one without the other.

Generally speaking, however, when the boards of directors of two companies agree to amalgamate in the interest of both, a merger is the right term. On the other hand, a company wanting to gain control of another business whose board does not recommend the change, is said to be attempting to take over that company.

Differences in corporate structure result from takeovers and mergers.

A takeover bid refers to an offer which may be made either to the whole of a company's shareholders or those owning ordinary shares, to purchase their existing stock holding. The price will be sufficiently over the current Stock Exchange quotation to induce them to sell out in return for quoted shares in the bidding company, debentures, cash, or some combination of these. If the bid succeeds then the corporate identity of the business taken over may disappear.

A merger between two or more companies often results in a new company being created, and a reorganization of the capital structure takes place, for example Trust Houses and Forte in 1970 merged to become Trust Houses Forte group, later Trusthouse Forte PLC, and now Forte PLC.

Gearing (leverage in USA)

The ideal capital structure for a company is difficult to determine since it is largely a matter of opinion. The capital structure is measured by relating the medium- and long-term fixed interest capital to total capital employed. The company is said to be high geared if a large proportion of its capital is in fixed interest securities such as preference shares and debentures. Company gearing may be measured in a number of ways, a common method is

$$\frac{\text{Fixed interest capital}}{\text{Total long term capital}} \times 100$$

There is no ideal standard percentage, much depending upon the type of industry and whether fixed assets are owned or leased. What is important, however, is the effect on ordinary shareholders' earnings of increasing the gearing as shown in Exhibit 15–1 of two companies with opposite gearings:

Exhibit 15–1

	Low Geared Ltd at 31/12/90	High Geared Ltd at 31/12/90
	£	£
Ordinary shares of £1	1,300,000	750,000
Loan 10%	200,000	750,000
	1,500,000	1,500,000
Year ended	31/12/90	31/12/90
	£	£
15% return before interest	225,000	225,000
Less: 10% loan interest	20,000	75,000
Equity earnings before tax	205,000	150,000
Less: Corporation tax (35%)	71,750	52,500
	133,250	97,500
Earnings per share	£0.1025	£0.130
Gearing	13.3%	50%
	(Low geared)	(High geared)

A high-geared company has extreme effects on ordinary shareholders' earnings. If High Geared Ltd was successful in 1991 but failed in 1992 to the extent shown in Exhibit 15–2, the fortune of ordinary shareholders can be traced.

Exhibit 15–2

	High Geared Ltd 31/12/91	High Geared Ltd 31/12/92
Return on capital employed before interest	25%	5%
	£	£
Profit before interest	375,000	75,000
Less: 10% Debenture interest	75,000	75,000
	30,000	Nil
Less: Corporation tax (35%)	105,000	
	195,000	

Earnings per share $\dfrac{£195,000}{750,000}$ = £0.260   Nil

It may be seen that with return before interest on capital employed going up from £225,000 in 1990 to £375,000 in 1991, an increase of 67%, equity earnings have risen by 100% from £0.130 to £0.260 per share because of high gearing. However, when low profits are earned as in 1992 the ordinary shareholders are worse off in a high-geared company than a low-geared one. High Geared shareholders are left with no return when profit before interest drops to £75,000, whereas Low Geared shareholders would have received £75,000

Less: 10% interest   £20,000

£55,000

Less: 35% Cpn. tax   £19,250

£35,750

If a company is confident of its future prospects it should seek to maximize its gearing subject to limitations to ensure that it does not become over-geared. One guide is that the interest charge should be covered four times by earnings.

An alternative gearing measurement:

$$\frac{\text{Fixed interest capital}}{\text{Equity}} \times 100$$

would show Low Geared Ltd 15.4%
High Geared Ltd 100%

(See page 221 for gearing ratios.)

Questions and problems

15-1 Explain what is meant by the term 'gearing' and why certain companies in particular fields tend to be more highly geared than industry as a whole.

15-2 What advantage, if any, accrues to ordinary shareholders when a company issues debentures.

15-3 Why, under the present taxation system, are preference share issues out of favour, but debenture issues popular with company boards of directors? Illustrate with assumed figures.

15-4 A large hotel and catering company is considering raising additional capital for expansion. List the various forms of capital which are available, and give a brief description of each.

(HCIMA)

15-5 A successful and expanding but relatively small private company, which owns two hotels and has a profit before tax of £45,000, finds its rate of growth restricted by lack of capital.

You are required to set out the advice which you would give as to how and where the company may obtain both additional working and fixed capital.

Assume such further facts concerning the company as are necessary for your answer.

(HCIMA)

15-6 Explain some of the reasons for companies in the hotel and catering industry amalgamating.

15-7 Compare mergers with takeovers by discussing their similarities and differences.

15-8 Calculate goodwill on purchase of Company A, given the following information:

Company A
Forecast profit – Year 1 £15,000
2 £20,000
3 £25,000

Net assets valued at £100,000
Average return for the industry 15%
You are to use two methods known to you.

15–9 The Golden Restaurant is up for sale. The capital employed amounts to £100,000 and recent profits are:

1982:	£15,000	1985:	£20,000
1983:	£16,000	1986:	£18,500
1984:	£17,500		

The profits quoted do not include a figure for proprietor's salary which is reckoned to be about £7,500 p.a.

A close look at the accounts reveals that the 1985 figure included £1,500 exceptional income but the 1986 profit was determined after £4,000 had been written off, whereas £5,000 would have been a more reasonable figure.

The proprietor indicates that he wants the goodwill to be valued on the basis of 3 years' purchase of the average net profits for the past five years as shown in his accounts.

Assuming a reasonable return for this type of business is 10%, you should put forward your views as to which method ought to be the basis for negotiations.

Further reading

1. Clarkson, G. P., and Elliot, B. J., *Managing Money and Finance*, Gower (1986); Chapters 9 to 13.
2. Higson, C. J., *Business Finance*, Butterworths (1986).

Chapter Sixteen
Source and Application of Funds

The statement of source and application of funds or 'funds statement' is now established as an end of year statement alongside the balance sheet and profit and loss account. It provides a link between the balance sheet at the beginning of the year, the profit and loss account for the year and the balance sheet at the end of the year.

Control of profit performance and liquidity are two of the most important financial aspects of a successful business. Accounting emphasis has always been on profit and the many ways it may be defined and used for various purposes. Indeed the operating statement we have seen helps keep management aware of the profit performance of sections of the business whilst the profit and loss appropriation account shows, *inter alia*, how profit has been used. The growing importance placed upon the reporting of liquidity and changes in liquidity has led to the funds statement which is designed to show how movements in assets, liabilities and capital in a period have changed the company's net liquid fund position. Net liquid funds are defined as cash at bank and in hand and cash equivalents, e.g. investments held as current assets, less bank overdrafts and other borrowings repayable within one year of the accounting date.

Enterprises with turnover or gross income of £25,000 and over are recommended to include a funds statement as part of their audited accounts for periods beginning on or after 1st January 1976.*

Explanation of funds

A funds statement is prepared from balance sheets at the beginning and end of a period taking account also of further information available in the profit and loss account and elsewhere. First it must be understood what items are regarded as sources of funds and applications of funds, secondly a format for presentation is necessary

* Statement of Standard Accounting Practice (SSAP) No. 10.

into which each item may be slotted, and thirdly the object of the statement should always be borne in mind, that is to show how net liquid funds (cash and equivalents) have been generated and absorbed by the operations of the business in the period.

To help in the initial understanding, an example follows consisting of:

(a) basic data – being a summary of a first year's operations (Exhibit 16–1);
(b) notes on the data;
(c) the resulting funds statement (Exhibit 16–2).

This approach has been chosen because with no starting balance sheet, the end of period figures given reflect changes in the period, which makes for simplicity.

A further example is used (Exhibit 16–3) to show the more usual situation of preparing a funds statement from balance sheets at two points in time. Here further aspects are developed.

Exhibit 16–1

Summary of first year's operations

			Source of funds	Application of funds
Note references		£000	£000	£000
(a)	Cash from share issue		100	
(b)	Equipment bought for cash			60
(c)	Sales	600		
	Expenses (excluding depreciation)	560		
	Cash from operations	40 ———►	40	
	Depreciation	10		
	Profit from operations	30		
(d)	Debtors increase			20
(e)	Creditors increase		30	
(f)	Stocks increase			40
(g)	Tax provision	10		
(h)	Dividends paid			10
(i)	Cash balances (increase)			40
			170	170

Notes on first year's operations

(a) Cash from debentures is similarly a source. Any premium obtained is an additional source. Cash paid to redeem debentures will be an application.

265

(b) Cash from the sale of fixed assets will be a source. Profit or loss on sale is disregarded.

(c) Cash from operations is not strictly correct as a description because £20,000 is still outstanding as Debtors increase. However, it is called in the funds statement funds 'generated from operations'.

Depreciation does not provide cash for replacing fixed assets which lose value. It is not a cash transaction but merely an accounting entry apportioning a part of the historical cost to an accounting period.

(d) Debtors increase is an application because cash has been sacrificed. If debtors decreased, cash will have flowed in, the amount of the decrease being a source of funds.

(e) Creditors represent a short-term source of funds.

(f) Stocks increase means that money has been diverted to build up stocks, an application of funds. When stocks are unnecessarily high, their reduction provides cash by avoiding having to purchase so much for operations.

(g) Provisions and reserves do not involve movement of cash and are, therefore, neither source nor application of funds. Tax paid in a period, however, is an application of funds.

(h) In the same way as the treatment of tax, dividends are taken into the statement when they are paid.

(i) An increase in the cash balance, like any other asset increase, is an application of funds. A bank overdraft is clearly recognized as a source of funds.

Exhibit 16–2

Statement of Source and Application of Funds* Year 1986

	£000	£000
Source of funds		
Profit before tax		30
Adjustments for items not involving movement of funds:		
Depreciation		10
Total generated from operations		40
Funds from other sources		
Issue of shares for cash		100
		140
Application of funds		
Dividends paid	(10)	
Purchase of fixed assets	(60)	(70)
		70

Increase/decrease in working capital

Increase in stocks	(40)	
Increase in debtors	(20)	
Increase in creditors – excluding taxation and proposed dividends	30	
Movement in net liquid funds:		
Cash balances	(40)	(70)

* Symbols: () = application of funds; other figures are sources.

Funds statement preparation

There are two methods of preparing a funds statement from two balance sheets and additional internal information, a short-cut method and a longer systematic method. The first method will be demonstrated and the second shown in outline. Information available are the balance sheets and three notes as follows:

Balance Sheets at 31st March

	1987 £000	1986 £000
Assets		
Fixed assets at cost	240	220
Depreciation	14	12
	226	208
Current assets:		
Stocks	55	40
Debtors	35	20
Bank and cash balances	10	30
	326	298
Liabilities		
Issued share capital	150	150
Revenue reserves	40	30
Retained profits	16	18
Loan capital	60	40
Current liabilities:		
Creditors	36	38
Current taxation	8	7
Proposed dividends	16	15
	326	298

Notes:
(a) Equipment was purchased for £60,000.
(b) Equipment was sold for £41,000. Depreciation of £5,000 was included in £12,000 charged to 1986. Original cost was £40,000.
(c) £10,000 was transferred to revenue reserves in 1987.

Short-cut method (Exhibit 16–3)

1. Draft the main headings of a funds statement leaving plenty of space under each heading.
2. Any balance sheet differences which need no adjustment are inserted in the statement. This will take account of loan capital, creditors, taxation paid, dividends paid, stocks, debtors, bank and cash balances. Tax and dividends are the 1986 current liabilities assumed to have been paid in 1987.
3. Use the above notes to determine further items such as equipment purchases and sales.
4. Completion of the statement requires the calculation of depreciation for the year if this is not supplied. To insert totals simple deduction is used. Increase in working capital of £12,000 added to other application of funds totalling £82,000 gives £94,000 which is the total source. Total generated from operations is the sum of funds from other sources taken away from total sources giving £33,000. Depreciation deducted from this figure gives profit before tax.

Exhibit 16–3

Statement of Source and Application of Funds Year 1987

	£000	£000
Source of funds		
Profit before tax		26
Depreciation		7
		—
Total generated from operations		33
Funds from other sources		
Loan capital		20
Sale of equipment		41
		—
		94
Application of funds		
Tax paid	(7)	
Dividend paid	(15)	
Purchase of equipment	(60)	(82)
	—	—
		12

Increase/decrease in working capital

Increase in stocks		(15)
Increase in debtors		(15)
Decrease in creditors		(2)
Movement in net liquid funds:		
Bank and cash balances	20	(12)

5. The advantage of speed in preparation must be weighed against the chance of errors creeping in which would make the balancing figure of profit inaccurate. If, however, the profit and loss account is to hand then this creates no problem for the profit before tax figure – the important first item in the statement – is available. The reconstructed account for this example is as follows:

Appropriation Section of the Profit and Loss Account for the year to 31st March 1987

	£		£
Tax provision	8,000	Unappropriated profit from	
Proposed dividend	16,000	1986	18,000
Transfer to Reserve	10,000	Profit on equipment sale*	6,000
Balance c/d	16,000	Balancing item = Profit	
		before tax (1987)	26,000
	£50,000		£50,000

* Normally profit or loss on sale of assets will feature in the main body of the profit and loss account.

Systematic method (Exhibit 16–4)

This method ensures a balanced statement by starting with columns for balance sheet differences and applying adjustments which are self-balancing. The adjustments are to take account of sale of fixed assets and of profit and loss account items so that one is left with profit before tax and depreciation.

Notes:

(a) Cash from equipment sale.
(b) Original cost of sale item.
(c) Depreciation of sale item.
(d) Profit on sale added back.
(e) Tax dividends (current liabilities) added back.
(f) Resulting figure is cost of purchase.

Exhibit 16-4

Balance sheet items	Balance sheet differences		Adjustments		Final figures for statement	
	Source £000	Application £000	Source £000	Application £000	Source £000	Application £000
Assets						
Fixed assets at cost		20		+ 40(b)		60(f)
Depreciation	2		+ 5(c)		7	
Stocks		15				15
Debtors		15				15
Cash	20				20	
Liabilities						
Shares						
Revenue reserves	10		+ 16(e)	+ 6(d)	26	
Retained profit		2	+ 8(e)			
Loan capital	20				20	
Creditors		2				2
Current tax	1			+ 8(e)		7
Proposed dividends	1			+ 16(e)		15
	54	54				
Fixed asset sale			+ 41(a)		41	
			+ 70	+ 70	114	114

Review

Only one form of presentation has been used in this chapter to avoid confusion. However, a wide variety of forms are encountered in practice ranging from one which simply lists and totals the sources and applications, to one which may start with the opening net liquid funds and end with the equivalent closing balance. The tendency is to highlight favourable aspects, and the latter form might be used where the improvement in net liquid funds may be negligible whilst the opening and closing balances might each by significantly large. The minimum amount of 'netting off' of, say, purchase and sale of fixed assets is recommended although some 'netting off' may be inevitable through the lack of information. In published accounts the funds statement should show figures for both the period under review and for the previous period.

Relationships between individual sources and applications can sometimes be recognized such as a long-term loan raised in the period providing funds to expand shown as the purchase of fixed assets and increases in stocks and debtors.

Finally a statement of source and application of funds, or funds statement for short, is important as a budget taking its place beside the budgeted balance sheet as an indication of the financial policy of the enterprise.

Questions and problems

16–1 Describe the meaning of the terms 'cash flow' and 'profit' and explain their differences.

16–2 Indicate by a tick whether each of the following financial changes effects a cash inflow, outflow or no change:

Financial change	Cash inflow	Cash outflow	No effect on cash
Share capital issue			
Decrease in creditors			
Sale of investments			
Annual depreciation charge			
Loan repayment			
Decrease in debtors			
Increase in general reserve			
Increase in stock			
Goodwill written off			
Decrease in cash			
Purchase of fixed assets			

16–3 It is sometimes desirable to ascertain from the balance sheet how changes in the liquid resources of a limited company have arisen.

List the factors which may have caused:

(a) a decrease in the liquid position;
(b) an increase in the liquid position.

16–4 Is it possible for a company to achieve a net profit in a period and yet show a net cash outflow?

16–5 The annual accounts of the Aldo Hotel Co. Ltd are as follows:

Balance Sheet as at 31st May 1993

1992 £000		£000	1992 £000		£000
80	Authorized and issued capital	80	170	Fixed assets – at cost	180
5	Reserves	10	10	Additions in year at cost	40
10	Unappropriated profits	8	180		220
—	Loan	12	99	Less depreciation	105
			81		115
			9	Cash	2
15	Current liabilities	30	20	Other current assets	23
110		140	110		140

Profit and Loss Account (including appropriations) for the year ended 31st May 1993

8	Directors' remuneration	10	14	Profit b/d	20
4	Depreciation	6	8	Unappropriated profits b/f	10
—	Loan interest	1			
—	Transfer to reserves	5			
10	Unappropriated profits c/f	8			
22		30	22		30

You are required to:
(a) Prepare a source and application of funds statement reconciling the cash at bank at 1st June 1992 with the cash at bank at 31st May 1993;
(b) Compare and contrast the information which can be established from the annual accounts above with that in your source and application of funds statement for the Aldo Hotel Co. Ltd.

(HCIMA)

16–6 The following is the balance sheet of a company at 31 December 1992.

31st Dec. 1991		1992
£		£
100,000	Paid up capital	100,000
25,000	General reserve	25,000
3,000	Proposed dividend for year	4,000
	Profit and loss account balance	
4,500	carried forward	10,500
3,000	Sundry creditors	2,100
135,500		141,600

£			£
30,000	Buildings at cost		30,000
60,000	Plant at cost	£80,000	
24,000	Less depreciation	£30,000	
36,000			50,000
38,300	Stock		42,600
10,100	Sundry debtors		12,400
21,000	Cash		6,600
135,500			141,600

Prepare a cash flow statement to explain the change in the cash balance since the end of the previous year.

16–7 The balance sheet of the Silver Lining Hotel Ltd for the year ended 30th April 1985.

Silver Lining Hotel Ltd
Balance Sheet as at 30th April 1985

£ 1984	£	£		£ 1985	£
			Fixed assets		
500,000			Freehold hotel at valuation		500,000
	80,000		Equipment at cost	100,000	
	45,000		*Less*: Depreciation	40,000	
35,000					60,000
535,000					560,000
			Less: Working capital deficit:		
			Current assets:		
	90,000		Stocks	130,000	
	35,000		Debtors	50,000	
	8,000		Bank	—	
	133,000			180,000	
			Less: Current liabilities:		
		79,000	Creditors	110,000	
		71,000	Corporation tax	60,000	
		—	Overdraft	50,000	
	150,000			220,000	
17,000					40,000
518,000			Net assets		520,000
			Represented by:		
			Shareholders' interest:		
400,000			Issued share capital		400,000
60,000			Reserves		60,000
58,000			Unappropriated profit		60,000
518,000					520,000

Movements on the equipment account during the year were:

	1984	Sold	Purchases	Depn. charge	1985
Cost	80,000	30,000	50,000	—	100,000
Depn.	45,000	20,000	—	15,000	40,000
	35,000	10,000			60,000

Sale proceeds	4,000
Loss charged to profit	6,000

You are required to prepare:
  (a) a source and application of funds statement reconciling the opening cash at bank with the closing overdraft; and
  (b) a critical report on your source and application statement and the balance sheet.

(HCIMA)

16–8 The summarized balance sheets of the Alpine Post House at 31st March 19X2 and 19X3 are below:

	19X2 £	19X3 £
Issued share capital	200,000	230,000
Share premium	20,000	22,000
Capital reserves	35,000	35,000
Retained profits	17,000	28,000
7½% convertible loan stock	50,000	30,000
8½% mortgage debentures	40,000	64,000
Trade creditors	8,000	11,000
Overdraft	34,000	—
Corporation tax	3,000	4,000
Proposed dividends	11,000	15,000
	418,000	439,000

	£	£
Freehold land and building at cost	216,000	216,000
Equipment, furniture and fittings (net)	134,000	140,000
Investment at cost	60,000	29,000
Food and beverage stocks	4,000	10,000
Trade debtors	2,000	6,000
Cash at bank and in hand	2,000	38,000
	418,000	439,000

Additional information:

(a) Of the £30,000 increase in issued share capital, £20,000 had been in respect of the 7½% convertible loan stock.
(b) Corporation tax figures shown are payable early the following year.
(c) During the year furniture which had cost £12,000 had been sold for £900. Seven-eighths of its useful life had been written off. New equipment had been purchased for £22,000.

The net closing balances on equipment, furniture and fittings are made up as follows:

	19X2 £	19X3 £
Balances at cost	180,000	190,000
Accumulated depreciation	46,000	50,000
	134,000	140,000

(d) During the year investments which had cost £31,000 had been sold for £35,000.

You are required to prepare a statement accounting for the cash increase that has occurred during the financial year ended 31st March 19X3.

(HCIMA)

16–9 The summarized balance sheet of Seaton Private Hotel Ltd as at 31st May 1986 is as follows:

	£
Capital employed:	
Share capital	20,000
Profit and loss account	20,000
Shareholders funds	40,000
Long-term loan	40,000
	80,000

	£
Employment of capital:	
Fixed assets at cost	100,000
Less: Aggregate depreciation	40,000
	60,000

Current assets:			
Debtors	20,000		
Stock	15,000		
Cash	5,000	40,000	
Less: Current liabilities:			
Bank overdraft	10,000		
Creditors	10,000	20,000	20,000
			80,000

The company is experiencing trading difficulties and has drawn up a budgeted profit and loss account for the 12 months to 31st May 1987:

Summarized budgeted profit and loss account for the year ending 31st May 1987

	£
Contribution from food and beverage operations	19,000
Contribution from sale of accommodation	22,000
Profit on sale of antique furniture	500
	41,500

	£	
Less: Wages and salaries	17,900	
Establishment expenses	22,600	
Advertising expenses	800	
Depreciation	5,000	
Loan interest	3,200	
Amortization of lease	1,200	
Taxation provision	800	51,500
Net loss after taxation and interest		10,000

Further information:

In the year to 31st May 1987:

(a) No dividends will be paid.
(b) The antique furniture will be sold for £8,000. (Aggregate depreciation of £2,500 had been provided to 31st May 1986.)
(c) The directors have undertakings from a group of

investors that the proposed issue of £10,000 of loan stock will be fully subscribed at the end of August 1986.

(d) The issue of the loan stock is intended to finance new furniture and fittings costing £12,000, to be acquired in September 1986.

(e) It is expected that at 31st May 1987 debtors will have reduced to 75% of the previous year's level, stock value will have risen by a third and creditors will have increased by £3,500.

(f) The increase in the taxation provision is in respect of corporation tax which is payable on 1st July 1987.

You are required to prepare:

(i) A budgeted sources and applications of funds statement emphasizing the change in the cash balance assuming the bank overdraft remains at £10,000. The statement should commence with the expected loss after taxation and interest.

(ii) The budgeted balance sheet as at 31st May 1987.

(HCIMA)

Chapter Seventeen

Capital Investment Decisions

A business must earn profits over a period of years to be successful. Although there may be other goals, such as growth, profit dominates because survival depends on it.

Investment opportunities

A successful business must recognize opportunities which lead to profitable long-term investments. The larger the firm the more important it is to seek out and find opportunities by:

(a) forceful management with the persistence and personality to push forward proposals considered to be viable;
(b) appointment of staff to seek and find opportunities;
(c) contacts with other bodies such as trade associations which might stimulate the recognition of opportunities;
(d) Compiling statistics relating to changes in the activities of both customers and competitors;
(e) Comparing the changing market demand and facilities available to meet it, so that long term forecasts may be made.

Capital investment

Whether the opportunity involves building a new hotel, or acquiring an old one, capital investment is required involving a long term commitment.

In order to formalize data associated with a capital project, large companies produce a 'feasibility study' which involves the collection and assembly of forecast information. It becomes an 'economic feasibility study' when the project is financially appraised.

The study would include information on marketing forecasts, competition, physical facilities, Government regulations, and the project's financial appraisal.

The selection and financing of capital projects are indisputably two of the most important and critical decisions of management. Funds invested in fixed tangible assets are tied up for years, and once the decision to go ahead is made, there is no easy way of turning back.

Investment appraisal methods

An investment appraisal measures the worthwhileness of a proposal to spend money on a capital project. A project's financial prospects are measured against criteria laid down by management.

Four methods of appraising projects are generally available. The first one, the accounting rate of return, uses average annual project profit as a measure. Although useful as a starting point in considering financial measures, it will be seen to have limited value. Two important methods involve discounting cash flows, and the fourth, payback, requires the use of cash flows without discounting. None is exclusive; the two discounting methods and payback each contribute to the decision-making process of selecting projects. A simple example – Castle Project – illustrates all four methods.

Accounting rate of return

This was the first to be used historically and takes account only of the investment and average annual project profit.

A company is considering investing £1,620,000 in a four year project named Castle, which is forecast to produce a total profit of £380,000. The whole investment is for capital equipment which will be fully depreciated on a straight-line basis.

Castle Project

Year ended	Profit £
31/12/93	95,000
31/12/94	95,000
31/12/95	95,000
31/12/96	95,000
	380,000

Investment 1/1/93, £1,620,000

This method develops a percentage – average annual profit as a percentage of the investment. Average annual profit is £95,000 (£380,000/4) which is 5.86% of the investment (£1,620,000). This calculation is valid for investments such as land and buildings which retain their value over time. However, a depreciating investment such as equipment may have no value after four years; accordingly an average investment amount – that is half the investment – is used as the denominator in the calculation. Halving of the investment doubles the annual return to:

$$\frac{£95,000}{£810,000} \times 100 = 11.73\%$$

The method may be acceptable for assessing short lived, low value investments of no more than a year or two. But for the vast majority of proposed projects it has two important failings:

1. An average annual profit figure can disguise great variations in profit for individual years. Profit generated early in a project's life is more valuable than a similar amount later as it attracts more interest and is less risky.
2. Annual profit is in any case the wrong medium for assessing investment benefits. Annual cash flow should be the basis of assessment, for it is cash that generates interest. Profit rarely coincides with cash because of depreciation charges.

Discounted cash flow (DCF) technique

Discounted cash flow technique describes how future cash flows are discounted to present values by using present value factors. DCF is used in two methods of investment appraisal, net present value (NPV) and internal rate of return (IRR), also called discounted cash flow yield.

Cash flows

It is important that the time value of money – interest – is considered in any investment appraisal. This requires the forecast of cash flows in as much detail as necessary for the needs of decision makers. Cash flows used in an investment appraisal may consist of:

1. Fixed capital investments and disinvestments.
2. Working capital investment and disinvestment.
3. Annual operating cash flows.

Each of the above should represent incremental cash flows of the business; cash specific to the project. Investments both fixed and working capital are regarded as a cash outflow, taking place at point in time Year 0.

At the end of a project, any fixed capital may have a residual value which is regarded as an inflow. Working capital will then no longer be needed and shown as an inflow.

The first operating annual cash flow is one year later than the investment, Year 1 and consists of the first year's forecast profit PLUS any depreciation deducted in arriving at this profit.

Depreciation does not appear in a cash budget because it is not a cash item. Similarly it has to be ignored from cash flows. As depreciation is already deducted from sales revenue in the profit and loss account in arriving at profit, the position must be reversed by adding depreciation to profit. Forecast profit for the Castle Project is £95,000 per annum and depreciation is £1,620,000/4 = £405,000. The annual operating cash flows is therefore £500,000:

Castle Project

Year	Year ended	Profit £	+	Depreciation £	=	Cash Flow £
1	31/12/93	95,000		405,000		500,000
2	31/12/94	95,000		405,000		500,000
3	31/12/95	95,000		405,000		500,000
4	31/12/96	95,000		405,000		500,000
		380,000		1,620,000		2,000,000

Establishing true return on investment

The concept of return on investment is well illustrated by borrowing from a building society.

As cash is received by a firm it becomes available for either reducing amounts borrowed or for other profitable uses. If cash received from a specific project is used to reduce the loan that funded it, true profit arises only after the investment has been repaid (with appropriate interest). Suppose the £1,620,000 is borrowed for the Castle Project with interest at 9% chargeable at the end of each year. Also that at each year end, operating cash generated is used to help repay the loan. The calculations are as follows:

			£000
1/1/93	Loan		1,620
31/12/93	Interest payable on loan outstanding at 9%	+	146
			1,766
	Repayment	−	500
			1,266

31/12/94	Interest payable at 9%	+	114
			1,380
	Repayment	–	500
			880
31/12/95	Interest payable at 9%	+	79
			959
	Repayment	–	500
			459
31/12/96	Interest payable at 9%	+	41
			500
	Repayment completing repayment of loan	–	500

The following table shows that repayment consists of interest and capital repayment. This is the manner in which a building society operates.

Year	Cash flows	Interest @ 9%	Capital repayment	Capital outstanding
	£000	£000	£000	£000
0	1,620			1,620
1	500	146	354	1,266
2	500	114	386	880
3	500	79	421	459
4	500	41	459	—
		380	1,620	

These calculations indicate that repayments have swallowed up all cash proceeds from the project, leaving no profit. Profit of £380,000 only equals interest paid.

From the lender's point of view a return of 9% has been made on the loan (less its own borrowing and administration costs). Similarly it may be said that Castle Project has earned the business 9% less its own cost of borrowing which has not been included in annual operating cash flows.

The whole point of assuming the cash proceeds have been used to pay back the loan, with interest, is to establish the true percentage return on the investment, namely 9%. If the business had borrowed at 6%, having made 9% it would have generated a surplus of 3% making the project worthwhile. If however the cost of borrowing were 11% the project would not have been worthwhile.

Discounting to present value

To establish whether a project's return exceeds the percentage cost of funding it (i.e. whether the project is profitable) DCF procedure is to:

1. Eliminate interest from future cash flows. The sum of the resulting cash flows is called present value.
2. Compare present value of future cash flows with the investment.

Exhibit 17–1   Present value model

Future value of £1 invested Year 0
with compound interest @ 9%

	Year 1	OR	Year 2	OR	Year 3
£1 invested now $\times (1.09)$ = £1.0900					
(Year 0) $\times (1.09)^2$ =			£1.1881		
(with compound $\times (1.09)^3$ =					£1.2950
interest)					

Divided by compound
  interest factor
= £1 Present Value

$$\frac{£1.0900}{(1.09)}$$

$$\frac{£1.1881}{(1.09)^2}$$

$$\frac{£1.2950}{(1.09)^3}$$

A simpler way of finding present values is to multiply future values by present value factors* shown in tables, e.g. @ 9%	£1.0900 $\times$	£1.1881 $\times$	£1.2950 $\times$
Year 1	0.917		
Year 2		0.842	
Year 3			0.772
= Present Value (rounded)	£1	£1	£1

*Present value factors are the reciprocals of compound interest factors

$$\frac{1}{(1.09)} \qquad \frac{1}{(1.09)^2} \qquad \frac{1}{(1.09)^3}$$

Compound interest is a convenient way of explaining present value, for present value is in a way the opposite of compound interest.

Exhibit 17–1 demonstrates a simple way of eliminating compound interest from future cash flows by using present value factors to discount cash flow.

Present value tables are usually rounded to three decimal places. Using the table on page 350 for 9%, the PV of cash flows from Castle Project may be calculated:

Castle Project

Year	Cash flows	PV factor @ 9%	Discounted cash flows
	£000		£000
0	−1,620	1.000	−1,620
1	500	0.917	459
2	500	0.842	421
3	500	0.772	386
4	500	0.708	354
	+380		nil

The project returns 9% interest as explained earlier. This however is the standard type DCF calculation which confirms it.

Use of annuity tables

When there are constant annual cash flows as with Castle Project, use of the annuity table (p349) speeds up calculations. The table consists of cumulative present value factors starting at Year 1. With Castle project, multiplying £500 by each year's factor is replaced by multiplying the constant cash flow of £500 once only by the annuity factor for the appropriate number of years. The four year factor at 9% is 3.240, and 3.240 × £500 = £1,620. There may be small differences between the accumulated factors and the annuity table due to rounding to three decimal places.

Net present value (NPV)

This method is used when management wish to know whether a project will achieve a required rate of return they have set. The required rate will be at least the estimated cost of capital to ensure a profit can be expected. (See page 294 for workings.)

The future cash flows are discounted at the required rate and the resulting present value compared with the investment. If present

285

value exceeds the investment there is said to be a positive net present value and the project is financially acceptable. A negative net present value would lead to a rejection of the project.

Mill is a project to be appraised by the NPV method using a required rate of 11%. The calculation is shown in Exhibit 17–2.

Exhibit 17–2

Mill Project

Year	Cash flows	PV factor @ 11%	Present value
	£000		£000
0	−1,620	1.000	−1,620
1	—	0.901	—
2	500	0.812	406
3	500	0.731	365.5
4	1,000	0.659	659

Net present value −£189.5

This simply informs management that Mill Project falls short by £189,500 of the 11% looked for and would be rejected.

Internal rate of return (IRR) also called DCF yield method

This form of the DCF technique seeks to establish the actual rate expected to be returned on the investment by finding a percentage rate of discount that will result in a zero or near zero net present value.

The first guess at finding the internal rate might be based on the accounting rate of return (average investment method) which is 11.7%, or on the required rate. The net present value using 11% has been calculated already in finding the NPV at the required rate (Exhibit 17–2). This resulted in an NPV of negative £189,500. A negative NPV means that the rate is too high – too much interest has been taken from the cash inflows. A second, lower rate say 5% is then used to calculate a second NPV, preferably one that gives a positive NPV. It might be noted that 0% discount is the lowest possible rate, providing a positive NPV of positive £380,000 because no interest has been deducted. The wider apart the two discount rates the less accurate the resulting true rate, as the relationships are not linear. A 5% rate calculation shows a positive NPV of £88,500 (Exhibit 17–3).

The true rate is calculated by taking the lower rate and adding a proportion of the range of both rates, represented by NPVs, that would result in an NPV of £0. The calculation is shown in Exhibit 17–4. It amounts to $5\% + [(£88,500/£278,000) \times (11\% - 5\%)] = 6.9\%$.

286

Exhibit 17–3   Net present value calculations

Mill Project

Year	Cash flows	PV factor @ 11%	Present value	PV factor @ 5%	Present value
	£000		£000		£000
0	−1,620	1.000	−1,620	1.000	−1,620
1	—	0.901	—	0.952	—
2	500	0.812	406	0.907	453.5
3	500	0.731	365.5	0.864	432
4	1,000	0.659	659	0.823	823
Net present values			−£189.5		+£88.5

Exhibit 17–4

	Range of 6%		
Rate	5%	?	11%
NPV	+£88,500	£0	−£189,500
		Range of £278,000	

The difference in rates used is 6% (11% − 5%).
The difference in NPV is the addition of £189,500 and £88,500 = £278,000.
The rate to add to 5% so that NPV = £0 is:

$$\frac{£88,500}{£278,000} \times 6\% = 1.9\%$$

Therefore the DCF rate of return, the true rate is 6.9%.

Although 6.9% is said to be the true rate, it is still only a close approximation of it. The true rate to two decimal places is 6.75% which may be checked by calculating and using 6.75% present value factors. The internal rate may also be found by using a graph and of course in practice is the subject of computer packages.

One proposed project only

Any independent proposed project is regarded as financially acceptable if:

NPV method shows a positive NPV

and/or IRR shows a rate of return above the cost of capital.

Given that the NPV method discounts cash flows at or near the cost of capital – the required rate – both methods leads to the same accept/reject decision.

One project required from two or more proposals

Several projects may be proposed to meet an objective such as using land to further a hospitality business. In many cases use of NPV and IRR will lead to the same project being recommended, criteria being the one with the highest NPV and highest IRR.

Exclusive use of IRR would lead to the same conclusion as NPV by evaluating incremental investments. Starting with the project with the smallest investment and working upwards through each incremental level, the rate of return on the incremental investment is calculated. If the incremental investment returns more than the required rate then the higher investment is better than the lower alternative. This continues until the next incremental investment returns less than that required. This cumbersome procedure only confirms the result of using NPV in identifying the best project from a financial point of view.

Ranking of projects

When a number of projects can be undertaken, viable projects may be initially ranked using a profitability index (PI) which relates PV to £1 of investment. The PI for each project is found by dividing discounted inflows by the investment and then projects are ranked according to the value of each index number. For instance the profitability index for Mill Project at required rate of 11% is £1,430.5/1,620 = 0.88. Projects with an index number lower than 1 would not be considered viable as they would have negative NPVs. A project with a discounted inflow of £2,500 and investment of £1,890 would have a PI of 1.32 and would be preferred to a project with a PI of 1.25.

When capital is rationed such that some viable projects have to be rejected, adjustments may need to be made to the mix of projects in order to maximize their total NPV.

Non-financial project data

As in other business decisions, financially measured data cannot hope to account for all factors to be considered when evaluating a project. Financial evaluation is a vital ingredient to be supplemented with non-financial data before decisions are made.

Evaluating NPV and IRR methods

Many organizations use both methods because the necessary calculations are carried out easily by computer. The time consuming task is preparing the basic forecast cashflows.

If only one method were to be used, NPV is to be recommended for the following reasons:

1. Maximizing net present value is a realistic objective coinciding with maximizing of shareholders' wealth.
2. It is appropriate in all circumstances, unlike IRR.

IRR merits include:

1. The financial measurement of a project, a percentage return, may be said to be easier to understand than a negative or positive NPV.
2. There is no need to estimate the cost of capital as with NPV.

Payback method of appraisal (PB)

Payback period is defined as the number of years it takes for an investment to generate sufficient cash to recover its initial capital outlay in full. Its popularity is mainly due to its simplicity of application. Other reasons for its use are:

(a) a business with liquidity problems will be aided in the short term if projects with low PB periods are preferred;
(b) using a low PB period is said to reflect a dynamic management who want quick returns;
(c) it allows for a special type of risk which will bring the cash flow to a halt, such as foreign intervention or sudden competition.

Its chief draw-back is that it takes no account of the project's overall earnings or of the significance of cash flows within the PB period. It is not therefore a measure of profitability because one project might have a rating of two years and be unprofitable with no further net cash inflows whereas another project may have a three year PB period with high net cash inflows for another three years.

The payback period for Castle Project is calculated as follows:

Year	Cash flow £000	Cumulative £000
0	−1,620	−1,620
1	500	−1,120
2	500	− 620
3	500	− 120(a)
4	500(b)	+ 380

Payback $= 3$ years $+ a/b = 3 + 120/500 = 3.24$ years.

Cumulative cash flows show investment will be recovered after 3 years but before 4 years. Payback is therefore 3 years plus the unrecovered investment at year 3 as a proportion of year 4 cash flow.

The payback period of 3.24 years would still apply if further inflows were expected after Year 4.

Basic DCF considerations

1. Cash flow assumptions:
    (a) initial investment is reckoned to be at the beginning of the period and designated Year 0;
    (b) annual operating cash flows start one year after initial investment at year 1.
2. Working capital is an outflow of cash when it arises. After this only changes to working capital are relevant. It is shown as cash inflow at the end of a project when it is no longer required.
3. Cash flows relevant to an investment project are incremental cash flows. If fixed administration overhead is not expected to rise then it is not a project cash flow.
4. Taxation often has a marked effect on a project's cash flows so that after-tax cash flows should be used where possible.
5. Inflation is usually ignored so that forecast cash flows are in present day terms. Only if inflation is expected to affect income and costs differently should it be taken into account.
6. Benefits of DCF include a more consistent financial appraisal and the discipline required means greater care is taken.

DCF example (Exhibit 17–5)

Golden Hotels Ltd are considering purchasing a site and building an hotel. A feasibility study shows the following costs: site and building £1 million, furnishings and fittings £300,000, working capital £100,000, making a total initial investment of £1.4 million. Annual operating cash flows are forecast to be Year 1 £50,000, Years 2–4 £200,000 p.a., Years 5–10 £230,000 p.a. In Years 5 and 7, furnishings will cost £20,000 each year.

Ten years has been considered a reasonable life before drastic alterations will be required. Site and building will then be worth about £700,000. Working capital will still be worth £100,000. For this kind of investment the company has a required rate of 10%.

Further DCF considerations

Taxation

After-tax cash flows should be used in DCF calculations because tax payments constitute an outflow of cash, and competing projects may have different tax allowances and charges which might influence the investment decision.

Exhibit 17–5

Golden Hotels Ltd

Year	Cash flow	PV factors @ 10%	Present values @ 10%	PV factors @ 15%	Present values @ 15%
	£000		£000		£000
0	−1,400	1.000	−1,400.00	1.000	−1,400.00
1	50	0.909	45.45	0.870	43.54
2	200	0.826	165.20	0.756	151.20
3	200	0.751	150.20	0.658	131.60
4	200	0.683	136.60	0.572	114.40
5	210	0.621	130.41	0.497	104.37
6	230	0.564	129.72	0.432	99.36
7	210	0.513	107.73	0.376	78.96
8	230	0.467	107.41	0.327	75.21
9	230	0.424	97.52	0.284	65.32
10	230	0.386	88.78	0.247	56.81
10	800	0.386	308.80	0.247	197.60
			+67.82		−281.67

Evaluation: NPV @ 10% = + £67,820
*IRR = 11%
Payback = 7.4 years

*IRR = 10% + (67.82/349.49)5%

The following procedure is used for converting pre-tax cash flows to post-tax cash flows.

1. Determine the investment incentives available for the purchase, for example plant and machinery – which include office furniture and motor cars – attract a writing down allowance (WDA) of 25%, and the construction of new hotels, extensions and structural alterations to existing hotels (minimum ten letting bedrooms), qualify for an industrial building allowance (IBA) of 4% per annum. Note, however, that construction costs on new hotels will only attract IBAs if the hotel:
   (a) has at least ten letting bedrooms;
   (b) has letting bedrooms as the whole or main part of its sleeping accommodation;
   (c) offers ancillary services including at least breakfast, evening meal, cleaning of rooms, making of beds; and
   (d) is open for at least four months during the season April to October.
2. The allowances are deducted from the pre-tax cash flow (profit + depreciation) leaving a figure of taxable profit.

3. When the plant is disposed of, any residual revenue is shown as cash inflow, and the writing down allowance in the final year adjusted (called the balancing allowance or balancing charge) so that capital allowances in total equal net cost of the asset (original cost less residual revenue).
4. Corporation tax is chargeable on each year's taxable profit and on average reckoned to be paid 12 months later.
5. Post-tax cash flows which come in for discounting consist of pre-tax cash flows less tax paid.
6. It is usually assumed that there are profits being generated elsewhere in the company against which capital allowances may be offset. Therefore a cash inflow of tax may be recorded in respect of a project where insufficient profit is made on it to absorb tax allowances.
7. If no profits are available in the company to use up capital allowances they may be carried forward until such time as there are profits available against which to set the allowances.

Exhibit 17–6 is an example of the above procedure.

Exhibit 17–6

The AB Hotel Group are considering the purchase of four new vending machines which will cost £36,000 to buy outright. It is estimated that they will have lives of seven years at the end of which their scrap value will be £1,000. To operate them an average investment in working capital of £3,000 will be required.

After depreciation of £5,000 per annum, the forecast operating profits are:

	£			£
Year 1	3,000	Year 5		3,000
2	4,000	6		2,000
3	5,000	7		1,000
4	5,000			

The company required rate of return on this activity is 10% after tax and discounting. The machines will qualify for 25% WDA in respect of tax and the company pays corporation tax at the rate of 35%

One manager supports the purchase because it has been worked out that the accounting rate of return before tax is 15.3%, as follows:

$$\frac{\text{Average annual profit}}{\text{Average investment}} \quad \frac{£3,286}{£21,500} \times 100 = 15.3\%$$

where the average investment is calculated as:

(£36,000 + £1,000)/2 + £3,000 = £21,500.

However, the after-tax discounted rate is just over 9% (9.3%), worked out as follows:

Writing down allowance (WDA) computations

Year	Book value b/f	25% WDA	Book value c/f	
	£	£	£	
1	36,000	9,000	27,000	
2	27,000	6,750	20,250	
3	20,250	5,062	15,188	
4	15,188	3,797	11,391	
5	11,391	2,848	8,543	
6	8,543	2,136	6,407	
7	6,407	5,407	—	(6,407 − 1,000)

Tax calculation

Year	Profit + depreciation	WDA	Taxable profit	Corporation tax (35%)
	£	£	£	£
1	8,000	9,000	(1,000)	(350)
2	9,000	6,750	2,250	788
3	10,000	5,062	4,938	1,728
4	10,000	3,797	6,203	2,171
5	8,000	2,848	5,152	1,803
6	7,000	2,136	4,864	1,702
7	6,000	5,407	593	208
	58,000	35,000	23,000	8,050

DCF calculations
Operating cash flows ( ) = outflows

Year	Pre-tax cash flows	Tax payable	Post-tax cash flows	10% PV factors	DCF
	£	£	£		£
1	8,000	—	8,000	0.91	7,280
2	9,000	350	9,350	0.83	7,760
3	10,000	(788)	9,212	0.75	6,909
4	10,000	(1,728)	8,272	0.68	5,625
5	8,000	(2,171)	5,829	0.62	3,614
6	7,000	(1,803)	5,197	0.56	2,910
7	6,000	(1,702)	4,298	0.51	2,192
8		(208)	(208)	0.47	(98)
	58,000	8,050	49,950		36,192

Investment cash flows

Year				
0	Machines	(36,000)	1.00	(36,000)
	Working capital	(3,000)	1.00	(3,000)
7	Machines – scrap	1,000	0.51	510
	Working capital recouped	3,000	0.51	1,530
				36,960

Net present value @ 10%   (£768)

Net present value @ 9%   £347

9% + [347/(347 + 768)] (10% − 9%) = 9.3%

Cost of capital

One criticism of DCF is that although a percentage rate of return is at the heart of the technique, there is no universal method of calculating a minimum or a required rate for projects in different organizations. DCF tends to get singled out for this criticism but it applies to all percentage appraisal methods. Golden Hotels (Exhibit 17–5) mentions 10% as a required rate. This rate is subjective in that the company may set a different rate target for different investments based on various factors, for example risk involved, whether a replacement or an expansion project, and how desirable the project is. The required or minimum rate may be based on the cost of the firm's capital. One way is to determine the cost of each source of capital and weight each according to its proportion to total capital. For example 10% cost of capital would result from:

	Amount (1) £	Proportion (2) %	Source cost (3) %	Weighted cost (4) = (2 × 3) %
Ordinary shares – market value	150,000	75.00	11.0	8.25
10% Debentures (35% Tax)	50,000	25.00	6.5	1.63
	200,000	100.00		9.88

Rounded to 10%

The cost of debentures is straightforward, being the gross amount less the current corporation tax percentage because interest is allowable for tax purposes.

The cost of a capital derived from the issue of ordinary shares and likewise of equity is a difficult concept and one about which little agreement exists in practice. One method which appears to be useful is a variation of the price earnings ratio, namely the best estimate of what average future earnings per share would be if the proposed capital expenditure were not made, relative to the current market price of the shares.

The marginal cost of capital is another concept, but this is not generally recommended. If a debenture issue were made to fund a particular capital project, the cost of the issue and interest payable less tax could be regarded as the marginal cost. The danger is that a project returning only the marginal cost might lower overall company profitability.

It should be borne in mind that as some projects may be for non-profit-making purposes, the minimum rate for profitable new work must well exceed the average return from all investments.

Uncertainty in investment projects

Because there can be no certainty that forecasts will be achieved, attempts are sometimes made to take uncertainty into account to help the decision maker. Some methods employed are:

(a) *Adjusting the basic cash flows.*
(b) *Adjusting the rate required.* A higher rate of return may be required from projects of higher than average risk.
(c) *Three level estimates.* High, medium and low values of the estimated factors making up the cash flows are taken and rates of return are calculated based on the various combinations, giving optimistic, average and pessimistic estimates. These help the decision maker by showing up the possible extreme results.
(d) *Applying probabilities to factors.* If probabilities are applied to factors such as sales, costs, etc., then the probability of various returns being achieved may be calculated. This is a sophisticated method used mainly in conjunction with a computer.
(e) *Sensitivity analysis.* This term refers to a statement of the likely effects on the return of changes in the factors such as a 10% drop in sales, compared with the average forecast.

Capital expenditure control

Financial evaluation of investments is but one procedure in the system of capital expenditure control. A summary of a company's system of capital expenditure control might appear:

— Seeking out opportunities which fit in with corporate plans.
— Possible projects subjected to a feasibility study.

— Completion of capital investment proposal form for desirable projects.
— Submission to top management committee of financially evaluated proposals that meet laid down criteria.
— Approval by top management places a project in the capital budget which may cover five to ten years.
— Capital expenditure is authorized in relation to budget before being incurred.
— Periodic review of progress and costs compared with budget.
— Post-completion audit of a project where practical so that lessons may be learned.

Questions and problems

17–1   Why are capital investment decisions so important?

17–2   What do you understand by the term 'net present value'?

17–3   Explain the following methods of capital investment appraisal:

(a) average return on investment;
(b) payback period;
(c) discounted cash flow.

17–4   A company with £15,000 to invest internally has produced economic feasibility studies in respect of four projects whose life would in each instance be four years. The net annual cash flows are estimated as follows:

	Projects			
	A	B	C	D
Years	£	£	£	£
1	Nil	Nil	5,000	20,000
2	Nil	5,000	5,000	3,000
3	15,000	5,000	5,000	1,000
4	15,000	10,000	5,000	1,000

The company borrows capital at 10% and expects a project to return 20%.

You are required to rank the projects in order of merit under the following methods of appraisal:

(a) payback;
(b) average annual profit on average investment;
(c) net present value at 10%;
(d) net present value at 20%.

17-5 A catering organization is considering the purchase of a new washing-up machine at a cost of £80,000. It should save £16,000 in cash operating costs per year and has an estimated useful life of 8 years, with a zero disposal value.
You are required to calculate:

(a) the payback period;
(b) the net present value if the minimum rate of return desired is 10% and state with reasons whether or not the company should buy; and
(c) the DCF yield.

17-6 The Brighton Horizon Co. Ltd, has £40,000 to invest. Out of the investment opportunities available, two have been selected for special attention. The immediate initial cash outlay for both is £40,000. It is forecast that for project A the net cash inflows arising from this investment will be:

Year	Net cash inflows
	£
1	10,000
2	20,000
3	20,000
4	25,000

At the end of the 4th year the investment will be sold for £5,000.

For project B; net cost savings of £18,000 for each of the four years will be achieved.
You are required to:

(i) determine which project to recommend according to the

(a) payback period method; and
(b) net present value method, assuming a discount factor of 20%
(ii) compare the payback period and net present value methods of investment appraisal.

(HCIMA)

17-7 AM Co. Ltd requires a DCF return of 15% or more on any capital project it undertakes. Three projects have been presented to the Capital Projects Committee for consideration, supported by the following projections:

			Projects	
		X	Y	Z
		£	£	£
Expenditure	Year 0	10,000	15,000	20,000
Cash inflow	Year 1	3,000	11,000	10,000
	2	3,000	11,000	10,000
	3	3,000		10,000
	4	3,000		
	5	3,000		
	6	3,000		

Assuming only one project can be chosen, state which project you would choose and give your reasons.

17–8 The Golden Chain Restaurants have been buying Danish pastries from a baker at £0.04 each, but are now considering producing them themselves if this is likely to prove profitable.
Two possible machines are available, A and B, and the costs in respect of each have been forecast as follows:

	Machines	
	A	B
	£	£
Variable costs per pastry	0.02	0.125
Fixed costs:		
Annual cash costs	2,500	3,500
Initial machine costs	6,000	15,000
Residual value at end of life	Nil	3,000
Estimated life of machine	4 years	4 years

You are required to:

(a) Calculate how many pastries must be sold in order that total average annual costs equal the outside purchase costs in respect of each machine.
(b) Calculate the annual number of pastries at which the cost would be the same whether produced on A or B machine.
(c) Show which machine should be purchased on financial grounds if the annual sales forecast is 400,000 pastries, and the minimum desired rate of return is 10%.

17–9 The following information is given relating to a proposed capital expenditure project:

	£
Cost of project	250,000
Cash inflow per annum, prior to tax	80,000
Scrap/residual value	Nil
Working capital requirements:	
At commencement of project	10,000
After one year, a further	10,000
All released at end of the seventh year	20,000

Taxation assumptions:

   (i) corporation tax is at the rate of 35%;

  (ii) there is a writing down allowance of 25% and there are sufficient corporate profits available from other activities to absorb the whole amount of this allowance in the first year;

 (iii) tax payments are made and allowances are received in the year following that to which they relate.

     Expected life of equipment   6 years
     Company cut-off rate   18% after tax

You are required to:

  (a) compile a discounted cash flow (DCF) statement to ascertain whether or not the project is acceptable;

  (b) calculate the approximate DCF rate of return (internal rate of return) for the project.

17–10 The trustees of a museum, which has surplus accommodation, propose to provide for visitors a cafeteria service of light meals and refreshments on a break-even basis. They further propose to use existing funds to meet initial capital costs. These funds now earn an income of 12% per annum. A condition of granting the loan for the capital costs is that the funds should be repaid over a five-year period and provide the same rate of interest as is now being earned.

It is estimated that investment in cooking equipment and furniture with a five-year life will cost £64,000. A supervisor and four other staff will be needed at a annual cost of £24,000. Selling prices of the food and refreshments will be based on a 50% uplift from direct costs. The cafeteria will be charged £4,000 at the end of each operating year to cover heating, lighting and other property expenses.

You are required to:

  (a) estimate the annual sales necessary to meet the trustees' requirements, assuming a constant value of sales each year;

(b) assuming that business will build up gradually and annual sales in year one will be 40% of capacity, in year two 60% of capacity and in years three, four and five each at full capacity, estimate the annual sales necessary in each of the five years to meet the trustees' requirements;

(c) assuming (b) is the more realistic forecast, write a report to the trustees commenting on their proposal, mentioning areas you consider need further investigation.

You should ignore taxation and the effects of inflation.

(CIMA adapted)

17-11 (a) Motourist Ltd has the following investment opportunities and their respective internal rates of return (IRR).

Investment opportunity	Cost of opportunity £	IRR%
A	1m	16
B	3m	12
C	2m	9
D	0.5m	4
E	3m	17
F	4m	14
G	5m	6

The marginal cost of capital for the first £11m is 10%, from £11m to £20m it rises steadily to 17%.

Prepare a graphical representation of this information and explain what it means.

(b) (i) Calculate and rank according to the decision criteria, the net present value (using the discount factor of 15%) and IRR, for the two following investment opportunities, both of which have lives of two years and no scrap value:

Investment opportunity	Y	Z
Initial cost	£1,000,000	£500,000
Cash inflows: Year 1	800,000	303,865
Year 2	562,500	450,000

(ii) Comment on the rankings of investment opportunities Y and Z.

Further reading

1. *Profitable Use of Capital in Industry*, CIMA.
2. Lucey, T., *Investment Appraisal: Evaluating Risk and Uncertainty*, CIMA.
3. Merrett, A. J. and Sykes, A., *Capital Budgeting and Company Finance*, Longmans Green & Co.
4. Wright, M. G., *Discounted Cash Flow*, McGraw-Hill.
5. Cox, B. and Hewgill, J. C. R., *Management Accounting in Inflationary Conditions*, CIMA.

Chapter Eighteen

Building Computer Spreadsheet Models

As we have seen, an essential task performed by managers is the planning of future business activities. Among other things this may involve identifying potential markets and developing suitable products and services to satisfy demand, or perhaps consolidating the current share of an existing market. Whatever the case, planning is critical if our business is to remain competitive and profitable.

Having selected the proposed course of action to be pursued this is translated into monetary terms for the purpose of establishing the annual budget. Sales revenue and associated costs are estimated in order to ascertain whether or not the plan is acceptable.

In a case where our initial plan indicates an inadequate financial return we will usually wish to know how profit would subsequently respond to changes in particular revenue and cost components. For instance, how will profit be affected if selling price is reduced by 10%? What is the likely effect of this on demand and how does the combined effect of these possible changes influence profit? Until recently, the answers to these and other similar questions could only be determined by laborious calculation and recalculation of the various revenue and cost items in the original budget. However, with developments in computer technology and the widespread availability of electronic spreadsheets, these 'what if' kind of questions raised by managers can be answered with greater ease and effectiveness than was previously possible. By using a standard computer spreadsheet package it is possible for us to design and build an effective model which facilitates the routine financial planning requirements of a particular undertaking.

The aim of this chapter is, therefore, threefold. Firstly, to show how a simple financial model can be created and tested. Secondly, to outline the essentials of spreadsheet design and relate the principles to the simple model. Finally, to incorporate the design principles into a simulated restaurant business broadly following the format recommended in the Uniform System of Accounts for Restaurants.

A brief review of the electronic spreadsheet

An electronic spreadsheet takes the form of a large grid which comprises columns and rows where labels and mathematical values are keyed in and processed with the aid of a computer. Once the spreadsheet program is loaded, labels, values and formulas can be entered at any point on the grid. This is similar to entering words and numbers on accounting analysis paper. The difference is that the spreadsheet allows formulas to be entered and then if a value is changed the computer facilitates the recalculation of the associated values via the appropriate formulas.

From our viewpoint as a user the major benefits derived from the implementation of a spreadsheet package are as follows:

(a) *Absence of programming.* We can develop a spreadsheet model without the knowledge of how to program. The command structure of the particular package has to be learned, but most of the packages are similar in principle and relatively straight-forward to operate.

(b) *Rapid computation.* A key feature of the spreadsheet is the speed at which the program calculates data. For instance, values can be changed in a profit statement and the new position calculated within a few seconds; a powerful facility when considering the different options available to managers.

(c) *Instant feedback.* As numerical or mathematical data are entered in a spreadsheet the rapid computation provides an instantaneous result. If a result is unrealistic then the error will usually become apparent.

(d) *Flexibility.* If the spreadsheet is required to be adapted the rows and columns can easily be manipulated to facilitate a new and improved layout.

(e) *Documentation.* Once the spreadsheet model has been created it can be printed out (hard copy) and retained for easy reference.

(f) *Data presentation.* Many spreadsheet programs not only allow the numerical layout to be viewed on screen and hard copied, but in addition will facilitate the display of the formulas in the same configuration. This makes interpretation of the model simpler for other readers.

A three-stage approach to creating a simple financial model

For those with limited experience of computer spreadsheets, a simple way of building a model is to construct it in three distinct stages, as follows:

— Stage one: enter labels and values;
— Stage two: enter formulas;
— Stage three: test the spreadsheet for correct functioning.

303

In order to explain the approach in detail the assumed data for the Hamble Restaurant, given in Exhibit 18–1, will be used.

Exhibit 18–1   Annual Budget

Hamble Restaurant

No of covers	10,000
Selling price per cover	£5
Variable cost per cover	£2
Fixed costs for the period	£24,000

Stage one

The first step to be taken in building the model is to decide upon an appropriate layout of the financial information. From an accounting standpoint the data may ideally be presented in the form of a marginal cost (or contribution margin) statement. The annual budget data for the Hamble restaurant can be entered on to the spreadsheet grid by typing in the relevant labels and values, as per Exhibit 18–2a. The break-even point in terms of the number of covers has been included on the grid as it is an important intermediate target for the restaurant to achieve. At this stage the spreadsheet is not a model because it does not contain the formulas which form the mathematical relationships between the separate decision variables (items of data that could change).

Stage two

The next step, therefore, is to enter the formulas for the Hamble Restaurant thereby creating the spreadsheet model. This is effected by selecting a value from the spreadsheet and deciding on a formula that will give the result. For instance, £50,000 sales revenue in cell B5 was determined by 10,000 covers × £5 selling price per cover, i.e. cells B2*C5. The formula may now be entered at cell B5 along with formulas appropriate to other cells on the grid (see Exhibit 18–2b). The formulas do not normally appear visually on the screen in their respective cell positions. They are stored in the computer memory, but will appear on the cell indicator line when the cursor is moved on to a cell which contains a formula. Note that as it is not possible to display a value and a formula simultaneously in a cell, Exhibit 18–2b and other similar figures show the formulas separately. Essentially, however, the formulas sit unseen in their respective cells.

The two fundamental steps to building a financial model, depicted in Exhibits 18–2a and 18–2b, assist the first-time user in relating

Exhibit 18–2a   Spreadsheet Grid (showing values)

	A	B : Hamble	C : Rest Cover
1.	Model 1	10000	
2.	No. covers sold		
3.			
4.		£	£
5.	Sales revenue	50000	5
6.	Less: Variable costs	20000	2
7.			
8.	Contribution margin	30000	3
9.			
10.	Less: Fixed costs	24000	
11.			
12.	Net profit/loss	6000	
13.			
14.			
15.	BEP in covers	8000	
16.			
17.			

Exhibit 18–2b   Spreadsheet Grid (showing formulas)

	A	B : Hamble	C : Rest Cover
1.	Model 1	10000	
2.	No. covers sold		
3.			
4.		£	£
5.	Sales revenue	+B2*C5	5
6.	Less: Variable costs	+B2*C6	2
7.			
8.	Contribution margin	+B5−B6	+C5−C6
9.			
10.	Less: Fixed costs	24000	
11.			
12.	Net profit/loss	+B8−B10	
13.			
14.			
15.	BEP in covers	+B10/C8	
16.			
17.			

Note: Commas are added to the sterling values using a format command, explained later.

accounting principles to the mechanics of the spreadsheet. Theoretically, however, the first step of entering the given accounting data (Exhibit 18–2a) can be omitted. Instead, it is possible to build the spreadsheet model directly by typing in labels and formulas at the outset (Exhibit 18–2b). However, by entering the values, such as the £50,000 sales revenue, prior to entering the formula provides a useful check on the accuracy of the formula. If the formula is correct then the £50,000 will not change. On the other hand, if the value does change the formula is likely to contain an error and should be checked. Once this is completed the decision variables, i.e. number of covers, selling price per cover, fixed costs, etc., can be added to the spreadsheet and the computer will then calculate the appropriate profit and break-even point.

Stage three

Having created the spreadsheet model by whichever means the final step is to test that it is working correctly. Using the restaurant model this can be effected by changing each decision variable in turn and observing the effect on profit and break-even position: For instance, increase the number of covers sold from 10,000 to 12,000. The computer should recalculate the position to show a new net profit of £12,000, an increase of £6,000 on the previous profit. The break-even point is, of course, not affected by changes in numbers of products sold. Another check would be to increase the fixed costs from £24,000 to £27,000. This should have the effect of reducing net profit from £12,000 to £9,000 and increasing the break-even point from 8,000 to 9,000 covers. Hence, assuming each change in a decision variable results in the correct outcome in the appropriate formula cells, the spreadsheet can be judged to be working correctly. Restaurant management can now try out various 'what if' situations and evaluate the subsequent effects on sales, costs and profit.

Building a simple spreadsheet model

Although the exercise that follows is based on the Microsoft Works spreadsheet other packages are fairly similar to operate, e.g. Lotus 123, Excel, Supercalc. Where the instructions given here do not exactly match refer to your package manual. After loading the program and arriving at the spreadsheet grid, the 'menu' is usually accessed by pressing either the Alt key or the slash (/) key.

Microsoft Works
Spreadsheet exercise: Cost–Volume–Profit Analysis

What to do	How to do it (Everything you key in is underlined)
1. Increase width of Column A to 20 spaces.	ALT FormaT Column Width 20 <R> (<R> = Return)
2. Reduce width of Column D.	Move the cursor (using the arrow keys) to column D. ALT FormaT Width 6 <R>
3. Reduce width of column F.	Move cursor to column F. ALT FormaT Width 6 <R>
4. Format Column D to two decimal places.	Move the cursor to Column D. ALT Select Column ALT FormaT FiXed 2 <R>
5. Format Column F to two decimal places.	Move the cursor to column F. ALT Select Column ALT FormaT FiXed 2 <R>

Now for Company 1 only

6. Enter name of exercise.	Move cursor to cell A1. CVP1 <R> (Note that labels left justify)
7. Enter 'number of covers sold' label.	Move the cursor to cell A2. No. covers sold <R>
8. Enter number of covers (**do not** use commas when keying in numbers).	Move cursor to cell C2. 10000 <R> (Note that numbers right justify)
9. Enter cover label.	Move cursor to cell D2. Cover <R>
10. Enter broken underline.	Move cursor to cell C3. "........ <R>
11. Enter £ under broken line.	Move cursor to cell C4. "£ <R>
12. Centre the £ sign.	ALT FormaT Style press down arrow three times <DArrow> <DArrow> <DArrow> <R>
13. Enter remaining labels and numbers for Company 1.	See spreadsheet on page 311 (Exhibit 18–3).

14. Enter the formulas for Company 1.

See spreadsheet on page 311. (Each cell formula begins with a plus-sign +)

Example: Enter formula into C5

Move cursor to cell C5. +C2*D5 <R>

15. Check that your spreadsheet is functioning correctly. Increase number of covers sold to 11,000.

Move cursor to cell C2. 11000 <R> Observe net profit changes from £2,000 to £2,500.

16. Reduce number of covers sold.

9000 <R> Observe net profit changes from £2,500 to £1,500.

17. Increase selling price per cover to £2.50.

Move cursor to cell D5. 2.5 <R> Note that net profit increases to £6,000 and BEP reduces to 3,000 covers.

18. Reduce fixed costs to 2000.

Move cursor as required. 2000 Note net profit increases to £7,000 and BEP decreases to 2,000 covers.

19. Increase number of covers sold to 10,000. Reduce SP to £2. Increase fixed cost to 3,000

Enter numbers in appropriate cells as above. Note that profit statement has returned to its original form, i.e. NP £2,000, BEP 6,000 covers.

20. Save your spreadsheet on disk.

ALT File Save A:CVP1 <R>

21. **Now enter the numbers and formulas for Company 2.**

Proceed as before referring to page 311 (Exhibit 18–3).

22. Check Company 2 spreadsheet by increasing covers sold to 12,000 and SP to £3 per cover.

Proceed as before. Note that the final result should be NP = £16,000, BEP = 4000 covers

23. Save your spreadsheet again.

ALT File Save (It will be saved under the same name.)

You have now created a spreadsheet. If you wish to stop now and exit Works type ALT File Save A:CVP1<R>; or if you have already saved your spreadsheet to exit from Works type ALT File eXit.

We now want to produce a break-even graph for Company 1 using Work's Graphic facility. To do this you need to add an additional column to Company 1 based on (say) zero covers sold, thus creating a 'range' for the spreadsheet to be able to draw the break-even graph.

24. Enter the following numbers into the cells indicated. This reflects the position if zero covers of Company 1 are sold.

    B2 0 B5 0 B6 0 B8 0 B10 <u>3000</u>. B12 <u>−3000</u> B15 <u>3000</u>

25. Select a data range.

    Move to cell B2. Press <u><F8></u> press the right arrow key <RArrow>

26. Create the graph.

    <u>ALT</u> <u>View</u>. <u>New</u> Chart. A graph appears. Press <u><Esc></u> Note that the menu at the top of the screen changes to the chart menu.

27. Choose the type of graph.

    <u>ALT</u> Forma<u>T</u> Line

28. Assign the selected range B2:C2 to the X axis.

    <u>ALT</u> Data <u>X</u>-Series

29. Select the sales revenue range.

    Move to cell B5. Press <u>F8</u> <RArrow>

30. Assign the selected range to the 1st Y axis range.

    <u>ALT</u> Data <u>1</u>st Y-Series

31. Display graph on the screen.

    <u>ALT</u> <u>View 1</u> (Chart 1). Note: sales revenue line on graph.

32. Return to the spreadsheet.

    Press <Esc>

33. Select the fixed cost range.

    Move to cell B10. Press <u>F8</u> <RArrow>

34. Assign the selected range to the 2nd Y axis range.

    <u>ALT</u> Data <u>2</u>nd Y-Series

35. Select the total cost range.

    Move to cell B15. Press <u>F8</u> <RArrow>

36. Assign the selected range to the 3rd Y axis range.

    <u>ALT</u> Data <u>3</u>rd Y-Series

37. Display graph on the screen.

    <u>ALT</u> <u>View 1</u> Note the break-even point on the graph and compare it to that calculated by the spreadsheet.

38. Return to the spreadsheet.

    Press <Esc>

39. Label graph.

    <u>ALT</u> <u>Data</u> <u>Title</u>

40.	Enter the chart title	Breakeven graph <TAB> <TAB> (press tab twice)
41.	Enter X axis label	Number of covers sold <TAB>
42.	Entry Y 1 axis label	Sales and costs <R>
43.	Save graph by simply saving spreadsheet again	ALT File Save
44.	You are now going to print your spreadsheet	ALT Print Print <R>
45.	Print your graph	ALT Print Chart <R>

Printing your graph will take some time. A % figure at the bottom left of the screen shows you how much of your graph has been sent to print.

46.	Exit from Works.	ALT File eXit

Designing a spreadsheet model

Creating a spreadsheet model such as the one presented in Exhibits 18–2a and 18–2b is fairly straightforward because it fits within a single computer VDU (visual display unit) screen, i.e. the model does not extend beyond 6–8 columns in width or 20–30 rows in depth. However, in practice this is rarely the case as the model is more likely to extend over several screens thus preventing the user from viewing it all at the same time.

In order to build a larger spreadsheet model a more formal approach to spreadsheet design is required which will reduce the possibility or errors and facilitate a logical and well organized series of entries and presentation of data. To this end a number of principles and guidelines have evolved which form the basis for the effective design of a working spreadsheet model. The main ones are explained below.

1. Prepare the initial spreadsheet model design on paper.

Understandably, we usually want to design a spreadsheet model straight on to a computer. This, however, often proves to be a difficult and onerous task which results in error and frustration. It can be overcome by preparing the initial outline draft of the model on paper away from the computer. This will provide an overview of the model that can draw attention to what may otherwise be unforeseeable problems. In the long-run a paper design will probably save time and assist in the development of a more efficient model.

Exhibit 18–3 Spreadsheet model

Spreadsheet Grid (showing values)

	A	B	C	D	E	F
			Company 1	Cover	Company 2	Cover
1.	CVP1		10000		10000	
2.	No. covers sold					
3.						
4.			£	£	£	£
5.	Sales revenue		20000	2.00	20000	2.00
6.	Less: Variable		15000	1.50	10000	1.00
7.	costs					
8.	Contribution		5000	0.50	10000	1.00
9.	margin					
10.	Less: Fixed costs		3000		8000	
11.						
12.	Net profit/loss		2000		2000	
13.						
14.						
15.	Total costs		18000		18000	
16.	BEP in covers		6000		8000	

Spreadsheet grid (showing formulas)

	A	B	C	D	E	F
			Company 1	Cover	Company 2	Cover
1.			10000		10000	
2.						
3.						
4.			£	£	£	£
5.			+C2*D5	2.00	+E2*F5	2.00
6.			+C2*D6	1.50	+E2*F6	1.00
7.						
8.			+C5–C6	+D5–D6	+E5–E6	+F5–F6
9.						
10.			3000		8000	
11.						
12.			+C8–C10		+E8–E10	
13.						
14.						
15.			+C6+C10		+E6+E10	
16.			+C10/D8		+E10/F8	

311

2. Identify grid areas as input and output screens.

An input screen is an area which contains items (decision variables) which could change when the model is in use, e.g. covers sold, average spend per cover, food cost percentage of sales revenue. Input screens can contain cell references and formulas if required. An output screen is an area where all entries from other areas of the spreadsheet are referenced and calculated. Thus, input screens mainly contain decision variables and output screens only contain references and formulas.

3. Enter a decision variable directly only once

Ensure the spreadsheet model is designed so that the value of each decision variable is typed directly on to an input screen cell once only. If the cell value is also required in another part of the spreadsheet model then it should be entered by reference to the particular cell address as explained in the next principle.

4. Move between input and output screens by cell reference only.

If a decision variable cell value or formula cell value is required elsewhere in a spreadsheet model it should be entered by reference to the particular cell address. For example, assume that the number of covers sold for the first quarter of the year is entered in cell B4 on the input screen. If this figure is required on an output screen at cell B55 then the notation B4 is entered at cell B55. Therefore, if the number of covers sold is altered at cell B4 the change will automatically be reflected at cell B55.

5. Where practicable build input and output screens with parallel structures.

For instance, if column C represents the second quarter of the year in an input screen then it should also represent the second quarter in subsequent output screens. This will enable other users to follow the logic of the model more easily.

6. Never include a decision variable in a formula.

This is a crucial principle. For example, if the cost of sales is 40% of sales revenue the formula could be entered as B44*.4 at the appropriate cell (the B44 being the sales revenue figure reference from the input screen). However, this would mean that any cells containing the cost of sales percentage would have to be identified each time the percentage is changed. The effect would be to destroy the logic of the model. The correct approach is to enter .4 at cell (say) B12 in the input screen and multiply the two cells together by entering B44*B12 at a third cell in the output screen.

7. Include a summary of results screen.

In the case of large and more complex models it is sometimes desirable, though not essential, to create an output screen which contains key 'bottom line' results that can be viewed on a single screen. For example, if a profit planning model comprises a quarterly cash budget and profit statement, it might be helpful to view the net impact of all changes in decision variables on profits, cash balances and break-even thresholds on one screen. For ease of access the results screen is usually best located in close proximity to the input screen.

8. Incorporate appropriate instructions in the spreadsheet model.

Again, this is dependent upon the complexity of the model. For example, it may be useful to explain how to enter data on the input screen. Also, where the model extends over a large area of the spreadsheet grid it may be appropriate to include a table of contents with grid references in order for users to readily identify and locate the various input and output screens.

9. Test the spreadsheet model for proper functioning.

Clearly, the extent of testing will depend on the size and complexity of the model, but manual checks should be made before using it. For instance, change selected decision variables and check that the results are consistent with the changes. If simple figures are used to test the spreadsheet it will be easier to spot any errors.

Applying spreadsheet design principles

In order to illustrate the effect of building a financial model which incorporates the appropriate spreadsheet design principles discussed above, the simple Hamble Restaurant model has been reconstructed and presented in Exhibit 18–4a and 18–4b.

Notice the model input and output screens have been identified on

Exhibit 18–4a Spreadsheet grid (showing values)

	A	: B	: C :
		Hamble	
1.	Model 2	Rest	
2.	INPUT SCREEN		
3.	No. covers sold	10000	
4.	Selling price per cover (£)	5	
5.	Variable cost per cover (£)	2	
6.	Fixed costs (£)	24000	
7.			
8.	OUTPUT SCREEN	£	
9.	Sales revenue	50000	
10.	Less: Variable costs	20000	
11.		‾‾‾‾‾	
12.	Contribution margin	30000	
13.	Less: Fixed costs	24000	
14.		‾‾‾‾‾	
15.	Net profit/loss	6000	
16.		‾‾‾‾‾	
17.			
18.	BEP in covers	8000	

Exhibit 18–4b Spreadsheet grid (showing formulas)

	A	: B	: C :
		Hamble	
1.	Model 2	Rest	
2.	INPUT SCREEN		
3.	No. covers sold	10000	
4.	Selling price per cover (£)	5	
5.	Variable cost per cover (£)	2	
6.	Fixed costs (£)	24000	
7.			
8.	OUTPUT SCREEN		
9.	Sales revenue	+B3*B4	
10.	Less: variable costs	+B3*B5	
11.		‾‾‾‾‾	
12.	Contribution margin	+B9−B10	
13.	Less: Fixed costs	+B6	
14.		‾‾‾‾‾	
15.	Net profit/loss	+B12−B13	
16.		‾‾‾‾‾	
17.			
18.	BEP in covers	+B6/(B4−B5)	

Note: input and output screens appear on one VDU screen due to the small size of the model

314

the grid, but that due to its small size both screens are able to be displayed on a single computer VDU screen. However, as illustrated later, for larger models the input and output screens will usually take up grid space equivalent to several VDU screens which will prevent a complete model being viewed at one time.

Note in particular that our redesign shows that the input screen contains only decision variables, i.e. items that could change, whilst the output screen contains only formulas. Although the values in the cells which contain formulas will change, if the input screen variables are adjusted, the formulas themselves remain unchanged.

All movements between screens follow the cell reference principle and the screens have been built with parallel structures, i.e. input decision variables and output formulas follow through under column B. Also, formula cells do not contain any decision variables. Testing of the model should indicate correct functioning.

Spreadsheet graphics

In addition to facilitating the creation of financial models, spreadsheet packages normally include a graphics option. This allows us to display a graphical representation of results drawn from a particular model. For example, a manager may wish to view a break-even graph of a restaurant so as to gain an overall perspective of the cost structure and potential profits and losses at various levels of sales. To illustrate this the Hamble Restaurant model in Exhibit 18–4 has been modified, as shown in Exhibit 18–5, and presented in the form of a break-even graph in Exhibit 18–6.

A spreadsheet program produces a CVP graph in a similar manner to a graph drawn manually. The graphics option is usually based on a linear model and therefore the program will require two pieces of data in order to draw each straight line. To facilitate this it is necessary to introduce a second set of data for the Hamble Restaurant example, shown in Exhibit 18–5. The additional set of data entered is based on zero sales and thus provides a range of activity for the program to draw the break-even graph presented in Exhibit 18–6. Note that 'total costs' have been added to the model in order to allow the program to draw the total cost line on the graph.

Once the CVP graph has been created any changes made to the decision variables in the input screen will not only adjust the sales, costs and profit in the output screen, but will also adjust the graph to reflect the changes. Thus the effect of a variety of financial decisions can be displayed and evaluated on screen in both numerical and graphical forms.

Exhibit 18–5a Spreadsheet grid (showing values)

	A	: B :	: C :
		Hamble	Rest
1.	Model 3		
2.	INPUT SCREEN		
3.	No. covers sold	0	10000
4.	Selling price per cover (£)	5	5
5.	Variable cost per cover (£)	2	2
6.	Fixed costs (£)	24000	24000
7.			
8.	OUTPUT SCREEN	£	£
9.	Sales revenue	0	50000
10.	Less: Variable costs	0	20000
11.			
12.	Contribution margin	0	30000
13.	Less: Fixed costs	24000	24000
14.			
15.	Net profit/loss	−24000	6000
16.			
17.	Total costs	24000	44000
18.	BEP in covers		8000

Exhibit 18–5b Spreadsheet grid (showing formulas)

	A	: B :	: C :
		Hamble	Rest
1.	Model 3		
2.	INPUT SCREEN		
3.	No. covers sold	0	30000
4.	Selling price per cover (£)	5	5
5.	Variable cost per cover (£)	2	2
6.	Fixed costs (£)	24000	24000
7.			
8.	OUTPUT SCREEN	£	£
9.	Sales revenue	+B3*B4	+C3*C4
10.	Less: Variable costs	+B3*B5	+C3*C5
11.			
12.	Contribution margin	+B9−B10	+C9−C10
13.	Less: Fixed costs	+B6	+C6
14.			
15.	Net profit/loss	+B12−B13	+C12−C13
16.			
17.	Total costs	+B10+B13	+C10+C13
18.	BEP in covers		+C6/(C4−C5)

Note: input and output screens appear on one VDU screen due to the small size of the model

Exhibit 18–6   Hamble Restaurant break-even chart

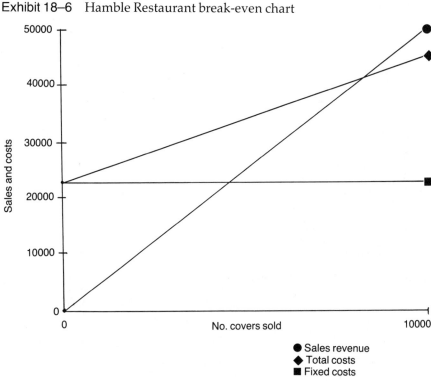

Developing a restaurant model

Having considered an approach to designing and building a simple financial model the principles and method can readily be applied to the creation of larger and more practical models relating to the hospitality industry. In order, therefore, to follow on from the earlier discussion an annual profit planning model for an assumed restaurant business has been developed and is presented in Exhibit 18–7.

Examination of Exhibit 18–7 reveals that in this case the large number of decision variables in the input screen completely fills a VDU screen. Also, the increased financial detail required with respect to sales, costs and profits necessitates the use of two output screens to contain the data. Thus, the restaurant model extends in total over three full screens. It is worth noting at this point that for still larger models an effort should be made to minimize the number of input screens as it is these which managers will wish to constantly view during their planning sessions.

The profit planning model illustrated in Exhibit 18–7 is based on the cost–volume–profit analysis (CVP) technique and so the decision variables in the input screen are separated into their fixed and variable components. The estimated fixed components relating to sales revenue and costs are entered as absolute annual amounts,

Exhibit 18–7   Restaurant Model

	A	B	C	D	E	F
					Classification	
1	Model 4a					
2	INPUT SCREEN: Decision variables			Fixed	Variable	
3	Number of covers			—	25000	13300
4	Average spend: food			—	8.5	per cover
5	Average spend: beverage			—	3.25	per cover
6	Shop and public room rental			6000	20000	
7	Cost of sales %: food			—	0.35	food sales
8	Cost of sales %: beverage			—	0.45	bev sales
9	Payroll and related			34000	0.15	total sales
10	Music and entertainment			9000	—	
11	Laundry			2400	0.005	,,
12	China, glass, linen, etc.			1200	0.01	,,
13	Paper supplies			—	0.005	,,
14	Menus, printing, etc.			1800	—	
15	Admin. and general			10300	—	
16	Marketing			4700	0.12	f&b sales
17	Repairs and maintenance			4200	0.004	,,
18	Energy			. 4300	0.008	
19	Fixed charges			34900	—	
20						
21	OUTPUT SCREEN No 1: Sales, gross profit and rental income					
22				Annual	Classification	
23				amounts	Fixed	Variable
24	Sales revenue:			£	£	£
25	Food			212500	—	212500
26	Beverage			81250	—	81250
27						
28	Total			293750		
29						
30	Cost of sales:					
31	Food			74375	—	74375
32	Beverage			36562	—	36562
33						
34	Total			110937		
35						
36	Gross profit			182812		
37	Shop and public room rental			26000	6000	20000
38						
39	Total income			208812		
40						
41	OUTPUT SCREEN No 2: Expenses, fixed charges and profits					
42	Controllable expenses:			£	£	£
43	Payroll and related			78062	34000	44062
44	Music and entertainment			9000	9000	—
45	Laundry			3869	2400	1469
46	China, glass, linen, etc.			4137	1200	2937
47	Paper supplies			1469	—	1469
48	Menus, printing, etc.			1800	1800	—
49	Admin. and general			10300	10300	—
50	Marketing			39950	4700	35250
51	Repairs and maintenance			5375.	4200	1175
52	Energy			6650	4300	2350
53						
54	Total			160612		
55						
56	Profit before fixed charges			48200		
57	Fixed charges			34900	34900	—
58						
59	Net profit or loss			13300		
60						

whilst the variable cost components are entered as percentages of the relevant sales items, as depicted under column E. This facilitates variations in sales, costs and profits, reflected in the output screens, which are prompted by changes in decision variables. Note that cell F3 in the input screen is the net profit figure read in from cell B59. This enables the user to see the profit that results from changes in decision variables whilst viewing the input screen.

The output screens have consciously been designed in the form of an accounting profit statement which broadly conforms to the Uniform System of Accounts for Restaurants. This is important because whether viewed on screen, or as a printed hard copy, outputs are more easily read and evaluated if they relate to the needs of the user – in this case restaurant management. The fixed and variable classification of revenue and costs in the input screen has been carried through to the output screens in order for management to be able to assess the magnitude of the figures in absolute (cash) terms.

As mentioned earlier, most spreadsheet packages have the facility to display and print formulas in the same configuration as the layout of the model. Reference to Exhibit 18–8 shows the formulas in the two output screens (the input screen remains the same as in Exhibit 18–7) and thus enables the user to understand, review and, if necessary, amend the model as appropriate. Furthermore, it can be seen that the restaurant model adheres to the relevant design principles discussed earlier.

With regard to improving the screen and printed copy presentation of the model a format command could be used. This allows sterling amounts in cells to be prefixed with the pound (£) sign, commas to be included in the figures and percentage signs where percentages are relevant. Note, however, that if these refinements are not entered using the format command the program will interpret the particular cells as labels (words) and be unable to use them for computation purposes.

An important point to bear in mind is that, during the process of building a model, the user should save the data on screen at regular intervals of between 15–30 minutes in case of power failure or some other unforseeen occurrence. Finally, after each building session the model should be copied on to a backup disk to ensure that a spare copy is always available in the event of the initial disk being mislayed, damaged or corrupted.

Spreadsheet Applications

Once the fundamentals of spreadsheet design and construction have been understood the principles can be applied to a wide variety of financial planning and control situations faced by managers. These include cost–volume–profit analysis, routine rooms, food and

Exhibit 18–8 Restaurant Model: output screens (showing formulas)

	A	B	C	D	E	F
21	OUTPUT SCREEN No 1: Sales, gross profit and rental income					
22		Annual		Classification		
23		Amounts		Fixed	Variable	
24	Sales revenue:	£		£	£	
25	Food	+E25		—	+E3*E4	
26	Beverage	+E26		—	+E3*E5	
27		————				
28	Total	+B25+B26				
29		————				
30	Cost of sales:					
31	Food	+E31		—	+E25*E7	
32	Beverage	+E32		—	+B26*E8	
33		————				
34	Total	+B31+B32				
35		————				
36	Gross profit	+B28−B34				
37	Shop and public room rental	+D37+E37		+D6	+E6	
38		————				
39	Total income	+B36+B37				
40		————				
41	OUTPUT SCREEN No 2: Expenses, fixed charges and profits					
42	Controllable expenses:	£		£	£	
43	Payroll and related	+D43+E43		+D9	+B28*E9	
44	Music and entertainment	+D10		+D10	—	
45	Laundry	+D45+E45		+D11	+B28*E11	
46	China, glass, linen, etc	+D46+E46		+D12	+B28*E12	
47	Paper supplies	+E47		—	+B28*E13	
48	Menus, Printing, etc	+D48		+D14	—	
49	Admin and general	+D49		+D15	—	
50	Marketing	+D50+E50		+D16	(B25+B26)*E16	
51	Repairs and maintenance	+D51+E51		+D17	+B28*E17	
52	Energy	+D52+E52		+D18	+B28*E18	
53		————				
54	Total					
		@SUM (B43..B52)				
55		————				
56	Profit before fixed charges	+B39−B54				
57	Fixed charges	22500		+D19	—	
58		————				
58		————				
59	Net profit or loss	+B56−B57				
60		————				

beverage budgeting, flexible budgetary control, comparative analysis, stock control, credit management, cash forecasting, menu engineering, profit sensitivity analysis, budget variance comparisons, market share analysis, pricing decisions and so on. Spreadsheets do not have to be large and complex to be effective. If a model is logically designed and built with care it will prove a powerful aid to management decision-making.

Questions and problems

18–1 As a hospitality management consultant you have been discussing with a client the possibility of developing a financial model using a computer spreadsheet package.

Your client is unfamiliar with electronic spreadsheet packages and she has asked you to explain the following details:

(a) The principles and methods of operation of an electronic spreadsheet package suggesting the benefits to be derived from its use.

(b) The key design principles that should be followed when building a financial model, outlining the purpose of each one.

(c) The areas of financial planning and control in which electronic spreadsheets can be used to assist management in decision making.

Your explanation should be expressed in layperson terms.

Chapter Nineteen

Published Accounts of Limited Companies

At the end of its financial year a company is required, under the Companies Act 1985, to prepare a profit and loss account and balance sheet in a prescribed manner, and obtain a directors' report and an auditor's report. One of each of these three documents must be sent to each shareholder and debenture holder and filed with the Registrar of Companies.

The Companies Acts to 1985 require a considerable amount of disclosures to be made in the annual accounts and directors' report. Perhaps the most important provision is the one which states that every profit and loss account of a company shall give a true and fair view of the profit or loss of the company for the financial year, and every balance sheet of a company shall give a true and fair view of the state of affairs of the company as at the end of its financial year. To provide these final accounts, proper sets of accounting records and the preparation and auditing of final accounts are compulsory for both private and public companies.

All large companies and public companies of whatever size must file full accounts approved by their auditors. Medium and small sized companies may file modified accounts.

Small companies are defined as companies satisfying any two of the following three criteria:

(a) annual turnover not more than £1.4m;
(b) gross assets not more than £0.7m;
(c) average number of employees per week not more than 50.

For medium sized companies the equivalent figures are:

(a) £5.75m;
(b) £2.8m;
(c) 250 employees.

Published balance sheet

The Companies Act 1985 sets out two formats for the balance sheet, one horizontal and the other vertical. Once a company has chosen a format it must adhere to it for subsequent financial years unless, in the opinion of the directors, there are special reasons for a change. Exhibit 19–1 is an example of a vertical balance sheet.

Exhibit 19–1

Balance Sheet 31st March 1992

	1992	1991
EMPLOYMENT OF CAPITAL	£m	£m
Fixed assets:	788.7	
Intangible assets	264.2	
Tangible assets	505.6	
Investments	18.9	
Current assets:	1,092.8	
Stocks	363.2	
Debtors	498.8	
Investments	45.9	
Cash at bank and in hand	184.9	
Creditors – amounts falling due within one year:	(520.8)	
Debenture loans	(20.2)	
Bank loans and overdrafts	(53.4)	
Other	(447.2)	
Net current assets:	572.0	
Total assets less current liabilities	1,360.7	
CAPITAL EMPLOYED		
Creditors – amounts falling due after more than one year:	317.2	
Debenture loans	228.4	
Bank loans	65.9	
Other	22.9	
Provisions for liabilities and charges:	51.5	
Capital and reserves:	992.0	
Called up share capital	158.6	
Share premium account	228.3	
Other reserves	32.1	
Profit and loss account	573.0	
	1,360.7	

Note: 1992 figures have been shown for illustrative purposes only. Comparative figures would be shown for 1991 in published accounts.

Published profit and loss account

The Companies Act 1985 sets out two horizontal and two vertical profit and loss account formats. Format 1 shows costs analysed by type of operation (i.e. operational format) while Format 2 shows cost analysed by type of expenditure. As with the balance sheet a company must adhere to a format for subsequent financial years. Exhibit 19–2 is an example of an operational format profit and loss account.

Exhibit 19–2

Profit and Loss Account year ended 31st March 1992

	1991/92	1990/91
	£m	£m
Turnover	1,928.8	
Cost of sales	(1,353.6)	
Gross profit	575.2	
Distribution costs	(94.0)	
Administrative expenses	(144.4)	
Research and development expenditure	(59.0)	
Profit before interest and taxation	277.8	
Interest (net)	(19.8)	
Profit on ordinary activities before taxation	258.0	
Tax on profit on ordinary activities	(110.6)	
Profit attributable to shareholders	146.4	
Dividends	(70.5)	
Profit retained for the year	75.9	

Note: Comparative figures would be shown for 1990/91 in published accounts.

Director's report

The following is a list of items which must appear in the directors' report:

(a) the state of affairs of the company;
(b) the company's principal activities;
(c) post-balance sheet events;
(d) likely future developments;
(e) employee involvement;
(f) details of own shares purchased or charged;
(g) proposed dividends and transfers to reserves;
(h) fixed assets;
(i) health and safety of employees and employment of disabled persons;
(j) political and charitable contributions;
(k) details of directors.

Standard Statements of Accounting Practice (SSAPs)

Whilst financial statements are prepared on the basis of fundamental accounting principles, many figures are based on judgement in putting principles into practice. In order to narrow the areas of difference occasioned by different people's judgement, Statements of Standard Accounting Practice have been published since 1971. SSAPs are intended to be authoritative documents containing recommendations and are applied as follows:

(a) they apply to all accounts with a 'true and fair view' audit certificate;
(b) significant departures from standards should be disclosed, explained and, where appropriate, quantified;
(c) auditors should refer to departures in the audit certificate.

Principal amongst the 23 SSAPs are:

SSAP 2 Disclosure of accounting policies
        3 Earnings per share
        5 Accounting for value added tax
        9 Stocks and work in progress
     10 Statements of source and application of funds
     12 Accounting for depreciation
     13 Accounting for research and development
     21 Accounting for leases and hire purchase contracts

Accounting policies (ref. SSAP 2)

A variety of accounting bases have developed which allow consistent and fair ways of dealing with such problems as depreciation of fixed assets and valuation of stocks. In order to provide a better understanding of the annual accounts, a statement of accounting policies followed for dealing with items which are judged material or critical in determining profit or loss for the year and in stating the financial position should be disclosed by way of a note to the annual accounts.

Four fundamental accounting concepts are defined in SSAP 2, viz the 'going concern' concept, the 'accruals' concept, the 'consistency' concept and the concept of 'prudence'. In the absence of a clear statement to the contrary, there is a presumption that these concepts have been observed in preparing annual accounts.

An example of accounting policies is shown in Exhibit 19–3.

Exhibit 19–3

NOTES ON ACCOUNTING POLICIES

1. *Basis of consolidation*
   (a) *Acquisitions and disposals*
   The Group balance sheet includes all the assets and liabilities of subsidary companies including those acquired during the year. The Group profit after taxation includes only that proportion of the results arising since the effective date of control, or in the case of companies or interests disposed of, for the period of ownership.
   (b) *Associated companies*
   The Group profit for the year before taxation includes the Group's proportion of the profits and losses of associated companies and the taxation charge correspondingly includes taxation on those results.
   (c) *Goodwill*
   The amount by which the consideration paid differs from the values attributed to net tangible assets of subsidiaries acquired is written off on acquisition.
   (d) *Overseas companies*
   In certain countries legislation or local practice prevents some subsidiaries from conforming with all these policies and, therefore, appropriate adjustments are made on consolidation in order that the Group accounts are presented on a consistent basis.

2. *Deferred taxation*
Provision is made for deferred taxation arising from timing differences between profits as computed for taxation purposes and profits as stated in the accounts except to the extent that the liability will not be payable in the foreseeable future. Timing differences are due primarily to the excess of tax allowances on fixed assets over the corresponding depreciation charged in the accounts and stock appreciation relief. In previous years full provision was made for deferred taxation calculated on the deferral method.

3. *Interest, internal professional fees and pre-opening expenses*
Interest on capital employed on land awaiting development and in the construction of new hotels and also internal professional costs incurred until the hotel starts to trade are capitalized as part of the costs of construction. In addition pre-opening and development expenses incurred up to the date of opening are deferred and written off over five years.

4. *Properties and investments in joint ventures*
Properties and investments in joint ventures are revalued at intervals of not more than seven years and the resultant valuation is included in the balance sheet unless the surplus or deficit is immaterial.

5. *Depreciation*
No depreciation is provided on freehold properties or properties held on leases with fifty years and over to run at the balance sheet date. Properties held on leases of less than fifty years are amortized over the unexpired term. All other fixed assets are depreciated over their estimated useful lives.

6. *Stocks*
Stocks are stated at the lower of cost and net realizable value.

7. *Foreign currencies*
Overseas trading results and net assets and United Kingdom loans in foreign currencies are expressed in sterling at the average rates of exchange ruling during one week prior and one week subsequent to the balance sheet dates. Currency translation differences are adjusted on the retained profits brought forward from the previous year. In previous years such differences were included as extraordinary items.

8. *Trading receipts*
Trading receipts represent the amounts receivable for goods sold and services provided, excluding inter-group sales.

Added value statements

An added value statement is included in the annual report and accounts of many large companies. A discussion document called *The Corporate Report* was published in 1975 by the Accounting Standards Committee. The report concerned the need for and use of financial reports, and one recommendation was the preparation and presentation of an added value statement.

Added value is defined as 'sales less bought-in goods and services'. It is a performance measure of the wealth created by a business in a period and emphasizes the return to those creating the wealth (or added value), namely shareholders, lenders, workers and the government.

The term profit has many meanings and communicating financial information to employees and shareholders in profit terms can be confusing. Added value is regarded as a simple concept in that it measures the value added to the cost of purchases and services.

Exhibit 19–4 provides an opportunity to compare a profit statement with an added value statement.

Varying interpretations exist of what is meant by bought-in materials and services. Whilst the popular version has been incorporated in Exhibit 19–4, there are arguments in favour of regarding depreciation as a bought-in item deducted from sales. Depreciation could for this purpose be regarded as no different from stocks of materials which are used up in a period to generate sales.

A potential problem concerns the danger of overemphasis by management on value added, leading to a reduction in profit. Profit would seem to be the more important ultimate objective.

Exhibit 19–4

Profit Statement for the Year 1992

	£000	£000
Sales		650
Less: Materials used	260	
Wages	180	
Purchased services	50	
Depreciation	30	
Interest paid	20	540
Profit before tax		110
Corporation tax		55
		55
Dividend paid		20
Retained profit for the year		35

Added Value Statement for the Year 1992

	£000	£000
Sources of added value		
Sales		650
Less: Bought-in materials & services		310
Value added by manufacturing and trading		340
Disposal of added value		
To employees		180
To providers of capital		
Interest on borrowings	20	
Dividends to shareholders	20	40
To Government – corporation tax		55
Re-investment in the business		
Depreciation	30	
Retained profit	35	65
		340

Advantages of added value statements

(a) An added value objective instead of a profit objective shows employees the teamwork required in creating wealth from which they benefit. Profit sharing schemes operate which are designed to reward employees with a share of increased added value.

(b) The sum of retained profit and depreciation represents funds generated internally to replace and extend fixed assets. This combined figure is not shown in the profit statement.

(c) Size of companies may be measured in a number of ways. Measurement by added value has advantages over a turnover measurement as added value ignores variations in material prices which could distort sales figures. It is a better measure than capital employed, for in the hotel and catering industry this may include leased and owned properties which distort comparisons.

Inflation accounting principles

Adjusting for inflation

Businesses with the following characteristics stand to lose from inflationary conditions unless care is taken: those

— owning high-cost fixed assets which depreciate,
— holding high stock values,
— borrowing only a small proportion of capital requirements.

There is a danger that the increased money needed to replace fixed assets and stocks in order to maintain the same volume of business, will have been distributed to shareholders. This would result in erosion of capital.

Clearly, many hotel and catering businesses are not in this position. Freehold land and premises tend to appreciate in value rather than depreciate, and stocks are relatively low in value. Nevertheless inflation does mean that their profit is likely to be overstated if only traditional accounting concepts are used in preparing final accounts.

The term inflation accounting refers to the presentation of final accounts which have been adjusted to take into account the effects of inflation on expenses charged in arriving at profit.

Final accounts are always prepared on an historical cost basis, which under inflationary conditions tends to show a higher profit than really exists. This is because, for instance, stocks used up are charged against revenue at their historic cost although the cost of replacing them may be far higher. Items of stock remain in the books at their original transaction price until used up or disposed of; the objectivity concept in particular applies here in that suggestions of bias and estimation in the valuation of assets are avoided. Stocks are valued at cost or net realization value whichever is the lower in accordance with the prudence concept and SSAP 9.

Satisfactory financial statements resulted from this practice until the monetary unit, the pound, became unstable through inflation.

329

Current value accounting (CVA)

This is a general description of methods of 'inflation accounting' which state economic events in market values at the date financial statements are prepared. This compares with the traditional valuation based on historical costs which are related to dates of purchase. The market value of assets considered by UK methods is associated with a replacement cost (so-called entry value) as compared with sales value of assets (exit value).

Valuation of fixed assets using the accepted historical cost convention is recommended in SSAP 9 to be the lower of cost or net realizable value. As cost is generally the lower, some means is necessary to adjust cost to current values. Annual professional valuations being mainly unnecessary and costly, price indices are generally recommended which take account of inflation over time. Alternatives are to use only the Retail Price Index (RPI) or to use a variety of indices to suit different assets. The CPP (current purchasing power) method would use only the RPI whilst CCA (current cost accounting) (ref. SSAP 16) would use specific indices.

Arguments may be put forward in favour of each method, but a single way of using indices to provide more useful final accounts information has not found favour. With inflation in the mid eighties very low, there is not the same urgency to deal with the matter as when inflation was in double figures.

Questions and problems

19–1 Describe, as if to a layman, the main differences between 'published' and 'internal' annual accounts as prepared by a limited liability company.

19–2 The following statement was made by an irate shareholder of a limited liability company. 'It is seemingly absurd that directors and management who are only employees have full access to the annual figures of a limited company whereas we, the shareholders, who are the owners receive only certain disclosures, laid down by law.' Discuss.

19–3 Westminster Hotels Ltd, which has an authorized capital of £700,000 divided into 500,000 ordinary shares of £1 each and 200,000 12% preference shares of £1 each, makes up its accounts on 30th June each year. Its trial balance at 30th June 1991, was as follows:

	£	£
Issued and fully paid-up capital:		
Ordinary shares		350,000
Preference shares		150,000
Profit and loss account balance 1.7.85		40,000
General reserve		90,000
Freehold land and buildings, at cost	720,000	
Unquoted investment, at cost		
(Directors valuation £70,000)	55,000	
Quoted investment, at cost		
(Market value £30,000)	33,400	
Equipment at cost	75,000	
Provision for depreciation on		
equipment 1.7.85		50,000
Stock 30.6.86, at cost or net realizable		
value whichever lower	30,000	
Debtors and creditors	140,000	110,000
Balance of cash at bank and in hand	48,500	
Profit for year ended 30.6.86 subject to		
the adjustments noted below		280,000
Preference dividend for half year –		
paid 1.1.86	9,000	
Interim dividend of 5% on ordinary		
shares – paid 1.3.86	17,500	
Income from investments:		
Unquoted		5,400
Quoted		3,000
Corporation tax payable on previous		
year's profits		50,000
	1,128,400	1,128,400

Notes and adjustments:
1. The profit for the year ended 30th June 1991 has been arrived at after charging £1,500 for audit fee, managing director's salary £8,000 but before charging depreciation and directors' fees which should be provided for as follows:

   (a) Depreciation of equipment for the year at 20% of cost; and
   (b) Directors fees as below:
   — Chairman £2,000
   — Three other directors including the managing director £1,000 each.

331

    2. Corporation tax based on assessable profits for the year at 35% is estimated at £100,000 and this should be provided for.

    3. The directors recommend:

       (a) Payment of a preference dividend for six months on 1.7.86

       (b) A final dividend of 10% on the ordinary shares

       (c) Transfer of £80,000 to general reserve.

    4. The turnover of the company for the year was £1,800,000.

You are required to prepare the profit and loss account for the year ended 30th June 1991 and a balance sheet as at that date in a form suitable for circulation to members and to conform, as far as the information given will permit, with the requirements of the Companies Act 1985.

19–4 The following list of balances was extracted at 31st March 1991 from the books of the Blossom Hotel Co. Ltd.

	£
Ordinary shares, fully paid	195,000
Preference shares, fully paid	30,000
Reserves	10,965
Freehold property at cost	330,000
Leasehold property, cost less amortization	60,432
Furniture and equipment, at cost less depreciation	52,293
Quoted investments, at cost	24,000
6% debenture stock	225,000
Wages and salaries	204,000
Rates and insurance	13,500
Fuel and light	18,690
Repairs and replacements	7,230
Depreciation charge for the year	5,340
Amortization charge for the year	4,000
Gross profit for the year (Sales £521,500)	312,925
Other expenses	21,160
Unappropriated profit at 1st April 1985	17,050
Stock	26,800
Debtors	15,705
Cash and bank balances	13,040
Deposits received in advance	1,500
Trade creditors	18,300
Preference dividend paid	1,050
Debenture interest paid	13,500

Take the following information into account:

(a) The authorized capital of the Blossom Hotel Co. Ltd is 250,000 ordinary shares of £1 each and 50,000 7% preference shares of £1 each.

(b) Provide for the outstanding preference dividend, and an ordinary dividend of 8%.

(c) Included in wages and salaries is £50,000 directors' remuneration.

(d) Provide for the estimated corporation tax liability of £18,000;

(e) The aggregate depreciation on kitchen and restaurant plant and equipment at 31st March 1991 is £16,707, and the amortization on the leasehold property is £14,568.

(f) Provide for fuel and light charges due at 31st March 1991 of £810.

You are required:

(i) to prepare the profit and loss account, the appropriation account for the year ending 31st March 1991, and the balance sheet as at that date.

(ii) indicate four other items of information which could be required to be disclosed in the annual accounts by the Companies Act. 1985.

(Ignore taxation on distributions).

(HCIMA)

19–5 Discuss the ways in which added value can be increased in an hotel company. Which ways would you favour, and why?

Further reading

1. Recent published accounts of limited companies will prove useful in appreciating legal disclosures and general style of presentation.

Chapter Twenty

Consolidated Accounts of Limited Companies

Since so many public companies in the hotel and catering industry produce a group balance sheet and profit and loss account in addition to the usual company final accounts, some understanding is required of the reasons why and how group final accounts are prepared.

A company taking over control of another company by the purchase of shares giving majority votes becomes a holding company of the one bought, which itself becomes a subsidiary.

A company, S Limited, is said to be a subsidiary of another company, H Limited, if – but only if – the following hold true:

(a) H Limited holds more than one half in nominal value of the equity share capital of S Limited; or
(b) H Limited is a member of S Limited and controls the composition of its board of directors; or
(c) S Limited is a subsidiary of another company which itself, by virtue of (a) or (b) above, is a subsidiary of H Limited. In this case S Limited is said to be a sub-subsidiary of H Limited.

A holding company with its subsidiaries is known as a group of companies, giving rise to the term 'group accounts'.

Group accounts

The Companies Act 1985 requires the preparation of group accounts where a company has a subsidiary at the end of its financial year and is not a wholly-owned subsidiary of another company incorporated in Great Britain.

Preparation of consolidated balance sheets

Whilst the consolidation of final accounts in practice is likely to be the work of an accountant, and may be complicated when subsidiaries hold control themselves of subsidiaries, a simple

334

approach will suffice to enable published group accounts to be understood.

Certain rules are necessary to consolidate balance sheets, starting with the rule that the balance sheets of the holding company and its subsidiary are added together and any inter-company balances eliminated.

(In all four examples which follow in Exhibits 20–1 to 20–4 the balance sheet of the holding company 'H' remains unchanged, whilst four different subsidiaries are used, S(A), S(B), S(C), S(D).)

Exhibit 20–1 When all shares in the subsidiary are bought at nominal value and an inter-company loan exists

Balance Sheet of 'H' Co. Ltd on 31st December 1991

	£000		£000
Issued ordinary share capital	100,000	Fixed assets	55,000
Current liabilities	10,000	Investment in S(A)	40,000
		Loan to S(A)	3,000
		Current assets	12,000
	110,000		110,000

Balance Sheet of S(A) Co. Ltd on 31st December 1991

	£000		£000
Issued ordinary share capital	40,000	Fixed assets	42,000
Loan from 'H'	3,000	Current assets	7,000
Current liabilities	6,000		
	49,000		49,000

The investment of £40,000 and loan of £3,000 are eliminated in the consolidated balance sheet; all other items are added together.

Consolidated Balance Sheet of 'H' Co. Ltd and its subsidiary S(A) Co. Ltd on 31st December 1991

	£000		£000
Issued ordinary share capital	100,000	Fixed assets	97,000
Current liabilities	16,000	Current assets	19,000
	116,000		116,000

The above consolidated balance sheet is in summary form only for the sake of simplicity, but reference should be made also to the following which illustrates, with sample details, how the balance sheets are combined to form the consolidated balance sheet.

Consolidated Balance Sheet of 'H' Co. Ltd and its subsidiary S(A) Co. Ltd on 31st December 1991

	H £000	S(A) £000	H and £000	S(A) £000
Fixed Assets				
Property	45,000	35,000		80,000
Equipment	10,000	7,000		17,000
	55,000	42,000		97,000
Current Assets				
Stocks	8,000	5,000	13,000	
Debtors	3,000	1,500	4,500	
Cash and bank	1,000	500	1,500	
	12,000	7,000	19,000	
Less: Current Liabilities				
Taxation	2,000	1,000	3,000	
Creditors	3,000	2,000	5,000	
Overdraft	5,000	3,000	8,000	
	10,000	6,000	16,000	

Net Current Assets (working capital) £19,000 − £16,000 =	3,000
Net Assets (capital employed)	100,000
Share Capital 100,000 ordinary shares of £1 issued and fully paid up	100,000

Goodwill on consolidation

Exhibit 20–2 When purchase price is greater than the value of net assets, and all shares in the subsidiary are acquired

If the cost of acquiring control of a subsidiary is in excess of its net asset value then the difference is regarded as goodwill when consolidating. Net asset value is the total assets less liabilities to outsiders.

Instead of S(A) Co. Ltd let S(B) Co. Ltd be acquired:

Balance Sheet of S(B) Co. Ltd on 31st December 1991

	£000		£000
Issued ordinary share capital	20,000	Fixed assets	29,000
Revenue reserves	8,000		
Profit and loss account	2,000	Current assets	7,000
(Net asset value)	30,000		
Loan from 'H'	3,000		
Current liabilities	3,000		
	36,000		36,000

'H' Co. Ltd paid £40,000 for S(B) Co. Ltd's net assets worth £30,000, leaving a figure of £10,000 representing goodwill on purchase. Net assets may be calculated as shown in the balance sheet of S(B) Co. Ltd by the addition of issued share capital and reserves, or by taking total assets (£36,000) less any liabilities to outside interests (£6,000).

The resulting consolidated balance sheet is as follows:

Consolidated Balance Sheet of 'H' Co. Ltd with S(B) Co. Ltd on 31st December 1991

	£000		£000
Issued ordinary share capital	100,000	Fixed assets	84,000
Current liabilities	13,000	Goodwill on consolidation	
		(£40,000 − £30,000)	10,000
		Current assets	19,000
	113,000		113,000

Should the price paid for a subsidiary be less than its net asset value, then a capital reserve arises on consolidation.

Minority interests on consolidation

Exhibit 20–3 When not all shares in the subsidiary are acquired, but enough to gain control, minority interests result

A controlling interest in a company is achieved when over 50% of the ordinary shares are acquired, assuming each share carries one vote and other shares are non-voting. If between 50% and 100% of the shares in a subsidiary are acquired, those not acquired are called the minority interest, and the value of these attributed to shareholders outside the group must be calculated.

The rule in this situation is that the claims of the minority shareholders must be deducted from the net asset value before calculating the value of the holding company's interest and goodwill. Preference shares, because of limited voting rights, need not be acquired and are normally taken at nominal value.

Consolidation is therefore effected by calculating net assets and deducting nominal value of preference shares. The resulting figure represents the value of equity which is then proportioned according to holding company and minority shareholdings. The consolidated balance sheet is prepared as though 100% control had been achieved, as Exhibits 20–1 and 20–2 but the value of minority interests are shown as a liability.

'H' Co. Ltd bought 30,000 ordinary shares in S(C) Co. Ltd for £40,000 whose balance sheet is as follows:

Balance Sheet of S(C) Co. Ltd on 31st December 1991

	£000		£000
Issued preference shares	20,000	Fixed assets	79,000
Issued ordinary shares of £1	50,000	Current assets	7,000
Revenue reserves	8,000		
Profit and Loss account	2,000		
	80,000		
Loan from 'H'	3,000		
Current liabilities	3,000		
	86,000		86,000

	£
Net assets: £86,000 − £6,000	80,000
Preference shareholders' claim	20,000
Value of equity	60,000

'H' Co. Ltd bought 30,000 shares being valued at

$$\frac{30,000}{50,000}, \text{i.e. } 60\% \text{ of } £60,000 \qquad £36,000$$

Since payment of £40,000 is £4,000 more than the value of 30,000 shares, goodwill results.

Minority interest (including preference shareholders) is

£80,000 − £36,000 £44,000

The consolidated balance sheet will appear as follows:

Consolidated Balance Sheet of 'H' Co. Ltd and S(C) Co. Ltd on 31st December 1991

	£000		£000
Issued ordinary shares	100,000	Fixed assets	134,000
Minority interest	44,000	Goodwill	4,000
Current liabilities	13,000	Current assets	19,000
	157,000		157,000

Pre-acquisition profits

Exhibit 20–4 Consolidating at a date after the purchase of a subsidiary gives rise to pre-acquisition and post-acquisition profits

It has so far been assumed that the consolidated balance sheet was prepared at the time of the subsidiary's acquisition. Profits made by the subsidiary were taken into account in determining net assets and consequently goodwill or capital reserve on purchase. Pre-acquisition profits (undistributed) of the subsidiary have therefore been capitalized and are not available for distribution. If not all shares are purchased, then it has been shown that only the part of the profits belonging to the holding is capitalized, the remainder being part of minority interests.

If consolidated final accounts are prepared at the end of the financial year following acquisition, it is likely that the subsidiary will have made further profits. These profits made subsequent to acquisition are available for distribution.

Clearly, then, when consolidating some time after an acquisition the subsidiary's profit and loss account must be separated into:

(a) pre-acquisition profit;
(b) post-acquisition profit.

On 30th September 1991 'H' Co. Ltd bought for £40,000 60% (30,000) of the £1 ordinary shares of S(D) Co. Ltd whose balance sheet on 31st December 1991 was:

Balance Sheet of S(D) Co. Ltd on 31st December 1991

	£000	£000		£000
Issued preference shares		20,000	Fixed assets	79,000
Issued ordinary shares of £1		50,000	Current assets	7,000
Revenue reserve at 1/1/86		8,000		
Profit and loss account:				
at 30/9/86	1,500			
1/10/86 to 31/12/86	500			
	——	2,000		
Loan from 'H'		3,000		
Current liabilities		3,000		
		86,000		86,000

Calculation of goodwill is as follows:

	£000	£000
Purchase price		40,000
Less: Net assets purchased:		
Nominal value of acquired shares	30,000	
Revenue reserve purchased 60% × £8,000	4,800	
Profit purchased 60% × £1,500	900	
	——	35,700
Goodwill		4,300

Minority interest is therefore:

	£000	£000
Preference shares		20,000
Ordinary shares 20,000 @ £1	20,000	
Revenue reserve 40% × £8,000	3,200	
Profit: 40% × £1,500	600	
and 40% × £500	200	
	——	24,000
Minority interest		44,000

Consolidated Balance Sheet of 'H' Co. Ltd and S(D) Co. Ltd on 31st December 1991

	£000		£000
Issued ordinary shares	100,000	Fixed assets	134,000
Profit and loss account S(D)		Goodwill	4,300
from 1/10/86 − 60% of £500	300*	Current assets	19,000
Minority interest	44,000		
Current liabilities	13,000		
	157,300		157,300

* This represents 'H's' share of profit made by S(D) since acquisition.

When studying published consolidated balance sheets, two items commonly found which refer to the purchase of subsidiary companies, namely minority interests and goodwill on consolidation, should now be clear. What has happened, then, is that all assets and current liabilities of subsidiaries have been added to the holding company's balances, the value of these items belonging to share-holders who have not sold their shares to the holding company is deducted as a liability to minority interests, and any excess the company has paid for net assets taken over has been added as goodwill.

The shares bought by the holding company will have been paid for in shares, debentures or cash or some combination of these.

The balance sheet of the holding company only shows interests in subsidiary companies as an asset, and therefore presents few problems in preparation.

Consolidated profit and loss accounts

The preparation of these naturally follows a similar pattern to that required for consolidating the balance sheet, in that the group's figures are added together and necessary adjustments made to them. To be more specific:

   (a) previous years' undistributed profit of all companies making up the group *is added to* —
   (b) the past years' profit of all the group, *from which is subtracted* (c), (d), (e) and (f) below:
   (c) pre-acquisition profits of the subsidiary;
   (d) profits of the subsidiary belonging to minority interests;
   (e) unrealized profit on inter-company transfers;
   (f) inter-company dividends.

341

Exhibit 20–5 Showing the preparation of a consolidated profit and loss account covering the above points

H(A) Co. Ltd bought on 1st January 1991 12,000 ordinary shares in S(E) Co. Ltd out of a total of 16,000. Stock of S(E) includes £1,000 for goods invoiced by H(A) at cost + 25%. The following profit and loss accounts were extracted before eliminating the inter-company profit in the stock held.

Profit and Loss Accounts for year ended 31st December 1991

	H(A) £000	S(E) £000		H(A) £000	S(E) £000
Interim dividends paid	10,000	4,000	Balance b/f	20,000	6,000
Balance c/f	29,000	10,000	Net profit for year	16,000	8,000
			Interim dividend from S(E)	3,000	
	39,000	14,000		39,000	14,000

Notes on accounts above and below:

1. H(A) Co. Ltd has a 75% interest in S(E) Co. Ltd leaving a 25% minority interest.
2. Profit included in stock valuation is £200.
   (Cost of £800 + 25% profit = £1,000). Since the stock is partly owned by minority shareholders, that portion is regarded as being sold to outsiders and the related profit counted as part of group profit. Profit to be eliminated is therefore 75% of £200.

Much of the detailed consolidation work is not shown in published group profit and loss accounts, reference being limited usually to minority interests.

Consolidated Profit and Loss Account of H(A) Co. Ltd with S(E) Co. Ltd for year ended 31st December 1991

Debit side

	£000	£000	£000
Dividend paid by S(E)	4,000		
Less: Minority interest	1,000		
	3,000 (f)		
Less: Contra	3,000		
Dividend paid by H(A)		10,000	
Profit on goods sold to S(E)	200		
Less: Minority interest	50 (e)		
		150	
Balance c/f			
S(E)	10,000		
Less: Minority interest	2,500 (c) & (d)		
	7,500		
Less: Stock adjustment	150 (e)		
	7,350		
H(A)	29,000		
		36,350	
		46,500	

Credit side

	£000	£000	£000
Balance b/f			
S(E)	6,000 (a)		
Less: Minority interest	1,500 (c)		
	4,500		
H(A)	20,000 (a)		
			24,500
Net profit for year S(E)	8,000 (b)		
Less: Minority interest	2,000 (d)		
	6,000		
H(A)	16,000 (b)		
			22,000
Interim dividend from S(E)	3,000 (f)		
Less: Contra	3,000		
			46,500

Questions and problems

20–1 Show the consolidated balance sheet as at 30th April 1991.

Parent company
Balance Sheet as at 30th April 1991

	£000		£000
Capital	6,000	Investment in S. Ltd at	
Profit loss A/c	3,500	cost 1,000 shares	1,600
Creditors	1,500	Fixed assets	5,400
		Current assets	4,000
	11,000		11,000

Subsidiary Company
Balance Sheet as at 30th April 1991

	£000		£000
Capital	1,000	Fixed assets	1,800
Profit and loss A/c	350	Current assets	750
Creditors	1,200		
	2,550		2,550

20–2 The following are the balance sheets of A Ltd and its subsidiary B Ltd. On the date when A Ltd acquired the shares in B Ltd, the latter company had a credit balance on the profit and loss account of £5,000. Prepare the consolidated balance sheet at 31st March 1992.

A Ltd
Balance Sheet at 31st March 1992

	£000		£000
Capital – 270,000		Freehold land and	
£1 shares	270,000	buildings at cost	100,000
Creditors	10,000	Investment in B. Ltd at	
		cost (144,000 shares)	144,000
		Stock	25,000
		Debtors	3,000
		Balance at bank	8,000
	280,000		280,000

B Ltd
Balance Sheet as at 31st March 1992

	£000		£000
Capital – 200,000		Freehold land and	
£1 shares	200,000	buildings at cost	150,000
Profit and loss A/c	1,500	Stock	50,000
Creditors	43,500	Debtors	30,000
		Balance at bank	15,000
	245,000		245,000

20–3 The balance sheet of A Ltd on 31st December was:

	£000		£000
Share capital	14,000	Fixed assets	10,000
Debentures	2,500	Investment in B Ltd	
Profit and loss A/c	2,000	4,000 shares at cost	5,200
Creditors	1,500	Current assets	4,800
	20,000		20,000

The balance sheet of B Ltd on 31st December was:

	£000		£000
Ordinary shares		Fixed assets	5,000
capital	5,000	Current assets	4,200
6% preference			
shares	2,500		
Profit and loss A/c	1,000		
Creditors	700		
	9,200		9,200

On the date when A Ltd acquired the shares in B Ltd, the profit and loss account of B Ltd stood at £500 (Cr). No dividends have been paid during the year but one year's dividend due to the preference shareholders has not yet been provided for. Prepare the consolidated balance sheet.

20–4 The accounts of A Ltd and its subsidiary B Ltd are shown below. A Ltd acquired its holding in B Ltd two years ago when the balance on B Ltd's profit and loss account was £800 Prepare a consolidated profit and loss account and balance sheet. (Ignore taxation.)

Profit and Loss Accounts for the year ended 31st December 1991

	A Ltd £	B Ltd £		A Ltd £	B Ltd £
Auditors' remuneration	200	100	Trading profit	3,000	1,600
Depreciation	300	200	Dividend – B Ltd	300	
Directors' fees	1,000	400			
Net profit c/d	1,800	900			
	3,300	1,600		3,300	1,600
Income tax	800	380	Balance b/fwd	550	1,700
Proposed div'd (Gross)	550	220	Net profit b/d	1,800	900
Balance c/d	1,000	2,000			
	2,350	2,600		2,350	2,600

Balance Sheet as at 31st December 1991

	A Ltd	B Ltd		A Ltd	B Ltd
Authorized & issued capital	9,000	3,000	Fixed assets	5,000	3,000
Profit & loss account	1,000	2,000	3,000 shares in		
B Ltd	500		B Ltd at cost	4,000	
Sundry creditors	950	780	Current assets	3,000	2,500
Proposed dividend	550	220	A Ltd		500
	12,000	6,000		12,000	6,000

Note: The Stocks of B Ltd include £600 goods supplied by A Ltd, the cost to the latter company being £500.

20–5 (a) Torfe Hotels plc is considering making an offer for the following hotels whose capital structures are:

	Strute Hotel Ltd £000	Rofte Hotel Ltd £000
Issued £1 ordinary shares	1,600	1,000
Share premium	400	200
Reserves	1,000	600
Loans (see Note)	600	1,800

Note: The weighted average interest payable on the loans is, for Strute Hotel Ltd 13% and for Rofte Hotel Ltd 18%.

The profits before interest and other appropriation for both companies are similar and range between £300,000 and £900,000.

(i) Write a report to the Board of Directors of Torfe

Hotels plc on the advantages and disadvantages of taking over these companies (ignore taxation).

(ii) Discuss the ways in which Torfe Hotels plc could acquire all the shares in these companies.

(b) On 1st June 1984, Gigantic plc acquired 60,000 £1 shares in Tiny Ltd, when the balance on the retained profit and reserves accounts of Tiny Ltd were £30,000 and £80,000 respectively. On 31st May 1985 the balance sheets of both companies disclosed:

Gigantic plc

	£000		£000
Authorised and issued		Tangible assets	33,000
ordinary shares	10,000	Investments	850
Other reserves	12,000		
Retained profit	6,000	Investment in Tiny Ltd	150
Loans	15,000		
Current liabilities payable			
within 1 year	11,000	Current assets	20,000
	54,000		54,000

Tiny Ltd

	£000		£000
Ordinary £1 shares	100	Tangible assets	435
Other reserves	85		
Retained profit	35		
Loans	230		
Current liabilities payable			
within 1 year	30	Current assets	45
	480		480

Included in the current assets and liabilities, as appropriate, is the dividend of £20,000 payable to the shareholders of Tiny Ltd.

Included in the Investments of Gigantic plc is a loan of £30,000 to Tiny Ltd.

Prepare a consolidated balance sheet for Gigantic plc at 31st May 1985.

Present Value Table

Present value of £1 received at the end of n years $\left(P = \dfrac{S}{(1+r)^n}\right)$

n	1%	2%	3%	4%	5%	6%	7%	8%	9%	10%	11%	12%	13%	14%	15%	n
1	0.990	0.980	0.971	0.962	0.952	0.943	0.935	0.926	0.917	0.909	0.901	0.893	0.885	0.887	0.870	1
2	0.980	0.961	0.943	0.925	0.907	0.890	0.873	0.857	0.842	0.826	0.812	0.797	0.783	0.769	0.756	2
3	0.971	0.942	0.915	0.889	0.864	0.840	0.816	0.794	0.772	0.751	0.731	0.712	0.693	0.675	0.658	3
4	0.961	0.924	0.888	0.855	0.823	0.792	0.763	0.735	0.708	0.683	0.659	0.636	0.613	0.592	0.572	4
5	0.951	0.906	0.863	0.822	0.784	0.747	0.713	0.681	0.650	0.621	0.593	0.567	0.543	0.519	0.497	5
6	0.942	0.888	0.837	0.790	0.746	0.705	0.666	0.630	0.596	0.564	0.535	0.507	0.480	0.456	0.432	6
7	0.933	0.871	0.813	0.760	0.711	0.665	0.623	0.583	0.547	0.513	0.482	0.452	0.425	0.400	0.376	7
8	0.923	0.853	0.789	0.731	0.677	0.627	0.582	0.540	0.502	0.467	0.434	0.404	0.376	0.351	0.327	8
9	0.914	0.837	0.766	0.703	0.645	0.592	0.544	0.500	0.460	0.424	0.391	0.361	0.333	0.308	0.284	9
10	0.905	0.820	0.744	0.676	0.614	0.558	0.508	0.463	0.422	0.386	0.352	0.322	0.295	0.270	0.247	10
11	0.896	0.804	0.722	0.650	0.585	0.527	0.475	0.429	0.388	0.350	0.317	0.287	0.261	0.237	0.215	11
12	0.887	0.788	0.701	0.625	0.557	0.497	0.444	0.397	0.356	0.319	0.286	0.257	0.231	0.208	0.187	12
13	0.879	0.773	0.681	0.601	0.530	0.469	0.415	0.368	0.326	0.290	0.258	0.229	0.204	0.182	0.163	13
14	0.870	0.758	0.661	0.577	0.505	0.442	0.388	0.340	0.299	0.263	0.232	0.205	0.181	0.160	0.141	14
15	0.861	0.743	0.642	0.555	0.481	0.417	0.362	0.315	0.275	0.239	0.209	0.183	0.160	0.140	0.123	15

n	16%	17%	18%	19%	20%	21%	22%	23%	24%	25%	26%	27%	28%	29%	30%	n
1	0.862	0.855	0.847	0.840	0.833	0.826	0.820	0.813	0.806	0.800	0.794	0.787	0.781	0.775	0.769	1
2	0.743	0.731	0.718	0.706	0.694	0.683	0.672	0.661	0.650	0.640	0.630	0.620	0.610	0.601	0.592	2
3	0.641	0.624	0.609	0.593	0.579	0.564	0.551	0.537	0.524	0.512	0.500	0.488	0.477	0.466	0.455	3
4	0.552	0.534	0.516	0.499	0.482	0.467	0.451	0.437	0.423	0.410	0.397	0.384	0.373	0.361	0.350	4
5	0.476	0.456	0.437	0.419	0.402	0.386	0.370	0.355	0.341	0.328	0.315	0.303	0.291	0.280	0.269	5
6	0.410	0.390	0.370	0.352	0.335	0.319	0.303	0.289	0.275	0.262	0.250	0.238	0.227	0.217	0.207	6
7	0.354	0.333	0.314	0.296	0.279	0.263	0.249	0.235	0.222	0.210	0.198	0.188	0.178	0.168	0.159	7
8	0.305	0.285	0.266	0.249	0.233	0.218	0.204	0.191	0.179	0.168	0.157	0.148	0.139	0.130	0.123	8
9	0.263	0.243	0.225	0.209	0.194	0.180	0.167	0.155	0.144	0.134	0.125	0.116	0.108	0.101	0.094	9
10	0.227	0.208	0.191	0.176	0.162	0.149	0.137	0.126	0.116	0.107	0.099	0.092	0.085	0.078	0.073	10
11	0.195	0.178	0.162	0.148	0.135	0.123	0.112	0.103	0.094	0.086	0.079	0.072	0.066	0.061	0.056	11
12	0.168	0.152	0.137	0.124	0.112	0.102	0.092	0.083	0.076	0.069	0.062	0.057	0.052			12
13	0.145	0.130	0.116	0.104	0.093	0.084	0.075	0.068	0.061	0.055						13
14	0.125	0.111	0.099	0.088	0.078	0.069	0.062	0.055								14
15	0.108	0.095	0.084	0.074	0.065	0.057	0.051									15

Present value of £1 received annually at the end of n years $\left(P_n = \dfrac{1}{r}\left[1 - \dfrac{1}{(1+r)^n} \right] \right)$

n	1%	2%	3%	4%	5%	6%	7%	8%	9%	10%	11%	12%	13%	14%	15%
1	0.990	0.980	0.971	0.962	0.952	0.943	0.935	0.926	0.917	0.909	0.901	0.893	0.885	0.877	0.870
2	1.970	1.942	1.913	1.886	1.859	1.833	1.808	1.783	1.759	1.736	1.713	1.690	1.668	1.647	1.626
3	2.941	2.884	2.829	2.775	2.723	2.673	2.624	2.577	2.531	2.487	2.444	2.402	2.361	2.322	2.283
4	3.902	3.808	3.717	3.630	3.546	3.465	3.387	3.312	3.240	3.170	3.102	3.037	2.974	2.914	2.855
5	4.853	4.713	4.580	4.452	4.329	4.212	4.100	3.993	3.890	3.791	3.696	3.605	3.517	3.433	3.352
6	5.795	5.601	5.417	5.242	5.076	4.917	4.767	4.623	4.486	4.355	4.231	4.111	3.998	3.889	3.784
7	6.728	6.472	6.230	6.002	5.786	5.582	5.389	5.206	5.033	4.868	4.712	4.564	4.423	4.288	4.160
8	7.652	7.325	7.020	6.733	6.463	6.210	5.971	5.747	5.535	5.335	5.146	4.968	4.799	4.639	4.487
9	8.566	8.162	7.786	7.435	7.108	6.802	6.515	6.247	5.995	5.759	5.537	5.328	5.132	4.946	4.772
10	9.471	8.983	8.530	8.111	7.722	7.360	7.024	6.710	6.418	6.145	5.889	5.650	5.426	5.216	5.019
11	10.368	9.787	9.253	8.760	8.306	7.887	7.499	7.139	6.805	6.495	6.207	5.938	5.687	5.453	5.234
12	11.255	10.575	9.954	9.385	8.863	8.384	7.943	7.536	7.161	6.814	6.492	6.194	5.918	5.660	5.421
13	12.134	11.348	10.635	9.986	9.394	8.853	8.358	7.904	7.487	7.103	6.650	6.424	6.122	5.842	5.583
14	13.004	12.106	11.296	10.563	9.899	9.295	8.745	8.244	7.786	7.367	6.982	6.628	6.302	6.002	5.724
15	13.865	12.849	11.938	11.118	10.380	9.712	9.108	8.559	8.061	7.606	7.191	6.811	6.462	6.142	5.847

n	16%	17%	18%	19%	20%	21%	22%	23%	24%	25%	26%	27%	28%	29%	30%
1	0.862	0.855	0.847	0.840	0.833	0.826	0.820	0.813	0.806	0.800	0.794	0.787	0.781	0.775	0.769
2	1.605	1.585	1.566	1.546	1.528	1.509	1.492	1.474	1.457	1.440	1.424	1.407	1.392	1.376	1.361
3	2.246	2.210	2.174	2.140	2.106	2.074	2.042	2.011	1.981	1.952	1.923	1.896	1.868	1.842	1.816
4	2.798	2.743	2.690	2.639	2.589	2.540	2.494	2.448	2.404	2.362	2.320	2.280	2.241	2.203	2.166
5	3.274	3.199	3.127	3.058	2.991	2.926	2.864	2.803	2.745	2.689	2.635	2.583	2.532	2.483	2.436
6	3.685	3.589	3.498	3.410	3.326	3.245	3.167	3.092	3.020	2.951	2.885	2.821	2.759	2.700	2.643
7	4.039	3.922	3.812	3.706	3.605	3.508	3.416	3.327	3.242	3.161	3.083	3.009	2.937	2.868	2.802
8	4.344	4.207	4.078	3.954	3.837	3.726	3.619	3.518	3.421	3.329	3.241	3.156	3.076	2.999	2.925
9	4.607	4.451	4.303	4.163	4.031	3.905	3.786	3.673	3.566	3.463	3.366	3.273	3.184	3.100	3.019
10	4.833	4.659	4.494	4.339	4.192	4.054	3.923	3.799	3.682	3.571	3.465	3.364	3.269	3.178	3.092
11	5.029	4.836	4.656	4.486	4.327	4.177	4.035	3.902	3.776	3.656	3.544	3.437	3.335	3.239	3.147
12	5.197	4.988	4.793	4.610	4.439	4.278	4.127	3.985	3.851	3.725	3.606	3.493	3.387	3.286	3.190
13	5.342	5.118	4.910	4.715	4.533	4.362	4.203	4.053	3.912	3.780	3.656	3.538	3.427	3.322	3.223
14	5.468	5.229	5.008	4.802	4.611	4.432	4.265	4.108	3.962	3.824	3.695	3.573	3.459	3.351	3.249
15	5.575	5.324	5.092	4.876	4.675	4.489	4.315	4.153	4.001	3.859	3.726	3.601	3.483	3.373	3.268

Index